BAL GANGADHAR TILAK

BAL GANGADHAR TILAK

Edited by

M.K. SINGH

ANMOL PUBLICATIONS PVT. LTD.
NEW DELHI - 110 002 (INDIA)

ANMOL PUBLICATIONS PVT. LTD.
H.O.: 4374/4B, Ansari Road, Darya Ganj,
New Delhi-110 002 (India)
Ph.: 23278000, 23261597
B.O.: No. 1015, Ist Main Road, BSK IIIrd Stage
IIIrd Phase, IIIrd Block,
Bangalore - 560 085 (India)
Visit us at: www.anmolpublications.com

Bal Gangadhar Tilak

First Published, 2008
ISBN 978-81-261-3512-7

PRINTED IN INDIA

Printed at Mehra Offset Press, Delhi.

CONTENTS

Preface

For about three decades the liberals dominated political stage of India. They contributed in their own way in national struggle, but were pushed in the background by the extremists; in the forefront being Lokmanya Bal Gangadhar Tilak.

Lokmanya changed the very character of the Indian National Congress and had a different outlook and approach. He was a great journalist and a believer in Hindu traditions and way of life. Through his actions he tried to establish that the society had a right to control its leaders. He was humanitarian and a great legislator. He was also a believer in violence but not in armed violence. He was a critic of the government and wanted to change the very method of demanding rights but at the same time he desired to accept what was given and to demand for more. He did not wish that the arena should be left to be misused by those who were tools in the hands of British imperialism.

He was deported out of India on charges of sedition but the toils of jail did not deter him from the path of struggling for national freedom which he had decided for himself. He knew the significance of the proper education for training Indian youth who were the future citizens of India and for this purpose he founded various educational organizations.

In the social field also he had a hand on the pulse of the society and openly declared that it was no business of the government to interfere in our social set up. The life of the society comes to an end in itself when political institutions and organisations begin to intervene in social affairs. Though who were politically advanced who never claim social superiority as well and thus political leaders were not necessarily social reformers. He condemned such like institutions as child marriage, ban on widow marriage or caste system. He believed that swadeshi and boycott were effective weapons for solving our political problems and thus laid a sufficient stress on these weapons for achieving our ends.

The book is of great significance for the scholars, students, teachers and researchers.

1

TILAK : LIFE SKETCH

Bal Gangadhar Tilak was universally recognized as the Father of Indian Unrest. He was one of the prime architects of modern India and heralded Asian nationalism. His philosophy Could not survive after his death as India came under sway of Mahatma Gandhi. Tilak was a brilliant politician as well as a profound scholar who believed that independence is the foremost necessity for the well being of a nation and that to win it through extreme measures should not be dispensed with. He was the first intellectual leader to Understand the importance of mass support and subsequently became the first mass leader of India. He realized that the constitutional agitation in itself was futile against the British and that, moreover, India was ill prepared for an armed revolt. As a result, although he was helpful to revolutionaries such as Savarkar, Aurobindo Ghosh and Chaphekar, he did not venture into it himself. Instead, he martialled the extremist win(,, of Indian National Congress. His movement was based oil the principles of Swadeshi (Indigenous), Boycott and Education. It was he who, through his own example, gave prestige to imprisonment in freedom struggle. It is a tragedy that his work is not given the recognition due to it. Tilak is often misinterpreted. Perhaps it is so because of his style of operation which raised bitter controversies and still more bitter opponentes even outside the bureaucracy.

Violent arguments characterized his relationship with social reformists Such as Agarkar, Rana and moderates like Ferozshah Mehta. Many blame him for opposing the Age of Consent Bill which raised the age limit for marriage of girls to 12 (from 10). But is fact that at the same time he had signed a counter-proposal where in one of the clauses was hat the girls (boys) should not be married until they are 16 (20). He educated all of his daughters and did not marry them till they were over 16. There are instances when he privately paid for the education of women. Still it remains true that, he was a reactionary and did not use his considerable influence to give a much-needed support to the social reformists. Probably, he did not want to offend tile prevalent rigid system he, himself having been brought up in the culturally narrow surroundings of Pune. It seems as if his canvas presented him no room for active social reforms.

He had several discussions with Shankaracharya of Sankeshwar and asserted that like Swami Vivekananda, the modern Shankaracharya must be educated on modern lines. Tilak received Bachelor of Arts degree from The Deccan College, Pune in 1879 and L.L.B. from the Elphinston College, Mumbai in 1882. He was among the founders of the New English School, Pune (188,) of which Prof Chiplunkar became the Principal. He had a genius for organisation and with Agarkar, the then foremost social reformist, started the newspapers 'Kesari' and The Maratha' in 188 1 and in 1890's started the annual celebration of 'Shivaji Festival' and 'Ganapati Festival' which served a platform for people to join in the nationalist movement against the British. Soon he came to be regarded as the undisputed leader of Maharashtra and was honored with the title 'Lokamanya' in 1893 which became synonymous with him in the 1900. As the nation fumed Over the partition of Bengal (1905), Tilak assumed the national leadership with his extremist attitude and stated his Position unequivocally as "Swarajya (self rule) is my birth right and I shall have it,"

Ganesh Festival and Shiva Jayanti

In order to inspire the common man he started these two festivals which were celebrated across cast land creed. There are many festive days and different festivals in the Hindu religion but they are rate celebrate individually and privately. For national awakening Tilak initiated Ganeshotsav and Shivaji Utsav in 1894. Shivaji Utsav started on Fort Raigad in 1894 and reached as far as Japan by 1905. In 1896 Ganeshotsav attained national importance.

The next three years saw meteoric rise in his stature the. British power which had long since considered him their chief concern and had sent him to prison twice already, decided on a firmer measure. Much has been said of his trial of 1908. He utilized his time in prison in scholarly pursuits and wrote "Gita Rahasya", a commentary on the Gita. He returned to Indian political scene in 1915. The political situation was fast changing under the shadow of World War 1. Mahatma Gandhi's star was on rise with Satyagraha at Sabarmati in 1914. The British charged Tilak in 1918. He fought those charges both in India and England, and was judged guilty. Amidst rumors of yet another sentence, he headed the Home-Rule commission in England to debate India's constitutional demands.

By that time, Gandhi had made preparations of the first nation wide non-cooperation movement and, perhaps, it was to make way for Gandhi that Tilak left for England. Tilak was, probably, the only leader who could have put brakes on Gandhi. Both had conflicting approaches. Gandhi had the courage to address and solve the issue of untouchability once and forever. He, Unlike Tilak, was a fluent speaker in Hindi and could thus reach the masses more easily. It is no secret that he had little respect for Tilak's real politics and Tilak hated adopting means which killed self pride of the masses. Whereas Gandhi preached, "Overcome hatred with love", Tilak pooh poohed moderates saying, "There is no empire lost by a free grant of concession by the rulers to the ruled." In both world wars, Gandhi encouraged Indians to fight for the British Empire unconditionally whereas Tilak held that if Indians were to remain slaves then it mattered little whether they joined army or not.

The Mahatma was modern with novel methods. His was a welcome arrival both for the Moderates who needed an answer to the Extremists and Tilak, in particular, and the British who would rather acknowledge and have a saint as the foremost adversary. In the 20's many of Tilak's followers, Dadasaheb Khaparde and N.C. Kelkar being the most prominent among them, supported Gandhi but none could have his say in the new order. Aurobindo Ghosh had retired to an ascetic life and Savarkar was serving two life sentences in Andaman. The Lokamanya had no worthy successor. Tilak's health continued to deteriorate rapidly at end of July 1920 and he went delirious and was unconscious for 3 days. His last words in the final momentary recovery were, "This happened in 1818 (End of Peshwai) and this in 1918. A hundred years' history - what a life of servitude ... Unless Swaraj is obtained, India shall not prosper It is necessary for our very own existence."

On Aug 1, 1920, he was declared dead. It is said that the British made an extraordinary request that his brain be handed over to them so that it could be studied, preserved and exhibited. It was not complied with.

Balawant Gangadhar Tilak (July 23, 1856 - August 1, 1920), was an Indian nationalist, social reformer and freedom fighter who was the first popular leader of the Indian Independence Movement and is known as "Father of the Indian unrest." Tilak sparked the fire for complete independence in Indian consciousness, and is considered the father of Hindu nationalism as well.

Self Rule is our birthright, and We shall have it!

This famous quote of his is very popular and well-remembered in India even today. Reverently addressed as Lokmanya (meaning "Beloved of the people" or "Revered by the world"), Tilak was a scholar of Indian history, Sanskrit, Hinduism, mathematics and astronomy.

Early Life

He was born on in a village Chikhali, near Ratnagiri, Maharashtra, into a middle class Chitpavan Brahmin family. Tilak had a divisive philosophy. He was among India's first generation of youth to receive a modern, college education. After graduation, Tilak began teaching mathematics in a private school in Pune and later became a journalist. He became a strong critic of the Western education system, feeling it demeaning to Indian students and disrespectful to India's heritage. He organized the Deccan Education Society to improve the quality of education for India's youth. He taught Mathematics at Fergusson College in Pune. Tilak founded the Marathi daily Kesari (Lion) which fast became a popular reading for the common people of India. Tilak strongly criticized the government for its brutality in suppression of free expression, especially in face of protests against the division of Bengal in 1905, and for denigrating India's culture, its people and heritage. I le demanded the British immediately give the right to self-government to India's people. Tilak joined the Indian National Congress in the 1890s, but soon fell into opposition of its liberal -moderate attitude towards the fight for self-government.

In 1891 Tilak opposed the Age of Consent bill introduced after the death of a child bride from sexual injuries. The act raised the marriageable age of a child bride from 10 to 12 which was already 16 in Britain since 1885. This was one of the first significant reforms introduced by the British since Indian rebellion of 1857. The Congress and other liberals whole-heartedly supported it but Tilak raised a battle-cry terming it as 'Interference in Hindu Religion'. Since then he was seen as a hard-core Hindu nationalist. When in 1897 bubonic plague spread from Bombay to Pune the Government became jittery and Assistant Collector of Pune, Mr. Rand and his associates, employed extremely severe and brutal methods to stop the spread of the disease by destroying even 'clean homes'. Even people who were not infected were carried away and in some cases, the carriers even looted property of the affected people. When the authorities turned a blind eye to all these excesses, furious Tilak took up people's cause by publishing inflammatory articles in his paper Kesari, quoting Hindu Scripture Bhagwat Gita to take up arms. Following this, on 27 June, Rand and his assistant were killed. Tilak was charged with incitement to murder and sentenced to 18 months imprisonment. Tilak opposed the moderate views of Gopal Krishna Gokhale, and was supported by fellow Indian nationalists.

Bipin Chandra Pal in Bengal and Lala Lajpat Rai in Punjab. In 1907, the Congress Party split into the Garam Dal (literally, "Hot Faction"), led by Tilak, Pal and Lajpat Rai, and the Naram Dal (literally, "Soft Faction") led by Gokhale during its convention at Surat in Gujarat. On 30 April 1908 two Bengali youths, Prafulla Chaki and Kudiram Bose, threw a bomb on a carriage at Muzzafurpur in order to kill a District Judge Douglass Kenford but erroneously killed some women travelling in it. While Chaki committed suicide when caught, Bose was tried and hanged. British papers screamed for vengeance and their shrill cries became even more insistent when Police raided and found a cache of arms at Calcutta. But Tilak in his paper Kesari defended the revolutionaries and called for immediate Swaraj or Self-rule. The Government swiftly arrested him for sedition. He asked a young Muhammad Ali Jinnah to represent him. But the British judge convicted him and he was imprisoned from 1908 to 1914 in Mandalay, Burma. Upon his release, Tilak re-united with his fellow nationalists and re-joined the Indian National Congress in 1916. He also helped found the All India Home Rule League in 1916-18 with Annie Besant and Muhammad Ali Jinnah. Tilak, who started his political life as a Maratha Protagonist, during his later part of life progressed into a fine nationalist after his close association with Bengal nationalists following the partition of Bengal, When asked in Calcutta whether he envisioned a Maratha type of government for Free India, Tilak replied that the Maratha dominated Governments of 16th and 17th centuries were outmoded in 20th century and lie wanted a genuine federal system for Free India where every religion and race were equal partners. Only such a form of Government would be able to safeguard India's freedom he added

Philosophical and Social Contribution

Although he was basically a proponent of Advaita Vedanta, he differed from the classical Advaitin view that jnana (knowledge) alone brings release. Tilak added a measure of karma yoga (the yoga of activity) to this, not as subordinate to jnana yoga, but as equal and complementary to it. Tilak proposed various social reforms, such as a minimum age for marriage, and was especially keen to see a prohibition placed on the sale of alcohol. His thoughts on education and Indian political life have remained highly influential - he was the first Congress leader to suggest that Hindi, written in the devanagari script, should be accepted as the sole national language of India, a policy that was later strongly endorsed by Mahatma Gandhi. However, English, which Tilak wished to remove completely from the Indian mind, remains an important means of communication in India. But the usage of Hindi (and other Indian languages) has been reinforced and widely encouraged since the days of the British Raj, and Tilak's legacy is often credited with this resurgence.

Another of the major contributions relates to the propagation of Sarvajanik (public) Ganesh festival, over 10- 11 days from Bhadrapada Shukla (Ganesh) Chaturthi to (Anant) Chaturdashi (in Aug/Sept span), which contributed for people to get together and celebrate the festival and provided a good platform for leaders to inspire masses. He first observed the festival at Gwalior permuted by Sardar Khasgiwale. He found the idea innovative and later he wrote in Kesri about it on 26th September 1893. His call for boycott of foreign goods also served to inspire patriotism among Indian masses.

Later Years and Legacy

Tilak was a critic of Mahatma Gandhi's strategy of non-violent, civil disobedience. Although once considered an extremist revolutionary, in his later years Tilak had considerably mellowed. He favored political dialogue and discussions as a more effective way to obtain political freedom for India. His writings on Indian Culture, history and Hinduism spread a sense of heritage and pride amongst Indians for India's ancient civilization and glory as a nation. Some consider Tilak as the spiritual and political leader of Mahatma Gandhi. But Gandhi himself considered Gopal Krishna Gokhale. A contemporary of Tilak, as his political mentor. When Tilak died in 1920, Gandhi paid his respects at his cremation in Bombay, along with 200,000 people. Gandhi called Tilak "The Maker of Modern India". Tilak is also today considered the father of Hindu Nationalism. He was the idol of Indian revolutionary Vinayak Damodar Savarkar, who penned the political doctrine of Hindutva. Bal Gangadhar Tilak's contribution to modern India stands on par with that of Mahatma Gandhi's.

Tilak was a great Sanskrit scholar and astronomer. He fixed the origin and date of Rigvedic Aryans, which was highly acclaimed and universally accepted by orientalists of his time. His role in Congress and advocating Home Rule for India were enormous. His newspaper (Kesari) founded in 1881 is going strong even today. Hundreds of schools in India were result of his vision. We owe the mass celebration of the Ganesh festival (see: Ganesh Chaturthi) only to Tilak. He was Guru to Savarkar (biography) and hundreds of nationalists and thousands of Indians. Actually he set up the platform for Gandhiji's leadership. Although Gandhi accepted Gokhale as his mentor, in practice, he adopted all of Tilak's ideas of Swadeshi and of social reform. In 1920, when Tilak passed away, 200,000 mourners assembled on Chowpati beach of Bombay, without a single untoward incident. It is very hard to condense the great man's contribution to our country, but I have made an attempt below. "Swaraj is my birthright and I shall have it!" were the fiery words of Tilak which roused a sleeping nation to action, making Indian people aware of their political plight under a foreign rule.

Tilak did not question the British Sovereignty nor his demands rebellious or revolutionary. All he was asking was favorable conditions in India, to enable people to learn to govern themselves. May be all over the world, the separatist forces should follow his vision and define freedom as ability to govern one's land. But the handful rulers who ruled India's millions thought otherwise. They thought that Tilak was whipping a rebellion and lie was imprisoned twice; two years for the first and six during tile second. They said, he had committed treason. Born in

Ratnagiri, a small coastal town in 1856 in a middle class family, Tilak had to fend himself for college education. At an early age he was convinced that the educational system the British provided for the Indians was not at all adequate. After graduation and a law degree, he helped found a school which laid emphasis on nationalism. He started a news paper 'Kesari' which tried to teach Indians of their glorious past and reminded them to be self reliant (Swadeshi). The British used all the native raw materials to run their factories in England and sold the finished products to India, keeping the India an ever dependent country. In the process, all the self-employing industries of India like spinning, weaving, glass making, sugar, dyeing, paper making were destroyed. People became destitute for no fault of theirs to help an empire become richer and stronger.

Tilak tried to breathe life into the moribund nation through four mantras. (1) Boycott of foreign goods (2) National Education (3) Self Government (4) Swadeshi or self reliance. He realized that mere protest against British rule was not going to help and insisted on native production and reliance. "We have no arms, but there is no necessity. But our strong political weapon is boycott (of foreign goods) Organize your powers and then go to work so that they cannot refuse you what you demand" - he told the masses. It is strange that the British read treason in these words. He founded Deccan Education Society to give better education as per the country's needs. He wrote scathing articles over inhuman punishment meted out to the nationalist youth who protested the division of Bengal (Vanga Bhanga). Indian newspapers were not to criticize the British policy in those days and two articles titled "Has the Government lost its head ?" and "To Rule is not to wreak vengeance" appearing in Kesari landed him in jail, after a namesake trial.

For the first time in British history, intellectuals in England (including the great orientalist, Max Muller) were able to convince the Government that the trial was unfair. But the second time (1908) was no different. Tilak advocated his own case and when the judgment of six years of blackwaters (kalapani) imprisonment was pronounced, he gave the famous statement : "All I wish to say is that in spite of the verdict of the jury, I maintain my innocence. There are higher powers that rule the destiny of men and nations. It may be the will of Providence that the cause I represent may prosper by suffering than by remaining free" Tilak was immensely popular through writing and through social work. His idea of national festivals took shape in Shivaji Utsav and Ganesh Utsav which were instrumental in bringing people together Culturally irrespective of their caste and creed. His trial and punishment led to national upheaval. But the British were careful enough to arrange everything in secret and the judgment was delivered at midnight and Tilak was taken under military vigil to be deported to Burma (present Myanmar, which was also under British control) At 52, a diabetic and ailing Tilak wrote his famous commentary on Bhagavad-Gita, the sacred book of Hindus.

He stressed that Gita taught action (karma), nothing but action. Religion or spiritual message were secondary and the need of the hour was to arise and fight. This was Lord Krishna's message to Arjuna. Tilak's wife, his companion of 45 years died at Pune and the news reached him in Madalay prison Burma only after a week. He had sacrificed his personal life, his profession, name and fame for the sake of the country. By the time Tilak completed his six year prison term, he was the unquestioned leader of the Indians - the uncrowned king. He was known as the Tilak Maharaj. It is strange co-incidence that the last Burmese king Theba had to spend his last days in solitary confinement in Ratnagiri and this 'uncrowned king' from Ratnagiri had to spend prison days in Burma! There was unprecedented jubilation in India after Tilak was free and was back in India. Civil resistance, the concept of Swaraj, and nationalism had taken deep roots. Tilak's suffering did not go in vain. A band of leaders, full of zeal for nationalism and self-sacrifice had come up in India. National schools were coming up in all corners of India. He paved the way for Khadi (hand woven cloth), picketing against foreign goods and alcoholism. His death in 1920 brought Mahatma Gandhi on the scene and Gandhiji gave a concrete shape to Tilak's ideas of Swadeshi.

The court which convicted Tilak bears a plaque that says, "The actions of Tilak has been justified as the right of every individual to fight for his country. Those two convictions have gone into oblivion—oblivion reserved by history for all unworthy deeds". Lokmanaya Bal Gangadhar Tilak was born into a cultured, middle-class Brahman traditional family in Ratnagari in 1856. His father Gangadhar Pant was a school teacher. After obtaining a university degree, Tilak went to study Law but then decided to teach mathematics in a private school in Pune (Poona). Teaching in School became the foundation of his Political Career. He developed the school into a university college after founding the Decca Education Society in 1884. The aim was to educate the masses especially in English Language and to awake the political consciousness of the people. 'He started to publish two weekly newspapers: Kesari ("The Lion"), published in Marathi, and The Mahratta, published in English. Through these newspapers Tilak became widely known for his bitter criticisms of British rule and also of those moderate nationalists who advocated social reforms along Western lines and political reforms along constitutional lines. Tilak sought to widen the popular nationalistic movement, which at that time was confined to the upper class Hindus. He revoked Hindu traditions and religious symbolism by organizing two important festivals.

Tilak's activities soon brought him into conflict with the British government, which prosecuted him for sedition and sent him to jail in 1897. The trial and sentence earned him the title Lokamanya ("Beloved Leader of the People"). In Mandalay jail, Tilak settled down to write his magnum opus, the Bhagawadgita Rahasya ("Secret of the BhagavadGita"), an original exposition of the most sacred book of the Hindus. On his release in 1914, on the eve of World War 1, he once more plunged into politics and launched the Home Rule League with the rousing slogan "Swarajya is my birthright and I will have it." In 1916 he rejoined the Congress and signed the historic Lucknow Pact, a Hindu- Muslim accord, with Mohammed Ali Jinnah, the future founder of Pakistan. Tilak visited England in 1918 as president of the Indian Home Rule League. By the time Tilak returned home in 1919 to attend the meeting of the Congress at Amritsar, he had mellowed sufficiently to oppose Gandhi's policy of boycotting the elections to the legislative councils established as part of the Montagu-Chelmsford reforms. Instead, Tilak advised the delegates to follow his policy of "responsive cooperation" in carrying out the reforms, which introduced a certain degree of Indian participation in regional government. But he died before he could give the new reforms a decisive direction. In tributes, Mahatma Gandhi called him "the Maker of Modern India".

Address to the Indian National Congress

The Indian National Congress was created by a group of English-speaking urban intellectuals in 1885. The original "moderate" leadership was soon more "militant" group, led by Bal

Gangadhar Tilak (1856-1920), which demanded "Swaraj [self-rule] for India. What follows is an excerpt from Tilak's address to Indian National Congress in 1907 calling for boycott of British goods and resistance to British rule. Two new words have recently come into existence with regard to our polities, and they are Moderates and Extremists. These words have a specific relation to time, and they, therefore, will change with time. The Extremists of today will be Moderates tomorrow, Just as the Moderates of today were Extremists yesterday. When the National Congress was first started and Mr. Dadabhai's views, which now go for Moderates, were given to the public, he was styled an Extremist, so that you will see that the term Extremist is an expression of progress. We are Extremists today and our sons will call themselves Extremists and us Moderates. Every new party begins as Extremists and ends as Moderates. The sphere of practical politics is not unlimited. We cannot say what will or will not happen 1,000 years hence perhaps during that long period, the whole of the white race will be swept away in another glacial period. We must, therefore, study the present and work out a program to meet the present condition. It is impossible to go into details within the time at my disposal. One thing is granted, namely, that this government does not suit us. As has been said by an eminent statesman the government of one Country by another can never be a successful, and therefore, a permanent government. There is no difference of opinion about this fundamental proposition between the old and new schools. One fact is that this alien government has ruined the Country. In the beginning, all of us were taken by Surprise. We were almost dazed. We thought that everything that the rulers did was for Our good and that this English government has descended from the clouds to save us from the invasions of Tamerlane and Chingis Khan, and, as they say, not only from foreign invasions but from internecine warfare, or the internal or external invasions, as they call it.... We are not armed, and there is no necessity for arms either. We have a stronger weapon, a political weapon, in boycott. We have perceived one fact, that the whole of this administration, which is carried on by a handful of Englishmen, is carried on with our assistance. We are all in subordinate service. This whole government is carried on with our assistance and they try to keep us in ignorance of our power of cooperation between ourselves by which that which is in our own hands at present can be claimed by us and administered by us. The point is to have the entire control in our hands. I want to have the key of my house, and not merely one stranger turned out of it. Self-government is our goal; we want a control over our administrative machinery. We don't want to become clerks and remain [clerks]. At present, we are clerks and willing instruments of our own oppression in the hands of an alien government, and that government is ruling over us not by its innate strength but by keeping LIS in ignorance and blindness to the perception of this fact. Professor Seeley shares this view. Every Englishman knows that they are a mere handful in this country and it is the business of every one of them to befool you in believing that you are weak and they are strong. This is politics. We have been deceived by such policy so long. What the new party wants you to do is to realize the fact that your future rests entirely in your own hands. If you mean to be free, you can be free; if you do not mean to be free, you will fall and be for ever fallen. So many of you need not like arms; but if you have not the power of active resistance, have you not the power of self-denial and self-abstinence in such a way as not to assist this foreign government to rule over you? This is boycott and this is what is meant when we say, boycott is a political weapon. We shall not give them assistance to collect revenue and keep peace. We shall not assist them in fighting beyond the frontiers or outside India with Indian blood and money. We shall not assist them in carrying on the administration of justice. We shall have our own courts, and when time comes we shall not pay taxes. Can you do that by your united efforts? If you can, you are free from tomorrow. Some gentlemen who spoke this evening referred to half bread as against the whole bread. I say I want the whole bread and that immediately. But if I can not get the whole, don't think that I have no patience. I will take the half they give me and then try for the remainder. This is the line of thought and action in which you must train yourself. We have not raised this cry from a mere impulse. It is a reasoned impulse.

Try to understand that reason and try to strengthen that impulse by your logical convictions. I do not ask you to blindly follow us. Think over the whole problem for yourselves. If you accept our advice, we feel sure we can achieve our salvation thereby. This is the advice of the new party. Perhaps we have not obtained a full recognition of our principles. Old prejudices die very hard. Neither of us wanted to wreck the Congress, so we compromised, and were satisfied that our principles were recognized, and only to a certain extent. That does not mean that we have accepted the whole situation. We may have a step in advance next year, so that within a few years our principles will be recognized, and recognized to such an extent that the generations who come after us may consider us Moderates. This is the way in which a nation progresses, and this is the lesson you have to learn from the struggle now going on. This is a lesson of progress, a lesson of helping yourself as much as possible, and if you really perceive the force of it, if you are convinced by these arguments, then and then only is it possible for you to effect your salvation from the alien rule under which you labor at this moment.

Achievements : Considered as Father of Indian National Movement; Founded "Deccan Education Society" to impart quality education to India's youth; was a member of the Municipal Council of Pune, Bombay Legislature, and an elected 'Fellow' of the Bombay University; formed Home Rule League in 1916 to attain the goal of Swaraj. Bal Gangadhar Tilak is considered as Father of Indian National Movement. Bal Gangadhar Tilak was a multifaceted personality. He was a social reformer, freedom fighter, national leader, and a scholar of Indian history, Sanskrit, Hinduism, mathematics and astronomy. Bal Gangadhar Tilak was popularly called as Lokmanya (Beloved of the people). During freedom struggle, his slogan -Swaraj is my birthright and I shall have it" inspired millions of Indians. Bal Gangadhar Tilak was born on July 23, 1856 in Ratnagiri, Maharashtra. He was a Chitpavan Brahmin by caste.

His father Gangadhar Ramachandra Tilak was a Sanskrit scholar and a famous teacher. Tilak was a brilliant student and he was very good in mathematics. Since childhood Tilak had an intolerant attitude towards injustice and he was truthful and straight forward in nature. He was among India's first generation of youth to receive a modern, college education. When Tilak was ten his father was transferred to Pune from Ratnagiri. This brought sea change in Tilak's life. He joined the Anglo-Vernacular School in Pune and got education from some of the well known teachers. Soon after coming to Pune Tilak lost his mother and by the time he was sixteen he lost his father too. While Tilak was studying in Matriculation he was married to a 10-year-old girl called Satyabhama. After passing the Matriculation Examination Tilak joined the Deccan College. In 1877, Bal Gangadhar Tilak got his B.A. degree with a first class in mathematics. He continued his studies and got the LL.B. degree too. After graduation, Tilak began teaching mathematics in a private school in Pune and later became a journalist. He became a strong critic of the Western education system, feeling it demeaning to Indian students and disrespectful to India's heritage. He came to the conclusion that good citizens can be moulded only through good education.

He believed that every Indian had to be taught about Indian culture and national ideals. Along with his classmate Agarkar and great social reformer Vishnushastry Chiplunkar, Bal Gangadhar Tilak founded "Deccan Education Society" to impart quality education to India's youth. The very next year after the Deccan Education Society was founded, Tilak started two weeklies, 'Kesari' and 'Mahratta'. 'Kesari' was Marathi weekly while 'Mahratta' was English weekly. Soon both the newspapers became very popular. In his newspapers, Tilak highlighted the plight of Indians. He gave a vivid picture of the people's sufferings and of actual happenings. Tilak called upon every Indian to fight for his right. Bal Gangadhar Tilak used fiery language to arouse the sleeping Indians. Bal Gangadhar Tilak joined the Indian National Congress in 1890. He was a member of the Municipal Council of Pune, Bombay Legislature, and an elected 'Fellow' of the Bombay University. Tilak was a great social reformer. He issued a call for the banning of child marriage and welcomed widow remarriage. Through the celebrations of Ganapati Festival and the birthday of the Shivaji he organized people. In 1897, Bal Gangadhar Tilak was charged with writing articles instigating people to rise against the government and to break the laws and disturb the peace.

He was sentenced to rigorous imprisonment for one and a half year. Tilak was released in 1898. After his release, Tilak launched Swadeshi Movement. Through newspapers and lectures, Tilak spread the message to each and every village in Maharashtra. A big 'Swadeshi Market' was opened in front of Tilak's house. Meanwhile, Congress was split into two camps-Moderates and Extremists. Extremists led by Bal Gangadhar Tilak opposed the moderate faction led by Gopal Krishna. Extremists were in the favour of self rule while the moderates thought that time is not yet ripe for such an eventuality. This rift finally led to a split in the Congress. Tilak was arrested on the charges of sedition in 1906. After the trial, Tilak was sentenced to six years of imprisonment in Mandalay (Burma). Tilak spent his time in prison by reading and writing.

He wrote the book 'Gita-Rahasya' while he was in prison. Tilak was released on June 8, 1914. After his release, Bal Gangadhar Tilak tried to bring the two factions of Congress together. But his efforts did not bear much fruit. In 1916, Tilak decided to build a separate organization called the 'Home Rule League'. Its goal was swaraj. Tilak went from village to village, and explained the aim of his league to the farmers and won their hearts. He traveled constantly in order to organize the people. While fighting for people's cause Bal Gangadhar Tilak died on August 1, 1920. Tilak, Indian nationalist leader and orientalist, was born July 23, 1856, at Ratnagiri, where his father, a Chitpavan Brahman, was an educational officer. At the Deccan College, Poona, he graduated in arts with honours in 1876, and took the LL.B. degree in 1879. In the following year he took the lead in providing secondary and higher education in Poona under Indian direction by founding an English school and the famous Fergusson College. Tilak conducted law classes till 1890, by which time he had become the sole proprietor as well as the editor of the two weekly papers, the Mahratta (in English) and the Kesari ("Lion "in Mahratti) which he and his friends had founded in 1880. These were the chief printed media of his anti-Government propaganda; but he took every advantage of public activities, such as membership of the local municipality and the organizing of Shivaji and Ganpati celebrations, to work upon the prejudices and passions both of the masses and of the educated minority. Identifying himself with Brahmanical orthodoxy he bitterly opposed social reforms. His violent condemnation in 1897 of the plague prevention regulations was followed by the assassination of the local plague commissioner (Mr. Rand) and a young British officer driving with him at the time. Convicted of sedition, he was sentenced to 18 months' rigorous imprisonment, but he was released within a year under pledges of good behaviour. In prison he pursued the Vedic studies which had already given him a place in oriental scholarship. His elaborate paper on "The Orion, or Researches into the Antiquity of the Vedas," read at the International Congress of Orientalists, London 1892 (published at Poona, 1893), was followed in 1903 by his "Arctic Home in the Vedas expounding a theory of extremely remote Aryan origins which has failed to secure the acceptance of other scholars. Tilak was twice elected to the Bombay Legislature for triennial terms. Again indicted for sedition in June 1908, he was sentenced by a Parsi judge (Mr. Justice Davar) to six years' transportation, afterwards commuted on account of age and health to simple imprisonment at Mandalay. On release in 1914 he actively promoted the home-rule campaign, and at last succeeded, after the death in 1915 of G. K. Gokhale, in his prolonged struggle to secure for his party control of the Indian National Congress. A libel suit he instituted in London against Sir Valentine Chirol for statements made in Indian Unrest (1910) ended in a verdict for the defendant with costs (Feb. 21 1919).

On returning to India he refrained from definite association with the non-cooperation cult. His death in Bombay, Aug. 1 1920, was followed by demonstrations of mourning throughout India, showing his remarkable hold on the popular mind. Tilak's formative part in the cult of Indian unrest is shown in the Report of the Rowlatt Sedition Committee, 1918. His speeches are collected with an appreciation by Aurobinda Ghose in Lokamanaya B. G. Tilak, Madras, 2nd edition, 1920. One of the stalwarts of India's freedom movement, Bal Gangadhar Tilak also known as Lokmanya Tilak. He is known for his famous quote "Self Rule is our birthright, and We shall have it! "He was reverently addressed as Lokmanya (or "Beloved of the people" or "Revered by the world"). After completing his graduation, Tilak began teaching in a private school in Pune and went on to become a journalist. He was very vocal in his criticism of the Western education system and set up the Deccan Education Society to educate India's Youth. Tilak founded the Marathi daily Kesari (Lion). In the pages of which he actively propagated the cause of freedom. He joined the Indian National Congress.

He was known for his hardcore Hindu views. In 1907, the Congress Party split into the two factions. The British authorities charged Tilak with sedition and he was imprisoned from 1908 to 1914 in Mandalay, Burma. He rejoined the Indian National Congress in 1916 and helped to found the All India Home Rule League in 1916-18 . Tilak was not in favour of Mahatma Gandhi's strategy of non-violent protest. He wrote many books on Indian culture, history and Hinduism like The Orion or Researches into the antiquities of the Vedas (1893), Arctic Home in the Vedas, Geetarahasya and others. He passed away on August 1, 1920.

2

TILAK : HIS PERSONALITY AND PHILOSOPHY

The period extending from the last decade of the 19th and the first decade of the 20th centuries was marked in India by growth of extremism and agitation in every sphere of life against the British rule and domination. Through the medium of the Indian-owned press, of the Indian National Congress, of the speeches and actions of Indian leaders like Womesh Chandra Bonnerjee, Dadabhai Naoroji, Surendranath Bannerjee, Ananda Mohan Bose, Romesh Chunder Dutt, Lalmohan Ghosh and others who had visited or lived in England, of English people themselves like A.O. Hume, Charles Bradlaugh, Ms. Anne Besant, C.F. Andrews, Sir William Wdderburn and George Yule and above all on account of the activities of terrorists in Bengal and Bombay Presidency, the legitimate claims of Indians first to be associated on terms of equality in the Government of their country, later to be granted home rule and a status equal to the self-governing portions of the British Empire, were ceaselessly and forcefully demanded and advanced. The elemental force of this agitation in many parts of India took the Government of India completely by surprise. But the main man behind this national resurgence and national awakening was Bal Gangadhar Tilak. A man of fiery idealism and indomitable courage, he declared: 'Swaraj is my birthright'.

The crushing of the Indian Mutiny of 1857 led to a complete cessation of open agitation against or dissatisfaction with British rule. On the surface, the years after 1858 were ones of internal peace. From open rebellion, the British Government had nothing to fear. The Mutiny had, however, left a feeling of bitterness in many Indian minds which neither time nor the British Government did much to dispel. After the Mutiny, the British Government always tended to treat Indians not only as their inferiors but also as people who could not be trusted. It was not therefore surprising that great resentment persisted in the minds of educated Indians.

In the pre-Mutiny era marked by the heyday of the Brahmo-Samaj, the educated classes had been at one in embracing Western ideals. After 1858, they split into two camps. In the first camp were those who wanted to switch over to European culture in thought, word and deed viewing all things Indian as barbarous and superstitious. In the other camp were the people who maintained that though Western education must be utilised to the full, yet all that was best in thought and action was contained in the traditions and tenets of orthodox Hinduism. This point of view was typified by Swami Dayanand's Arya Samaj whose popular movement was for 'Back to the Vedas' and their followers execrated the foreigners as 'Melechhas', displaying a harsh intolerance towards anything that was not Hindu. Bal Gangadhar Tilak, to begin with, belonged to the second group in his early years and later became totally anti-British in every sense of the word. It is this fact that constitutes Bal Gangadhar Tilak's claims to his great pre-eminence and greatness among the great heroes of India.

Bal Gangadhar Tilak was by birth a Brahman, which was to be an important factor in his life. He belonged to the sect called 'Chitpavan', which was the predominant influence controlling his early activities in politics and public life. The Chitpavan Brahmans had been in the 18th and the early part of the 19th century's de facto rulers of the Maratha Kingdom, which had its capital in Poona. Poona was the Headquarters from which the resistance of the Maratha power to the English power in the latter half of the 18th and the first quarter of the 19th centuries. The Peshwas were Chitpavan Brahmans who skilfully conducted their opposition and resistance to the English power in India and it was more stubborn and more prolonged than that of any other Indian Kingdom, Hindu or Muslim. The Peshwas were defeated by the English in 1818. Towards their English rulers who had deprived them of their power and pre-eminence in society, many of them felt an animosity which was more bitter, sustained and purposeful than was noticed anywhere else in India.

Tilak was brought up in the strictly orthodox Brahman tradition. As a Chitpavan Brahman, he had behind him a glorious tradition of politics and public service. As a Maratha, he was told the heroic stories of the glorious days of Shivaji and the Maratha Empire. After completing his school and college studies, he was appointed Professor of Mathematics in the New English School at Poona. There, after a while, he became the Founder and Proprietor of two journals, the 'Maratha' printed in English and the 'Kesari' printed in Marathi. Kesari was the first vernacular-Marathi-journal to gain any noticeable and respectable circulation among educated Indians who were later destined to gain fame throughout the Peninsula. Tilak was a staunch advocate of education, more particularly school education, through the medium of the mother tongue and in Poona the Marathi language. He helped in establishing National Schools independent of Government control which were later suppressed by the English Government. His Marathi journal Kesari reached a circulation of more than 20,000 copies by 1895.

The first session of the Indian National Congress was held in December 1885 in Bombay. Bal Gangadhar Tilak was 29 years old at that time. Tilak was not present at this first meeting. Bal Gangadhar Tilak went as a delegate to the Fifth Session of the Indian National Congress at Bombay in 1889. In this session Tilak warned his countrymen not to act like beggars in dealing with English Authorities in India. In this session itself Tilak raised his famous cry: 'Freedom is my birthright and I will have it 'which awoke an emotional echo throughout India. His forthright and violent attitude aroused misgivings among many of the moderates like Mahadev Govind Ranade, Gopalakrishna Gokhale and Surendranath Bannerjee. At the same time it has to be noted that the public realised the force of his personality and the note of challenge and defiance in his writings and speeches. All this brought him an immense and unquestioning following. Outstanding and intellect, subtle as well as forceful in arguments, he could rouse in those with whom he came into contact the same violent emotion, whether of enthusiasm or hatred, which he himself felt. On any given public issue, he was passionately sincere and he had the gift that was to be later pre-eminently Mahatma

Gandhi's, of inspiring unquestioning devotion. He was given by common consent, the name of 'LOKAMANYA', which meant 'respected by the people'.

In 1893, he organised in Poona the first public festival in Lord Ganesh's honour. He founded Ganapathi Societies, banded the students in the towns and the youths in the villages into Melas, and Gymnastic Societies, giving to them a corporate feeling and a sense of their own importance. Simultaneously through his powerful column in the Kesari, he exhorted the youth and all the people of Maharashtra to deeds of self-denial and honour 'and by implication, violence' in defence of their ancient glory against the hated foreigner. In 1893 he also founded the Anti-Cow-Killing Society which was a direct challenge to Muslims. He followed this up by demanding at several meetings of the 'Sarvajanik Sabha', immediate action from the Government for the lifting of the ban on the playing of music by Hindu processions in front of Mosques.

Further to consolidate Maratha sentiment and activity, in 1895 Bal Gangadhar Tilak organised and presided over the first great Shivaji Festival at Raigarh, Shivaji's first capital. During the worst famine years in 1896 and 1897, Tilak was in the forefront organizing all kinds of relief work to relieve the distress. When there was an outbreak of plague in 1897, Tilak displayed great energy and unselfishness. At the same time he carried on a series of bitter attacks on the British Government in his journal 'Kesari'. In June 1897, two British Officials Rand and Ayerst were assassinated in Poona by a young Chitpavan Brahman called Damodar Chapekar. Though Tilak was in no way involved in this murder, yet he was prosecuted for sedition and convicted on a majority vote of six European Jurors against three Indians and sentenced to 18 months' imprisonment. Bipin Chandra Paul and Aurobindo Gosh became his disciples. When the Swadesi Movement began in Bengal in 1905, Tilak became the unquestioned leader of India.

In 1908, Tilak was charged with criminal conspiracy and sentenced to transportation for life which was later modified to 6 years imprisonment at Mandalay in Burma. During his stay in prison, he wrote his famous books on the origin of the Aryans and his commentary on the Baghavat Gita. On completion of his term of imprisonment in 1915, he joined hands with Mrs. Anne Besant and formed the Home Rule League. In 1919 Tilak visited England as the leading member of a deputation sent by Congress to put its point of view with regard to the new Government of India Act called 'Montague-Chelmsford Reforms'. Bal Gangadhar Tilak passed away in Bombay in August 1920 at the age of 64. A vast crowd, which included Mahatma Gandhi and Jawaharlal Nehru, followed the funeral procession.

In the India of 1905, he was a powerful factor in the creation of an All India Opinion on most vital matters governing the destiny of India. He was accorded by millions of India a hero worship which is given only to those who are capable of utmost sacrifice for advancing the cause of national glory and public welfare. He has rightly been called 'The Father of Indian Unrest'.

Lokmanya Bal alias Balwant Gangadhar Tilak like his father, he was also very well grounded in Sanskrit and Mathematics. He passed the Matriculation Examination in 1872 and joined the Deccan College for higher studies in 1873. He was a resident student in the college. Two professors had made a mark on Tilak's mind during his college career. They were principal William Wordsworth (the grandson of the well-known poet William Wordsworth) and Professor Kero Laxman Chhatre. Tilak's command over Mathematics and Sanskrit became known to all in the Deccan College. His striking originality and compendious method were noted with pride by Prof. Chhatre and his other colleagues. Tilak studied for one term at Elphinston College, Mumbai in 1875 but he did not feel comfortable in the Mumbai college and returned to Pune for the second term. As a young student of the scholastic career, he was patriotic to the core. He passed his first B.A. in 1875, another one in 1876 in first class and turned his attention to Law for two years. After securing first division in B.A., Tilak joined the Law College for the professional degree. Tilak came in contact with another young student Gopal Ganesh Agarkar during his stay in the Deccan College. Agarkar was doing his M.A. and was interested in the subjects moral philosophy and logic. Gopal Ganesh Agarkar was progressive in his views on religion and fought fearlessly against the conservatism. He waged a relentless war against the age-old customs like the sati, the child-marriages, etc. and the social system like the caste system.

The Hindu widows were the pitiable lot these days. Agarkar had strong views on the subject and felt that the country would go ahead only after eliminating the evil customs and beliefs from the Hindu society. The works of Spencer and Mill had tremendously influenced him. He felt very strongly about the degeneration caused by religious orthodoxy expressing itself in social institutions like the caste system, child-marriage and the almost barbarous treatment meted out to Hindu widows under the name of religion. He was of the opinion that the regeneration of the country could only come about by removing these evils from the Hindu society. Tilak, though agreed with Agarkar in this matter, felt very keenly the bondage into which his country had fallen and the poignant shame of it made him think of foreign means for the political emancipation of his enslaved countrymen. Tilak firmly believed that all social evils could be mended if the country attained political freedom.

Moreover, he held the view that social reforms can be brought about by the initiative of the Hindus themselves. Intervention by the British in the cause of social reform would increasingly divide the people only to the benefit of the colonial administration. Vishnushastri Chiplunkar was an eminent scholar and one of the recognised leaders of the intellectual world in Pune. He vehemently criticised the role of Christian missionaries and the social reformers. He often defended the history and civilization of Hindus and awaken to rouse the people. He pleaded that only because of ill-luck, the Hindus were reduced to slavery. Mahadeo Govind Ranade, was a mighty intellect, a man of great wisdom broad mind, prodigious industry and vast learning, an eminent economist and historian, and one of India's greatest thinkers of his day. He aimed at reorganising Hindu society on the basis of justice and reason, which implied a freedom from race, creed, and prejudices. He was for social reform in Hindu society. Both Ranade and Chiplunkar were instructors and inspirers of the two schools of thought they founded. In this battle Tilak sided with Chiplunkar whereas Agarkar with Ranade. However, about education, they held similar views. Agarkar and Tilak began to think out ways and means of establishing private schools on the model of missionary institutions. Ranade said that the country would not be emancipated unless it had, like America, its national press, national education and national church. When Agarkar and Tilak approached Chiplunkar, he welcomed the idea and agreed. Chiplunkar resigned from the job of a teacher in a government school at Chiplun and opened a school in Pune in January, 1880. This school, the New English School, was going to make history in the cultural and political life of Pune. Tilak joined on the first day as promised. Agarkar after his M.A. examination joined the school in January 1881.

The New English School prospered and brought fame to the founders, who were the men of undying faith determined to carry out their mission at all cost. Even the British officers admired the progress made by the school. At about the same time, the colleagues discussed the possibility of launching two weeklies _ one in Marathi and the other in English _ to educate the people on public affairs. Chiplunkar was very keen on this project. He had already purchased on instalments the press of Namjoshi, who was conducting the 'Deccan Star', his own paper. Now it was decided to name the Marathi weekly the 'Kesari' _ the Lion, and the English weekly the 'Mahratta', for a Mahratta has been known as an indefatigable fighter for the honour of his country. The declared objectives of the weeklies were to give a fearless account of the existing condition of the country, to give reviews of Indian books and to give correct estimates of political affairs in Britain. To begin with, the 'Kesari' was a co-operative concern and Chiplunkar, Agarkar and Tilak used to write in it. Agarkar was the first editor of 'Kesari' while Tilak was that of 'Mahratta'. The Kesari always had a soft corner for the rulers of Indian states and wanted to support them whenever possible. However, both Agarkar and Tilak, the young editors were found guilty in the case of Kolhapur princely state and were sentenced to four month's imprisonment and a fine of Rs. 1000. They were sent to Dongri Jail in 1882.

Both of them received a hero's welcome when they were released from the jail. This imprisonment brought added luster to the New English School and to the Kesari and they continued to prosper. In 1882, when the Education Commission, under the Chairmanship of Sir William Hunter visited the then Bombay Presidency, the workers of the New English School made such an impression on the commission and the prominent men of the Bombay University that they encouraged them to start a college to impart higher education to Indians. As a result, in 1885, the Ferguson college was started. Tilak taught Sanskrit and Mathematics with great ability in this college.

Starting of Conflict

The Kesari in its first issue clearly explained the objective of imparting political education to the people. It said, "Just as street lights and the rounds of police constables bring to light anything wrong or unjust happening on the roads in the dark, the editorial pen brings to light the injustices and the wrongs of the administration. In England, the doings of all, right from the Queen Empress down to the lowest servant of the crown, are brought before the eyes of the public through the columns of news papers, and thus no act of injustice goes unnoticed. It is our intention to write impartially about the way in which officials of Government perform their duty. Thus, the Kesari undertakes to keep a vigilant eye on the administration and give it praise or blame when due, without favour or fear. However, in the editorial board of the Kesari, there started an ideological conflict on the question of precedence of social reform. Agarkar wanted social reform even by government legislation. Tilak wanted political freedom first and opposed government's intervention in socio-religious institutions. He insisted that social reforms should come from within by the education of public opinion and should not be foisted upon the people by any act of coercion. It may be mentioned that principal Wordsworth and even Mr. Justice Telang held the same view. These differences on public matters affected the harmony in Kesari as well as in the New English School. There were also differences about the emoluments to be received by the life members of the society for work done by them outside the school and college. Tilak wanted complete dedication and selfless work like that of missionaries. But Agarkar, Apte and Gopal Krishna Gokhale opposed it. As a result Agarkar left Kesari in 1887 to start the new newspapers, Sudharak (the Reformer) a paper of his own and the Kesari was left to Tilak alone. Because of increasing differences Tilak left Deccan Education Society in 1890. While resigning he said, ' In leaving the school today I seem to have forsaken the goal of my life".

Wider Horizon

Tilak was now more and more attracted to public activities. Basically he was a born rebel and wore the rebel robe to the end of his life. He now entered into a wider field. He came forward as a public figure and a vigorous independent agitator who rebelled against all wrongs, and his boundless devotion to whatever cause he championed was witnessed by an admiring public. He must have felt very poignantly for having lost the occupation of his choice when he left the New English School. Forsaken by his colleagues Tilak must have spent sleepless nights in thinking of his future. But the courageous Tilak decided to convert this liberation from the narrow field into a blessing for the advancement of his country. Now the Kesari _ the lion _ began to roar in the cause of people against the tormenting bureaucracy, the missionaries and the social reformers. His first task was to reach the people because he knew that lasting change, that a rebirth of values, required change in the hearts of people and not, as the reformers believed, change in the forms of institutions. As an editor who had always dedicated himself to popular education he first reached the people. N.C. Kelkar, his chief colleague observed, "Through his paper, the 'Kesari', he exercised an immense influence over the masses; and it is this influence that is mainly responsible for the infusion of a new spirit among the people and the same influence was responsible for his two sedition cases and the subsequent imprisonments."

He was a sincere, forceful speaker, and he taught from both the class-room and the public platform his new message of awakening India.

Establishment of Congress

The Indian National Congress was established in 1885. Tilak welcomed it. He foresaw for the Congress a great future and visualised it as the future parliament of the country.

As an editor, Tilak was unsurpassed. The Kesari and the Mahratta under his guidance were always tremendously influential and came to be financially successful. His sincerity and unflinching sense of dedication led him to champion the causes of his people against any and all who would be unjust, autocratic or opportunistic. As editor of the Kesari, Tilak became the awakener of India.

. The Lion of Maharashtra, the most influential Indian newspaper editor of his day.

Tilak's Philosophy for the Nation

Lord Macaulay's Indian intellectuals, the leaders of Westernisation in social and political reform, based their programme of social and political action almost entirely on the philosophy of life and action of nineteenth century Europe. They were truly more the products of Western civilization than Indian. Tilak was not satisfied with the Western values and was not ready to reject India's own philosophy of life in order to imitate the philosophy of the British.

For Tilak, there was no reason for India to feel ashamed of her civilization when compared to the west. Just the contrary, India should feel great pride. Indian values were different from but not inferior to western values.

Dharma, according to Tilak was the integrative principal, and Swadharma the spiritual and social duty of each individual. Here was the guide to social and political action.

The Westernized intellectuals (mainly social reformers) wanted to change and remake India in an alien faith. But they were wrong. Tilak reminded them, "How can a man be proud of the greatness of his own nation if he feels no pride of his own religion?" It was the Bharadharma that provided an understanding of the moral purposefulness of the universe, which is the necessary basis of a philosophy of life. It provided Tilak and the nationalists like Ghose, Pal, and Lal with a guide to concrete action in personal, social and political matters.

From an Indian philosophy of life Tilak and the nationalist leaders began to construct an Indian philosophy of politics that was to become the political theory of the Indian Independence Movement. He became the chief architect of the political philosophy of the Indian independence movement as he was one of the most important leaders of India at that time.

Two Festivals

Perhaps the most effective way in which he reached the people was through the employment of national festivals. He was instrumental in popularizing two great festivals, one to Ganapati, the Hindu deity of learning and propitiousness, and a festival to revive the memory of glory of Shivaji, the liberator of Maharashtra, and the restorer of Swaraj through his battle with the Mughal Empire. He especially emphasised the dynamic spirit of Shivaji. He believed it was the spirit which actuated Shivaji in his doings that is held forth as the proper idea to be kept constantly in view of the rising generation. To keep this spirit constant, Tilak worked ceaselessly to reach the people and to educate them through the festivals. He carried his doctrine throughout Maharashtra and waged his battle. Education through religion and history, through the association in the popular mind with gods and heroes, through recreating an appreciation of the heritage of the past as a guide to the future. This was the way he educated the people.

First Sedition Case (1897)

Tilak was aggressive and writing very strongly through the editorials of Kesari against the British bureaucracy.

The British bureaucracy and the Anglo-Indian press realised that Tilak was an emerging leader of the people and of a new spirit in India. Those who lacked foresight began to fear him.

In the tense atmosphere of famine and a plague _racked Pune, a young man, Damodar Chaphekar assassinated Rand. Rand was the British official in charge of the plague. Those who feared Rand, were quick to blame Tilak for the death, and hinted at his complicity in a conspiracy for political assassination. Tilak was, of course, innocent of any knowledge of or collaboration in this crime. He had publically disagreed with Rand for his unsympathetic behaviour towards the plague stricken people.

Tilak had condemned the inhuman aspects of the British anti-plague campaign, but he had never contemplated or encouraged the assassination of the British official in charge. Tilak, nevertheless, was brought to trial in 1897, not as an accessory to assassination, not as being involved in the plot to commit murder, but rather on the charge of 'sedition'. The court allowed the prosecution to argue that he had written seditious matter and his criminal sedition constituted, in effect, 'dissatisfaction' with the British Raj. It was brought to the notice of the court that Tilak was not positively "affectionate for" British officialdom. This was one of the most unusual interpretations of 'sedition and disaffection' in the annals of British justice. Nevertheless Tilak was convicted and sentenced to two years' imprisonment. The British had miscalculated both the effect of this sentence on Tilak and on public opinion. N.C. Kelkar observes, "His arrest and prosecution in 1897 was a sensation that nearly pulled the mind of the country by its roots, as political prosecutions were then extremely rare, and Tilak was, in himself a man big enough to mark an epoch by his personal misfortune." But this was not Tilak's last imprisonment. The British Indian Government endeavoured to convict him of perjury in connection with the well-known Tai Maharaj case in 1904. They did not succeed as he was acquitted by the High Court. In 1908, he was sentenced to six years' imprisonment, again for sedition; but in 1916, he was acquitted of a similar charge. For two decades he was persecuted by the British Indian Government because they saw in him the greatest challenge to their rule over the Indian empire. The seditation case in 1897 roused sympathy not only in Maharashtra but also in Bengal. In Bengal, Shishir Kumar Motilal Ghosh and Surendranath Bannerjee started raising funds for the defense of Tilak.

The court found Tilak guilty but Tilak's prestige rose very high in the minds of the people. Max Mueller and Indian leaders submitted a memorial to the government for the early release of Tilak. The government also soon realised the mistake and released Tilak. Tilak emerged from prison in 1899 (first sedition) after serving eighteen months of his sentence. Now he became a national hero. He got following outside Maharashtra. He became the first all-India national leader. He had been persecuted for his political opinions. He was now the acknowledged political leader of the nation and the nation was prepared to heed his opinions. He had begun as an awakener of the people and as a critic of bureaucratic abuses. He emerged from prison with the responsibility of leading the Nationalist cause to political self-determination (Swatantrya). He was acclaimed the Lokmanya, the honoured and respected of the people. Tilak's knowledge and love of the great classical Indian values had prepared him with a personal philosophy and a frame of reference for his battles with social reformism and with the spirit of orthodoxy. It also provided him with the foundation of his emerging political philosophy. He had fought against injustice, he had argued against the placating policies of the moderates. Now he began to put forward a positive political programme centred around the concept of Swaraj, self-rule for India. He realised that the self-rule must precede the meaningful social reform. National self-rule, he believed, was the only enduring basis for national unity and national self-respect. He reminded people that Shivaji had recreated Swaraj as a necessary foundation of social and political freedom, progress and morality. He, therefore, declared, which in course of time became a famous slogan, that "swaraj is my birth right and I shall have it".

Tilak's Programme for Swaraj

He now vigorously took up the propaganda of Swadeshi, Boycott and National education. These were the three programmes for the achievement of Swaraj. The swadeshi movement spread in many states and was met with repression. Theprogramme of national education was a logical outgrowth of the Swadeshi and Boycott movements. The plan involved the establishment of schools throughout the country dedicated to giving young India a truly national education. Boycott moved from the economic into the political sphere. It moved from Bengal to all-India.

Second Sedition Case (1908)

There were bomb outrages and the government's attitude was becoming increasingly stiff towards them. The repression by the government breed conspiracies and political murders. Against this background Tilak wrote the editorial in Kesari on May 12, 1908 "the misfortune of the country". By this article Tilak was alleged to have brought into hatred and contempt the government established by law and also set one class of people against another. A prosecution was instituted against Tilak under section 124-A and 153-A. He was arrested on May 25, 1908.

The case came up for hearing before Justice Davar on July 17, 1908 and a jury of six Europeans and three Parsees was empanelled. On all charges Tilak was found guilty by a verdict of seven to two. He was sentenced for six years imprisonment. When asked just before sentence was passed if he had anything more to say, he spoke the immortal lines : "All I wish to say is that inspite of the verdict of the Jury I maintain that I am innocent. There are higher powers that rule the destiny of things and it may be the will of the providence that the cause which I represent may prosper more by my suffering than by my remaining free." He was placed in virtual solitary confinement in a prison cell in faraway Mandalay. In this solitary confinement he wrote his great philosophic treatise on the Gita _ the Gita Rahasya. He lived the life of a true scholar and knowledge seeker, and the Karmyoga of his Gita became the greatest monument to the success of his search.

Home Rule

Not only in India but in England also, there was widespread opinion that Tilak's imprisonment was a proof that the Government had resolved by hook or by crook to remove him from their path. The 'Manchestor Guardian', 'The Times', 'New Age' were very critical about the 'British justice'. He was released from jail in 1914, the year in which World war I started in Europe. Because of the war, British wanted internal peace in India about which Tilak gave personal assurance but stressed the passive nature of his campaign for Home Rule. Tilak and Mrs. Besant and their co-workers toured all of India. Home Rule Leagues became the effective organizations for the spreading of the new message of politically awakened India. Home Rule was linked to swaraj. Tilak repeatedly said,

> "I said that it was our 'right' to have Home Rule but that is a historical and a European way of putting it; I go further and say that it is our 'Dharma'; you can not separate Home Rule from us, as you can not separate the quality of heat from fire; both are inseparably bound up."

Tilak and Jinnah

During the year Tilak had worked closely with Mohammed Ali Jinnah, one of the prominent young Muslim leaders. As a matter of fact, when the government tried in 1916 again to convict Tilak of preaching seditious doctrines, it was Jinnah who represented him before the court and won his acquittal. Tilak knew that a united India, Hindu and Muslim, could best promote India's cause, and through his efforts the 1916 Lucknow session of the Congress witnessed the development of a common programme with the Muslim League. It is because of Tilak, the organised Muslim community worked with the Congress and demanded equal position to India in the British empire.

Tilak's England Trip Cancelled (1918)

The Home Rule League deputation consisting of Tilak, G.S. Khaparde, B.C. Pal, N.C. Kelkar and R.P. Karandikar wanted to go to England to present to the English people India's case for a more honoured place among the nations of the Empire. Tilak and the company, therefore, left Pune in March, 1918, went to Mumbai, Madras and Ceylon (Sri Lanka) to proceed to England. However, their passports were cancelled and in Ceylon, they were telegraphically informed not to proceed to England since England was waging a great war.

The Chirol Case and Tilak's Visit to England

Sir Valentine Chirol had made defamatory comments in his book, 'Indian Unrest', both about Tilak and about the independence movement in India. To Tilak the most objectionable thing was that Chirol interpreted his actions and writings as a direct or indirect incitement to deeds of violence, and some of his remarks on Tilak's personal character were based on the judgement of Mr. Justice Chandavarkar. Tilak brought a civil suit in London against Sir Valentine Chirol. In fact the suit was nominally against Chirol, in reality it was against bureaucracy. Obviously, Tilak lost the case. The British court feared that Tilak's victory would have amounted to the British withdrawn from India. Tilak lost the case but won many friends for India's cause. He had to spend £400 every day as fees. The fees for studying the brief amounted to £3,000. His experience in England had also convinced him of the value of 'foreign propaganda', of placing India's just case for self-rule before the people of the world. He hoped to see Indian leaders working not only in London but also in Tokyo, Paris and Rome, and he expressed a desire to go himself to the United States to further the cause of Indian independence. He also wanted to go to Paris in 1919, to attend the Paris peace settlement for the conclusion of World war I. He wanted, there, to advocate the application of the principle of national self-determination to India. But the British government refused permission.

Advent of Gandhi

In the meanwhile Gandhi had returned to India from South Africa and was now preparing the country for a non-violent struggle against the Government of India over the Rowlatt Act. He wished Tilak were a satyagrahi. Tilak wrote from London, "We should fully support Mr. Gandhi". Tilak returned to India on November, 26, 1919. He passed away in Mumbai on 1st August, 1920 because of malarial fever and pneumonia.

Legacy of Lokmanya Tilak

Undoubtedly the nation will ever remain grateful to Tilak for the deathless struggle he launched for the deliverance of his countrymen from political bondage and for the endless sacrifices and sufferings he made in the cause of the motherland. Indeed he was largely the maker of the Congress movement, and it was he who brought about a mass consciousness and changed the course of history. He taught the people that they need not humbly submit to alien conceptions of either the purpose of life or the right ordering of life. He reminded the nation of its history and its heritage. This pride in history and in classical values allowed a self-reliant India to grow strong and to take action to bring about a better way of life in accordance with India's own vision of life and the world. Dhananjay Keer, the welknown biographer of eminent leaders, observes, "Tilak was not only the first mass leader of India to rise in revolt in Asia against the British Empire, but also the herald of Asian nationalism who inspired the Asian leaders and nations that were suppressed under the iron heel of western imperialism.

Dr. Sukarno, the Indonesian President, testified to this fact when he said, during the course of a speech at Bombay that he derived inspiration from their freedom struggle from Tilak, Gandhi and Dadabhai Naoroji". This fact was also testified when the then Chief Minister of Maharashtra and later the Dy. Prime Minister of India, Mr. Yashwantrao Chavan stated in a public speech on 1st August 1961 in Pune that the Chief Minister of East Nigeria had told him that they held Tilak and Gokhale in very high esteem. Gandhiji, in his paper, 'Young India' wrote, " Lokmanya Bal Gangadhar Tilak is no more .... No man of our times had the hold on the masses that Mr. Tilak had. The devotion that he commanded from thousands of his countrymen was extraordinary. He was unquestionably the idol of his people. His word was law among thousands. A giant among men has fallen. The voice of the lion is hushed". Jinnah called him a selfless patriot and a unique figure. Maulana Hazrat Mohani said that Tilak was greater than and superior to every other leader in every respect. The Indian and the foreign newspapers were appreciative of Tilak's unique contribution for the growth of Indian nationalism. V.G. Bhat, who accompanied Tilak in his London tour says,

"Sons and daughters of India ! May the example of the Lokmanya inspire you to undertake work entailing service and sacrifice for the uplift of your countrymen and establishing the brotherhood of man all over the world. Do as much as you can unegoistically for these noble causes, in the fullest faith that such selfless work will lead you to God".

3

TILAK : AS THE FATHER OF UNREST

Bal Gangadhar Tilak (29th Couplet) Described by British as "The Father of Indian Unrest" Tilak was born on 23.07.1856. His slogan, "Swaraj (Self Rule) is my birthright", inspired millions of Indians. His book "Geetarahasya" a classic treatise on Geeta in Marathi was written by him, in prison at Mandalay. Great journalist- editor, an authority on Vedas, Sanskrit Scholar, mathematician and a natural leader of India. Died 0 1.08.1920 "Swaraj is our birthright," thundered Tilak, the Lion of India. He founded schools and published newspapers, all for his motherland. He rotted in a distant jail at Manda lay, in Burma. He wore himself out till his last breath, to awaken his countrymen. "If 5 sheep eat up all the grass in a meadow in 28 days, how many sheep will eat up the grass in 20 days?" "Seven sheep, sir," flashed back the answer even before the teacher finished his question. 'Who is it that answered without working out the sum?" Thundered the teacher. Two or three voices shouted, "Bal, sir." The teacher went near Bal. He took his note book and glanced through it. Should he not at least take down the problem, let alone work it out? Where have you worked the sum?" Bal, with a mischievous smile, pointed to his head with his index finger. "You should work the problem in your book," the teacher said. 'Why? I will do it orally," replied Bal. Bal's classmates found it difficult to under- stand certain problems even when the teacher did them thrice. But, to Bal Mathematics was as easy as drinking Water. Sanskrit, of course, was like peeled banana to him! Intelligent But Mischievous Bal's father Gangadhar Ramachandra Tilak was a Sanskrit scholar and a famous teacher. Because of his scholarship, he had become

'Gangadharpant' to every one. Bal learnt all the lessons at home and there was nothing left to learn at school. Though Bal was very intelligent, he was not his teachers' favourite because of his mischievousness.

From his childhood, he used to form independent views. He took an independent stand always. He was very much different from boys of his age. Those were the days of his schooling in the primary school at Ratnagiri. One afternoon the teacher entered the class after the interval and found groundnut shells scattered in the classroom. Naturally he grew angry. He took his cane and asked, "Who scattered the groundnut shells like this?" There was silence. The teacher's anger rose. "Speak, who ate the groundnuts?" No one confessed. The teacher lost his temper. He decided to punish the entire class. He began to give each boy two cuts with his cane. When Bal's turn came, he did not hold out his hand. "I did not eat the ground- nuts. So I will not receive the cuts." "Then who ate the groundnuts?" "It is said that carrying tales is bad. So I won't tell." Bal's straightforwardness and truthfulness made the teacher himself uncomfortable. He became angry, too. He sent him out of the school. And Bal's father Gangadharpant received a complaint against his son. Next day, the father brought Bal to the school. He said that what his son had said was true. Bal was not in the habit of eating anything outside his home and he, the father, never gave his son money to buy anything. Even at that young age it was Tilak's nature to protest against injustice.

Childhood

He liked stories very much. Soon after his studies, he would run to his grandfather to hear stories from him. His grandfather had lived in Kashi during the days of the 1857 Revolution (the first war of Independence). On hearing the stories about the revolutionaries like Nana Saheb, Tatia Tope and Jhansi Rani, Bal would be thrilled. Oh! What great men were they who sacrificed their lives for the country! When he grew up he, too, should serve his country like them and free Mother India from slavery this became his heart's desire. Bal was ten years old when Gangadharpant was transferred to Pune. Coming from Ratnagiri to Pune was a milestone in the life of Bal Tilak.

A New Place and New People

By joining the Anglo-Vernacular School in Pune, young Tilak was able to get good education from well known teachers. Bal's mother passed away only a few months after coming to Pune. Fasts and strict religious observances had made her weak and thin. She wished for a son, and undertook a strenuous from of the worship of the Sun God for eighteen months. The boy who was born by the grace of the Sun God, was instrumental in making the sunset in the British Empire! Bal lost his father also six years after his mothers death. Then he was 16 years old. He was studying in the Matriculation Class. He had been married to a ten-year old girl called Sathyabhama.

At College

Naturally one's responsibility increases after marriage. Now Ball Tilak became 'Bal Gangadhar Tilak'. After passing the Matriculation Examination he joined the Deccan College. His health was delicate as his mothers. How could he sacrifice his life for the country if his body was weak? So, Tilak decided to' improve his physique even at the cost of his studies during the first year at college. He used to do physical exercises every day. And his food was regulated but nutritious. In the course of one year, Tilak was first in all games and sports He became an expert swimmer and wrestler. He developed his body so well that all wondered at such radiant health. In 1877, Tilak got his B.A. degree. It was no wonder that he got first class marks in mathematics. He continued his studies and got the LL.B. degree also.

Dedicated to the Country

Tilak, being a double graduate, could easily have got a well-paid job like others, under the British. But, as he had decided when he was young, he dedicated himself to the service of his country. The concept of Swaraj had yet to blossom in the minds of the people. They had to be made to feel that thirst for independence. Patriotism had to be nurtured. To lay a strong foundation for a new way of life, an educational institution reflecting Indian culture had to be established. Every Indian had to be taught about Indian culture and national ideals. Good citizens can be moulded only through good education. Such were the views of' Bal Gangadhar Tilak. His classmate Agarkar gave him full support. As Tilak and Agarkar were working out the plans for a system of education which Would make students truly useful to the country, another great person, Vishnushastry Chiplunkar, joined them.

The New School—A Banyan Tree

Chiplunkar, himself a teacher, wished that at least the youngcr generations should receive the fight type of education. The people's blind faith that British rule was God's gift to India had to be wiped out. Tilak, Agarkar and Chiplunkar were three persons impelled by the same ideal. They joined hands to create an educational institution to develop moral strength in the pupils. The educational institution planned and founded by Tilak is like a banyan tree. The little seedling planted by him, has grown into a gigantic tree with many branches, and every branch has meant renewed life and a new educational institution. The New English School has now grown into the 'Deccan Education Society'. This society now runs the Fergusson College and the Greater Maharashtra Commerce and Economics College in Pune, the Willington College in Sangli and the Bombay College in Bombay as well as a number of high schools.

As the New English School started in 1880, progressed, attracted larger and still larger numbers of pupils. This was a school which reflected out culture and the ideals of our life and was thus our very own. It was also securing the best results in the examinations. Teachers Were so preparing their pupils for the examinations as to secure all the scholarships for their school. Tilak and his colleagues toiled not a little for the school. During the first year, neither Tilak nor Chiplunkar drew even a rupee as salary.

The World of Journalism

Now Tilak thought of expanding the field of national education. The school imparted education only to the students. It was necessary to bring home to the mind of every Indian the nature of the slavery of Indians. People had fo be organized and the people had to be roused to their condition and duty. Tilak thought that the newspapers were the most effective media. The very next year after the school was started, Tilak started two weeklies. 'Kesari' was the Marathi Weekly and 'Mahratta' was the English Weekly. The newspapers attracted the people. In just two years 'Kesari' had more readers than any Indian language paper. The editorials gave a vivid picture of the people's sufferings and of actual happenings. They called upon every Indian to fight for his right. The language was so sharp as to create in the most cowardly reader the thirst for freedom. Tilak used to say to his colleagues:

"You are not writing for the university students. Imagine you are talking to a villager. Be sure of your facts. Let your words be clear as day light."

Prison

After the death of Rajaram, Maharaja of Kolhapur State, his adopted son Shivaji Rao became the Maharaja. 'Kesari' published articles condemning the cruel way in which the British treated him. When the people came to know of the tyranny of the British, unrest gripped Pune and Kolhapur. The Government filed a case against 'Kesari' (for publishing the facts!). The young editors Agarkar and Tilak were sentenced to 4 months' rigorous imprisonment. Tilak went to the prison with his friend Agarkar.

Farewell to His Own Institution

As the New English School was progressing well, Fergusson College and Deccan Education Society were established. Tilak made a rule that no one should expect more than seventy-five rupees a month as his salary. But other members of the management opposed this. When differences of opinion on this issue became endless, Tilak made over to others the institution he himself had founded. Tilak was filled with immense grief, when he had to resign from the institution which he had started and for which he had toiled day and night for ten years. The weeklies 'Kesari' and 'Mahratta' also brought no profit. Tilak had to find part time work to maintain his family. Never would he work under the British. He started classes to coach students for the Pleaders, Examination.

The Significant Years

The period seven years between 1890, when Tilak left the educational field, and 1897, when he was imprisoned, was very significant in the life of Tilak. During this period, Tilak the Teacher became Tilak the Politician. The director of an institution became a national leader. The exceptional - energy, so far hidden in him, now raced forth in many directions. In seven brief years, he acquired the experience of seventy years.

In addition to the Two weeklies, he was running classes for students of Law. He actually waged a war against the Government for the sake of social reforms. He issued a call for the banning of child marriage and welcomed widow marriage. Through the celebrations of Ganapathi Festival and the birthday of the Shivaji he organized people. He was a member of the Municipal Council of Pune, a member of the Bombay Legislature, and ail elected 'Fellow' of the Bombay University. He was also taking a leading part in the Congress sessions. Added to these, he wrote and published his maiden work 'Orion'. Such were Tilak's achievements in this brief span of seven years.

That Tilak managed to transform the local festivities of Ganesha and Shivaji into national festivals, 'is proof of his organizing ability and shrewdness. If people are to feel in their very blood and bones that they are all one, they should meet often; they should have common ideals and there should be occasions, when they can 'forget all other differences and mingle together joyously. Tilak's plan made these festivities spread to every nook and corner of Maharashtra in a few years.

Government's Celebrations Amidst Corpses

In 1896, famine broke out in India. Tilak pressed the government to relieve the distress of the people at once. He helped the farmers affected by the famine. He collected information about the conditions in every district and published it in the 'Mahratta' and the 'Kesari'. Plague broke out while the people were still in the grip of famine. Tilak opened some hospitals and, with the help of volunteers, looked after the patients. Though the people were in the grip of famine and plague, the government was indifferent. The Viceroy himself said that there was no cause for anxiety. He also said that there was no need to start a 'Famine Relief Fund'! Revenue collection went on as usual. The government's indifference was severely criticized in the articles published in Tilak's papers. They published fearlessly reports about the havoc caused by famine and plague and government's utter irresponsibility and indifference. In the editorials, Tilak made appeals to the people and gave them advice.

He explained to them the 'Famine Relief Act'. He exhorted them to demand relief from the government as their right. "Are you cowards even while you are dying? Can't You gather courage?" So he questioned the people. He gave constructive suggestions to the government to arrest the plague. The government made preparations to celebrate the Diamond Jubilee of Queen Victoria's reign. On one side, people were busy cremating the victims of the plague; on the other side, the governments was busy making arrangements for the Diamond Jubilee Celebrations! At last, the government appointed a Special Plague Officer to arrest the havoc of the plague. His name was Rand and he was more terrible than the plague itself. He sent armed soldiers to make the people vacate the houses which plague had entered. The soldiers forcibly entered the houses and terrified the people with their guns. They admitted to the hospitals some one they could catch no matter whether he was suffering from plague or not. They took the remaining members of the family to distant camps; they burnt all their belongings on the assumption that they carded the infection. Rand Sahib became a worse plague than the plague itself. But, in his own hospitals, Tilak was toiling day and night to save the lives of plague-affected people. 'Has The Government Gone Mad?' A youth, enraged by the senselessness of the government's anti-plague measures, shot the Special Plague Officer Rand dead. The police reacted violently and acts of injustice and cruelty multiplied.

Tilak's Blood Boiled

Under the title "Has the Government gone mad?" Tilak condemned in the 'Kesari' the immoral acts of the govern merit. Tilak's pungent writings made the government tremble. The government came to the conclusion that if Tilak was free it could not survive. By some means or the other Tilak must be locked up behind the bars. The government suspected that Tilak might have had a hand in Rand's murder! It took objection to a poem and an article on Shivaji published in the 'Kesari', and imprisoned Tilak in 1897. Tilak was charged with writing articles instigating the people to rise against the government and to break the laws and disturb the peace. He was sentenced to a year and a half's rigorous imprisonment.

A Lion Even in the Cage

The cells in the jails in those days were actual, hell. The dark cell measured just 13 square feet, and the prisoner could not even turn from one side to another. Thc blanket was full of worms. Mosquitoes were innumerable. The bugs in the bed sucked the prisoners' blood as if to prevent the mosquitoes from flying away with the prisoner. The bread was mixed with sand. The clothes were coarse. Officers whipped the prisoners and mercilessly set them to work. Tilak had to make rope and mats from coir and his fingers got blisters. The fingers that wrote 'Orion', which won praise from great scholars like Max Muller, were made to do dreadful tasks which made them bleed. Tilak lost 30 pounds in weight in just four months. In the little leisure he had he read and wrote. His book 'The Arctic Home in the Vedas' written in the jail, is a priceless work. Scholars and statesmen from all over the world appealed to the government to release Tilak. The government insisted on two conditions to release him: he should not attend any reception arranged in his honour and he should not criticize the government. Tilak was ready to accept the first condition as lie did not desire anything for himself. But he would rather live as an outlaw in the Andamans than live as a coward in Maharashtra, admitting that he had done something wrong when he had not done so. So he rejected the second condition. Finally the government reduced his sentence from one and a half years to a year.

A National Leader

It was Deepavali in 1898; Tilak was released from jail. The joy of the people was beyond words. There were illuminations and fireworks everywhere. There was a heavy rush of people to have 'darshan' of Tilak. He was taken in a procession through the main streets of Pune. People shed tears of joy. Mothers and children worshipped Tilak's portrait in their homes by lighting incense and camphor. Tilak, who was a regional leader, now became the national leader. Every Indian's heart was filled with reverence for Tilak. His sufferings in the jail had made him very weak. His eyes were sunken and the bones in the cheeks protruded. But after his release in a few days his health improved.

The Sacred Word: 'Swadeshi'

At this time, the 'Swadeshi' movement grew intense. (This was a movement for "boycott of goods made in other Countries.) Gokhale, Ranade, Paranjape and others had shown the importance of the swadeshi principle. Through newspapers and lectures, Tilak spread the message to each and every village in Maharashtra. A big 'Swadeshi Market' was opened in front of Tilak's house. Swadeshi goods were sold in the fifty odd stalls of the market. The slogan of swadeshi was heard every where. Foreign clothes were reduced to ashes. Foreign sugar' was thrown away and local jaggery was used. Swadeshi cotton mills, paper mills and factories to manufacture matches were started. The students of Rajaram College, Kolhapur, were to take an examination. They tore the blank books given to them, saying they would not use foreign-made paper. These students were given six lashes cacti as punishment. And they pleaded that they should be beaten only with a local made cane 'Swadeshi, Swaraj (self-rule), Boycott and

National Education'- these were the sacred words preached by Tilak. And the people made weapons of these words. The tendency grew in Indians to defy slavery. Galvanizing people's love of their country was itself a revolution brought about by Tilak.

A Shameless Government

Fourteen years later Gandhiji started the non-cooperation movement against the British. The methods he placed before the people, Tilak had formulated as early as in 1906! During this time, the Government of India and some British newspapers harassed Tilak in many ways. A rich man, Baba Maharaj by name, had died. He had expressed the wish that Tilak should look after his property. So Tilak took charge of it. Baba Maharaj's wife was misled by some selfish persons. She complained against Tilak to the government. The government was waiting for an opportunity to crush a leader who had been fighting against it. It appointed special officers and held a mock trial; 'it decided that Tilak had tendered false evidence and was also guilty of forgery. He was handcuffed like thieves and murderers and sent to prison. Tilak, after coming out of the jail of bail, fought for fourteen years in different courts and finally got justice from the privy Council in England. The Privy Council rebuked severely the courts in India for the way they had tried this case. The 'Globe' of London and 'The Times of India' had writ ten that Tilak incited People to Commit Murders. Tilak did not rest till he made those papers apologize to him.

'The Country's Misfortune'

The British divided Bengal. Then the people of Bengal used boycott itself as powerful weapon. A powerful movement flared up to protest against the division of Bengal. There was a District Magistrate who was the embodiment of injustice. A revolutionary by name Khudiram Bose threw a bomb on him. The government used very harsh methods to break the will of the people. Aurobindo was arrested and taken to the police office in iron handcuffs, with a rope tied to his waist. Any one suspected of trying to use explosives could be sent to prison for 14 years! Such atrocities made the people revolt against the government Tilak's blood boiled. He wrote an article in the 'Kesari' under the title 'The Country's Misfortune' and took the government to task: 'It is unfortunate that bombs are being made in the country. But the responsibility for creating a situation in which it has become necessary to throw bombs, rests solely on the government. This is due to the government's unjust rule.' The British were like a pricked balloon. They concluded that their government would be in danger if Tilak remained free.

Exiled from the Country

The government made this article 'The Country's Misfortune', a pretext to charge Tilak with treason against the government. Tilak was arrested on 24th June 1908 in Bombay. He was sentenced to six year's imprisonment outside India. Tilak was then 52 years old. He had plunged into the struggle for freedom with no thought for his health and had grown weak. Diabetes had further weakened him. How could he withstand this severe imprisonment for six years far away from India? The Country was plunged in grief. Even foreign thinkers condemned this severe punishment to Tilak, who was a scholar, highly respected and honoured throughout the world.

A Scholar And a Hero Even In jai I The prison in Mandalay, Burma; a small room made of wooden planks; inside, a cot, a table, a chair and a bookshelf this was Tilak's room. There was no protection from wind and cold. And he was cut off from other men. By the time Tilak completed one year in this jail, he got a note through one of his friends. The note said that if he accepted certain conditions, then he would be released. Tilak wrote back saying, 'I am now 53 years old. If I live for another ten Years, that means I shall live for five years after I come out of the prison. I can at least spend those five years in the service of the people, if I accept government's conditions, I am as good dead'.

The rigorous imprisonment was reduced to simple imprisonment. So he was allowed to read and write. It was here that he wrote the book 'Gita-Rahasya'. It is a mighty work. Tilak wished to forget his loneliness and so was always immersed in reading and writing. By the time his term of six years in the jail was over, he had collected about 400 books. He learnt in the prison, German and French languages with the help of 'Teach Yourself, guides. He returned to his old daily routine, which he had given up for want of time. Every morning he used to pray to God, chant hymns like the Gayathri Manthra and perform religious rites; then, he would read and write. Tilak's wife passed away in India when he was still rotting in the jail in Mandalay. In India Tilak was released on 8th June 1914. He was brought to Pune on the

16th and was let off. Many organizations in Pune arranged public meetings in honour of Tilak. Tilak said. "Six years of separation from you has not lessened my affection for you. I have not forgotten the concept of swaraj. There will be no change in the programmes I had already accepted. They will all continue as before." By the time Tilak returned from Mandalay, there was a serious rift between the two Congress groups.

His efforts to unite them were in vain. Then Tilak decided to build a separate powerful organization called the '[ionic Rule League'. Its goal was swaraj. Tilak went from' village to village, explained the -aim of his league to the farmers and won their hearts. 'Home Rule' means that we ourselves should manage our homes. Should our neighbour become the master of our house? An Indian should have as much freedom in India as an Englishman has in England. This is the meaning of 'Home Rule' so Tilak explained. He travelled constantly, in order to organize the people. He spoke from hundreds of platforms about 'Home Rule'. And wherever he went he received a hero's welcome.

Swaraj—Our Birth Right

After his visit to Lucknow, he came to Kanpur. 'Swaraj—Our Birth Right' "We want equality. We cannot remain slaves under foreign rule. We will not carry for an instant longer, the yoke of slavery that we have carded all these years. Swaraj is our birth right. We must have it at any cost. When the Japanese, who are Asians like us, arc free, why should we be slaves? Why should our Mother's hands be handcuffed?" Swaraj's alter blazed. The government was again alarmed and troubled. As days passed, Tilak began to stamp the slogan 'Swaraj is our birthright' on the minds of every Indian. Lokamanya Tilak's popularity grew rapidly. Years Old In 1916, Tilak completed sixty years of a fruitful life. Scholars, leaders and friends thronged his house on the occasion of the sixtieth birthday celebrations. Tilak was honoured with the presentation of an Address of Felicitations and a purse of one lakh rupees.

The celebrations were on a grand scale. The Lokamanya gave away the money to be used in the service of the country. The government also gave him a present on the occasion of his sixtieth birthday! On the day before his birthday. The government served him with a notice; it ordered, him to give a surety of Rs. 20,000 for his good behaviour for one year ! His body gradually grew weaker.

His talks and writings were not as fiery as before. Yet he successfully tried to unify the divided Congress.

In England

When a journalist of England by name Chirol, visited India, he studied the movement directed by Tilak and made false allegations against Tilak. He charged that 'Tilak was the leader of a violent revolution in India!' Tilak claimed that this was an insult to him and went to court for damages, He had to go to England for the 'Chirol episode' and had to remain there for 13 months. On account of this, he had to spend his precious time and money. It was not solely for this case that Tilak visited England. His purpose also was to explain to the British government conditions in enslaved India. He addressed hundreds of meetings and intensified the 'Home Rule' movement. He won the friendship of leaders of the Labour Party. The Lion Of India Is No More In 'the World War, the British sought the help of Indians. Victory in the war intoxicated the British and tyranny was let loose in India. When the Rowlat Act was opposed, the 'Jailianwala Bagh Massacre' took place. The heartless government murdered in cold blood hundreds of unarmed civilians in a brutal way.

On hearing this, Tilak rushed back to India at once. He issued a call to the Indians not to stop their movement no matter what happened, till their demands were met. The Lokamanya had become very weak by this time. The body was tired and yet, he undertook tours to awaken the people. He visited Sangli, Hyderabad, Karachi, Sollapur and Kashi and lectured at all these places. Later he came of Bombay. In July 1920, his condition worsened. In the early hours of 1st August, the light went out. Even as this sad news was spreading, a veritable ocean of people surged to his house to have the last glimpse of their beloved leader. Two lakhs of people witnessed his last journey. Mahatma Gandhi, Lala Lajpat Rai, Shaukat Ali and others shouldered the bier by turns. Tilak's was a magnificent life and he was every way worthy of the people's homage. He led a simple life, and offered himself, body and soul, to the service of his country. Tilak had no property. His, clothes were very simple. A dhoti, a shirt, a shawl on the shoulder and a red 'Pagadi' (a marathi cap) on his head - this was all he wore. The Lokamanya's wife Sathyabhama also was very simple like her husband. She never wore costly dress. She spent all her life in working for the family and in looking after guests.

At the time of her death, she longed to see her husband. But that was not to be. Tilak was in the Mandalay jail at that time. Bal Gangadhar Tilak (July 22, 1856-Aug 1, 1920) is recognised as the Father of Indian Unrest.

He was one of the prime architects of modern India and heralded Asian nationalism. His philosophy could not survive after his death as India came under sway of Mahatma Gandhi. He believed that independence is the foremost necessity for the well being of a nation and that to win it extreme measures should not be dispensed with. He was the first intellectual leader to understand the importance of mass support and subsequently became the first mass leader of India. He realized that the constitutional agitation in itself was futile against the British and that, moreover, India was ill prepared for an armed revolt. As a result, although helpful to revolutionaries such as Savarkar, Aurobindo Ghosh and Chaphekar, he did not venture into it himself. Instead, he created and martialled the extremist wing of Indian National Congress. His movement was based on the principles of Swadeshi (reliance on indigenous products), Boycott and Education. Through his own example he gave prestige to imprisonment during freedom struggle. Violent arguments characterised his relationship with social reformists such as Agarkar, Ranade and moderates like Firozshah Mehta. Many blame him for opposing the Age of Consent Bill which raised the age limit for marriage of girls to 12 (from 10). But it is fact that at the same time he had signed a counter-proposal wherein one of the clauses was that the girls (boys) should not be married until they are 16 (20). He educated ail of his daughters and did not marry them till they were over 16. There are instances when he privately paid for the education of women, Still it remains true that he was a reactionary and did not use his considerable influence to give a much needed support to the social reformists. Probably, he did not want to offend the prevalent rigid system - he, himself, having been brought up in the culturally narrow surroundings of Pune. He had several discussions with Shankaracharya of Sankeshwar and asserted that like Swami Vivekananda, the modern Shankaracharya must be educated on modern lines. Tilak received Bachelor of Arts degree from The Deccan College, Pune in 1879 and L.L.B. from the Elphinston College, Mumbai in 1882.

He was among the founders of the New English School, Pune (1881) of which Prof Chiplunkar became the Principal. He had a genius for organisation and with Agarkar, the then foremost social reformist, started the newspapers Kesari and The Maratha in 1881 and in 1890's started the annual celebration of Shivaji Festival and Ganapati Festival which served a platform for people to join in the nationalist movement against the British. Soon he came to be regarded as the undisputed leader of Maharashtra and was honoured with the title Lokamanya in 1893 which became synonymous with him since 1900. As the nation fumed over the partition of Bengal (1905), Tilak assumed the national leadership with his extremist attitude and stated his position unequivocally as "Swarajya (freedom) is my birth right and I shall have it." The next three years saw meteoric rise in his stature and the British power which had long since considered him their chief concern and had sent him to prison twice already, decided on a firmer measure. Much has been said of his trial of 1908. He utilised his time in prison to in scholarly pursuits and wrote Gita Rahasya, a commentary on the Gita. He returned to Indian political scene in 1915. The political situation was fast changing under the shadow of World War 1. Mahatma Gandhi's star was on rise with Satyagraha at Sabarmati in 1914. The British charged Tilak in 1918. He fought those charges both in India and England, and was judged guilty. Amidst rumours of yet another sentence, he headed the Home-Rule commission in England to debate India's constitutional demands while Gandhi was finishing preparations of the first nation wide non cooperation movement. His health continued to deteriorate rapidly at end of July 1920 and he went delirious and was unconscious for 3 days. His last words in the final momentary recovery were, "This happened in 1818 (End of Peshwai) and this in 1918. A hundred years' history - what a life of servitude ... Unless freedom is won, India shall not prosper. It is necessary for our very own existence." At 00:40 on Aug 1, 1920, he was declared dead. It is said that the British made an extraordinary request that his brain be handed over to them so that it could be studied, preserved and exhibited. It was not complied with.

4

TILAK AND DEMAND FOR HOME RULE

Undoubtedly it is Tilak who made the people realise of their fundamental rights by ensuring their active participation in Indian politics against the Raj. The celebration of national festivals in a large scale was another shrewd measure of Tilak to engender in the heats of the people a feeling of oneness, self-respect, and self-sacrifice with a deep sense of national respect and honour. He was also greatly responsible to widen the implications of Swaraj and made it a most sacred slogan for realizing the goal of independence cherished by one and all. He is rightly called the Father of Indian freedom struggle as he dominated the Indian political scene for about three decades. Undoubtedly, Tilak was also the first Indian leader, who planned to make his movement mass-based. He himself went down to the masses dwelling in the remote villages and gave them the message of their rights and implications of the freedom struggle. He became the editor of the Kesari on 22 October 1887 and of the Mahratta on 3 September 1891. With the Kesari he was in his element. A weekly paper and with a circulation of over 35,000, it moulded the national life of Maharashtra.

The Kesari, as the name indicates, stood for manliness, strength. Its style was like the physiognomy of its, illustrious editor, plain, blunt and aggressive. It was 'reason fused and made red-hot with passion.' Tilsit's release in 1914 gave a new twist to the existing nationalist politics of India. It was a common belief earlier amongst the bureaucracy that he would not be able to survive the oppressive sentence he had to undergo in Mandlay.

Though nearly broken in health, he maintained a most formidable spirit which was yet to launch an anti-Raj movement. He was in receipt of numerous messages from his followers and well-wishers from India and abroad.

Tilak-Maharaj-Ki-Jai and Long Live Tilak were the spontaneous slogans of people, who happened to accord him a warm welcome on his release. He declared in an assembly of thousands of people, 'I can only assure you all that separation for six long years could not diminish my love for you and that I am ready and willing to serve you in the same manner, in the same relation and in the same capacity as I did before although I may perhaps have to modify the course a little.'

Pandit Motilal Nehru opined, 'I was always stuck with his remarkable grasp of the intricacies of difficult situations and the clear judgment he brought to bear on the subjects under discussion. I must however confess that I never found myself on the same plane of thought with him."

Mahatma Gandhi reminisced about Tilak thus: 'I admire Lokmanya like millions of his countrymen for his indomitable will, his vast learning, his love of country, and above all, the purity of his private life and great sacrifice. Of all the men of modern times, he captivated most the imagination of his people. He breathed into us the spirit of Swarajya. No one realised the evil of the existing system of government as Lokmanya did .

C.R. Das opined, 'Was Tilak a revolutionary ? Was Lokmanya Bal Gangadhar Tilak, the idol of his people, the implacable foe of the bureaucracy, an anathema to it, the worshipper of Shivaji, the greatest Mahratta since Shivaji, a revolutionary ? A passionate devotion to work, an energy that never wavered or halted, a supreme mastery of details, a grit, an utter callousness to, or disregard of, difficulties or dangers gave indeed to all his action a sharpness and an edge. ... He was by temperament incapable of the big jump, and a spirit that would take what it gets and fight for the rest cannot harbour that restlessness, that impatience, which is at once the habit and instrument of the born revolutionary.] He was conservative by instinct, compromise was the essence of his politics, but he never lost sight of the ideal to which his whole being moved. ... Action gave him the impulse of his life and it bred in him the will to suffer. ... Tilak won and laid the beginning a greater India reborn for self-fulfilment and the service of humanity.

Pandit Madan Mohan Malaviya reminisced about Tilak thus : 'Mr. Tilak made it clear so far back as the beginning of 1907 that self-government on colonial lines sufficed for him as a thing to work for. That was his attitude when he started the Home Rule movement in 1915 and joined hands with Mrs. Annie Besant for its realisation. One may safely say that was his attitude to the last. The means by which he sought to bring about self-government on colonial lines was the creation of a vigorous, clamorous public opinion in India which would not be satisfied until it saw self-government established, and continued agitation in England to make the English people realise the wisdom and justice of helping to establish it."

Rabindranath Tagore greatly praised the services of Tilak :

'He had more faith in Truth than in method. His ideal of the fulfilment of India's destiny was vast, and therefore, it had ample room even for a dreamer of dreams, ever for "music maker". He knew that freedom had its diverse aspects, and, therefore, it could be truly reached if individuals had their full scope to use their special gifts for opening out paths that were diverse in their directions.'

Annie Besant indeed had high opinion for him. 'He was a man filled with passionate and never weakening love for India, for whom every sacrifice for her was joy, every suffering was welcome. No physical bondage could bind that free spirit... In my own relations with him, I found him absolutely straight and loyal to his word."

C. Rajagopalachari stated, 'His plans remind one of Napoleon. He would be in his natural element in the fierce battle-field, amidst blood and ruin, and stand unmoved amidst physical pain and intense suffering. On the other hand Lokmanya Tilak who spoke the doctrine of Force, really could not beat to see a fly hurt, and would break down if he saw any slaughter of human beings whatever might be the end in view. ... His philosophy did not urge asceticism for politicians but he himself was an ascetic and saint as well as politician.

J.M. Sen Gupta stated that he was... a dauntless soldier in freedom's battle... Living a life of solemn consecration, he endeavoured to create in the nation a resolute will to be free and a dauntless determination to face all difficulties and sufferings that a struggle for freedom brings in its train pre-eminity, a man of action, with a supreme capacity for splendid organisation, he taught by his life that it was by action more than anything else that the will of the people could be trained and strengthened.'

M.A. Jinnah opined, 'Mr. Tilak was a shrewd practical politician.... [He] rendered yeoman services to the country and played a very important part in bringing about the Hindu-Muslim unity, which ultimately resulted in the Lucknow Pact in 1916. Subsequently he was one of the pioneers of the Home Rule League movement and established the Indian Home Rule League... He felt that we must work the constitution so far as it went and fight for more. He actually prepared a definite policy and programme of electioneering campaign and advised the people to be ready to see that our best representatives were returned to the various legislatures. ... He was a unique figure both in the political and social life of the country."

T. Prakasam stated, 'It was Lokmanya Tilak that laid the real foundation of Swarajya in India at a time when the rest of the people, educated as well as uneducated, were asleep; that he fully foresaw the trend of events that must follow the causes at work in full force in his day. His teachings and selfless work and devotion were based upon his undaunted courage, unbending patriotism and ungrudging suffering for the freedom of his country...'

In an article published in the Maharatta, Tilak put forward cogent reason for the necessity of the foundation of the Indian Home Rule League. 'It was generally recognized that the time had positively come for an organization to be started for educating public opinion and agitating for Home Rule throughout the country.

The Congress was the body which naturally possessed the greatest authority for undertaking such a work with responsibility. The scheme of self-government which the Congress is supposed to be intending to batch, served as a plausible excuse for most of moderates to negative a definite proposal to establish a Home Rule League. But the' Congress it is generally recognized, is too unwieldy to be easily moved to prepare a scheme for self-government and actively work for its practical success.

The spade work has got to be done by someone. It can afford to wait no longer. The League may be regarded as a pioneer movement and is not intended in any sense to be an exclusive movement. Tilak's speeches amongst the masses of western and central regions of India had direct and homely appeal which made him a hero of the people. His name became a household and this kind of popularity earned him the epithet of Lokmanya revered by the people. He became to be liked, praised rather worshipped like a god. Whenever he happened to tour, he was accorded a right royal reception. Me, on his part, earned their love and affection and appealed to them to imbibe the virtues of fearlessness, sacrifice of any kind and patriotism and advised them to hold out the national hero Shivaji as their model. In a meeting Tilak happened to address at Poona he stated, 'The British just want You to supply soldiers whom they want for the war. They tell us a calamity is hanging over India. What is that to us ? Why 'should we come forward to protect that India in which we have no rights, in which we are treated like slaves ?... Tile bureaucracy has overrun the whole nation; and we are not prepared to become soldiers in order to increase the power of these men. What are we to tell our men? Join the army to strengthen the Zulm of those English people ?' On the occasion of Shivaji Coronation Festival Tilak presided over a lecture on conscription. In his speech, he called the army as mercenary one which consisted of foreigners ready to shoot the people without compunction. At another occasion Tilak observed. 'History and reason are against the difficulties created by the bureaucracy, and we must triumph in the end. Be prepared to say that you are a Home Ruler. Say that you must have and I dare say when you are ready you will get it. There is nothing anarchial in this demand... Home Rule is the only remedy. Insist on your rights. India is your own house.' Tilak defined Swarajya during the course of his speech delivered at Belgaum on Ist May 1916. "What is Swarajya ? Many have a misconception about this. Some do not want it. Thus there are many kinds of People.

The idea of Swarajya is an old one. Of course when Swarajya is spoken of it shows that there is some kind of rule-opposed to swa i.c. ours and that his idea originates at that time. This is plain. When such a condition arrives, it begins to be thought that there should be Swarajya, and men make exertions for that purpose. You are at present in that sort of condition. Those who are ruling over you, do not belong to your religion, race or even country. The question whether this rule of the English Government is good or bad is one thing. The question of one's own and alien' is quite-another. Do not confuse the two, at the outset." For the first time after 1907, extremists happened to attend the session of the Indian National Congress at Lucknow. It was a significant phenomenon to note when 'A Home Rule Special' carried Tilak and the members of his party to the Lucknow Congress in 1916 and when they received unique ovations all along the way.

At Lucknow, their reception all over was proverbial in manner and style. It was indeed a royal reception. The tyres of his car were cut in order to force Reception Committee to plat him in a carriage which was unauthorised and dragged through the main bazars and streets of the town and the wild acclamation of a huge procession. So far so when he arrived at the pandal of the Congress, he was virtually carried on shoulders by his numerous followers and admirers. His speech, which was fairly comprehensive and effective in contents touching upon various crucial political facts of the time, I was greeted with deafening cheers. In supporting the resolution on self-government at the Lucknow Congress.

Tilak severely criticised the bureaucracy in India and put forward demand for self-government." 'We have to get these rights from powerful bureaucracy, an unwilling bureaucracy, naturally, unwilling because the bureaucracy now feels that these rights, these privileges, this authority, will pass out of their hands. I would feel the same if I were in that position, and I am not going to blame the bureaucracy for entertaining that natural feeling. But whatever the character of that may be it is a feeling which we have to combat against; it is a feeling that is not conducive to the growth of self-government in this country. We have to fight against that feeling. When we have to fight against a third party, it is a very important thing that we stand on this platform united, united in race, united in religion , united as, regards all different shades of political creed. That is the most important event of the day. 'Let us glance. As I said, ten years ago when Dadabhai Naoroji declared that Swaraj should be our goal : its name was Swaraj. Later on it came to be known as self-government or constitutional reform and we nationalists style it Home Rule. It is all the same, in three different names. It is said that as there is objection raised that Swaraj has a bad odour in India and Home Rule has a had odour in England we ought call it constitutional reform. I don't care to call it by any name. I don't care for any name. If you style it as A.B.C. reform scheme or X.Y.Z. reform scheme, I shall be equally content; I don't mind for the name, but I believe we have. But I believe you have hardly realised the importance and character of that scheme of reform. Let me tell you that it is far more liberal than the Irish Home Rule Bill, and then you can understand what possibilities it carries with it. It will not be complete Home Rule but more than a beginning of it. It may not be complete self-government but it is a far better than local selfgovernment. It may not be Swaraj in the widest sense of the word, but is far better than Swadeshi and boycott. It is in fact a synthesis of all Congress resolutions passed during the last 30 years, a synthesis that will help us on to proceed to work in a definite, in a certain responsible manner.' In a Home Rule conference held at the Aminabad High School, Lucknow on 30 December 1916, Tilak gave vent to his feelings about the functions of bureaucracy, concept of liberty and on the need of Home Rule for India."

'The fight at present is a triangular light you have to wrest the whole Self-government from out of the hands of a powerful bureaucracy. This body has already commenced to work in order to retain power in its own hands. It is but natural. You would do the same thing yourself if you were in possession. Possession is nine points of law. Bureaucracy in possession is nine points of law. Bureaucracy is in possession of power and why should it part with it ? Rights cannot be obtained by yearly resolutions. There are difficulties in the way of carrying out these resolutions, but These difficulties must strengthen us in our beliefs and in our actions. 'We now want liberty. Similarly, we educate our children and expect them to take our position later on in life. So is the case with Englishmen.

They have united us, they have educated us and they must expect us to take the position we are fit for. History and reason are against the difficulties ,created by the bureaucracy and we must triumph in the end. The only thing that comes in our way is that we are not yet prepared. No shilly, shallying will do. Be prepared to say that you are Home Ruler. Say that you must have it and I dare say when you are ready you will get work for it ? 'Home Rule is the synthesis of all Congress resolutions. Home Rule is the only remedy. Insist on your rights. India is your own house. Is it not ? Then why not manage it yourself ? Our domestic affairs must be in our own hands. We do not want separation from England.' 'The Lucknow Congress in 1916 led to the unity of Tilak and his associates on one side and the moderates on the other.

Besides the Congress and Muslim League jointly sponsored resolutions which had full support of the cause of self-government.

In fact the agreed resolutions aimed at the establishment of provincial autonomy, the provision of election of about four-fifths of the members of central and provincial legislatures, the introduction of the clement of responsibility in not less than half members of executive and foreign affairs in the hand of the central government, and last but not the least, the grant of Dominion Status for India." Over the Muslim representation, it was agreed that they should have separate electorates. While in the centre, their representation was to be one-third, in the provincial level, they should have 50 per cent in Bengal, 25 per cent in Bihar and Orissa, 33.13 per cent in Bombay, 30 per cent in UP, 15 per cent in C.P. and 15 per cent in Madras. With this kind of understanding between the Hindus and Muslims, and moderates and extremists, the tempo of the ,Home Rule Movement was greatly exhilarated. The Kesari observed. 'Friday 29th December, 1916 is a day in India British relations worthy to be written with golden letters.

On that day on the banks of the sacred river Gomati the standard of Indian swaraj was unfurled. The resolution of swaraj passed on that day was an act of historic importance, the aspirations of India were crowned on that day, so I speak, and all her subjects came there to pay their homage to Mother India. Case distinctions, differences of opinion, personal jealousies and everything that was gross and went to destroy the unity of the nation was, finally drowned in the waters of the Gomati and India assumed, a new sacred form. At a very well attended meeting of the citizens of Kanpuron January 1, 1917, Bal Gangadhar Tilak spoke on Home Rule for India as follows" : 'Gentlemen : It is extremely unfortunate that I am not addressing you in your mother-tongue Hindi which claims to be the lingua franca of India. I am sorry for it the more when I see the large crowd that have assembled here to welcome me on this occasion. I am sorry because I am one of those who hold that Hindi should be the lingua franca of India in future. But unfortunately, not being able to speak in Hindi I have thought it fit to address you in English on this occasion, a few words which relate to a subject in which all of us were engaged at Lucknow. Gentlemen, you must have all probably heard that the Lucknow Congress was a memorable Congress, a momentous step being taken therein as regards Home Rule. You will be able to learn that after 30 years of deliberation we have at last come to the conclusion that nothing will save us except Home Rule. As I have said in the Congress, it is a synthesis of all the resolutions hitherto passed to the Congress during the last 30 years. Whatever side you may look at the question from, you will be convinced that the freedom which Home Rule implies is necessary for the regeneration of this country. 'Every thing the moral, material or intellectual sphere of this nation depends upon the freedom which at present we are deprived of. You can not do anything which in your opinion is [calculated to raise your status to that of a civilized nation according to the modern standard. It has been pointed out by more eloquent speakers than myself and men who are entitled to your respect and veneration for more than I am. I say it has been pointed out to me several times that unless we get a part of the freedom for which we are trying, for a part of the power which rests in the bands of the bureaucracy at present, it is impossible for us to attain that position to which we are entitled as a birthright. If you see what is your position at present, if you look around, you will see that you are crippled in every respect. Whether you like the question of industry, whether you take the question of education, or any other question, everywhere there is a stumbling block in your way, so that you have not the power to carry out what you wish. We must be prepared to face this one important question before we can hope to make any progress-progress that is worth the name. Many of the objections of the attainment of Home Rule have already been answered in the Congress and out of the Congress. I would only take ore or two of them because I am afraid that speaking in English I shall not be understood by this large audience and, secondly, because the time at our command is very short. You, who are assembled here to listen to me and to do honour to me well, I think agree that in honouring me you are honouring the cause of Home Rule. The very fact of here to hear a speaker who has devoted some to this question shows that you are all interested in that important question. They say that there is no public opinion in India in favour of Home Rule. This is a proposition which if our opponents were here will find contradicted by the presence of you all. I do not think that you have come here to respect my person but I think you have come here to respect the cause of Home Rule : and a very large gathering like this a splendid refutation of the objection that we are not prepared for Home Rule, that we are unable to exercise influence over the masses in this country, that we can take no interest in it and that it will take several decades of years if not hundreds of years according to our opponents to render us fit for Home Rule. 'This meeting is in itself, as I said, a refutation of the charges that are brought against us. Another objection that is raised is that we Hindus never enjoyed Home Rule.

Nothing can be more incorrect more erroneous and false, I may say, than a statement like this. Many of you in Northern India enjoyed Home Rule in ancient days. The Hindu polity which is included in the King's duties in the Manusmriti text lays down a kind of social organization which is known-at Chatur Varna. Many of you now believe that Chatur Varna consists merely of different castes. That divide us at present. No one thinks of the duties belonging to these castes. A Kshatriya will not take food with Brahmin and a Brahmin will not take food with a Vaishya and a Vaishya will not take food with a Sudra. It was not so, let me point out, in the days of Manu and Bhagvatgita. Bhagvatgita expressly states that this division was not by birth but by the quality and by the profession which were necessary to maintain the whole society in those days. The Kshatriyas defended the dominion and defended the people against foreign aggression and against internal interruptions. Where are those ? The whole of that class is gone off and their duties devolve upon the British who have taken charge of the duties of Kshatriyas.

'Take again commerce. You think this is a commercial town. There are many labourers but you find that the country is exploited for the benefit not of India but of other nations. Raw products are exported and refined products are brought in to the sacrifice of several industries for which India was famous in ancient times. See the Vaishya class-that too is now being dominated by the British people or British merchants. Take the Brahmins, I am a Brahmin. We boasted that we were the intellectual heads of the community, we were the brain in fact-but that brain is now rendered so dull that we have but to import into this country foreign philosophy at the cost of our ancient learning in every department of life. What I consider is that Chatur Varna divides the whole society into so many departments of life and every one of these departments you have been a loser every year every decade. 'I want you now to recognize this fact and to try for gaining the position which we occupied in our own society. We have been deprived of volunteering, we have been deprived of the right to the higher grades in service.

The men remain, but the duties are gone and all your feeling at present is that I am a Kshatriya and you are a Brahmin and that he is a Sudra. All have lost their titles. I am not partial to one or other. I want you to realise the fact that although you may claim the blood of Kshatriya although you may claim the blood of a Brahmin, you do not claim that polity, those qualifications which the Sudras are enjoying which should have been yours at this moment. Now one aspect of Home Rule is to encourage you to acquire the freedom which you enjoyed in these various departments of life and to come up to that standard by the co-operation of and under the sovereignty of the British rule. 'This result is not to be achieved by any unlawful and 'unconstitutional means, but I am sure by a desire and interest to raise your status to achieve this goal by means of the sympathy of the British people and by remaining a permanent part of the Empire.

But this part is of two kinds. In a household, servants from part of a household and children from part of a household. We went to occupy 'the part of children and not to servants not a dead part but an equal part in that greatest Empire which the world has seen. We are quite willing to remain a part but not a dead part which will be a burden to the Empire but a living member, and a living member is expected to develop all the qualities which you find in the department of social life. It is with this view, gentlemen, that the Home Rule agitation had been started to make you masters in your house and not servants. This is the real sense of that situation which every one is bound morally and intellectually to attain. 'Home Rule is nothing else, but to be masters of your houses. Have you ever thought of such a simple question, what am I in my house-am I a dependent or am I master ? And if India is your house, I want to ask you gentlemen whether there can be any ground or reason to tell your that you ought not to be masters so far as your domestic affairs are concerned. 'When an Englishman has been deprived of his'right he will not be content unless he gets back his rights. Why should you lag behind, why should you not in the name of religion, in the name of polity, in the name of the polity which was cultivated in the past to the largest extent the history of the world has yet produced in the name of that philosophy that is religious, I appeal to you to awaken to your position and do your birth-right—I mean the right of managing your own affairs in your own home. If you do not do it, who will do it for you ? Do not be hypnotised. You are fit for it, only you have not seen it. You can get your object by your own efforts, by your own action, and this is the self-realization that I want you to feel. If you once realise that you are the master of your domestic affairs as other men are, as in the colonies and as men in the other parts are, I dare say nothing can stand between you and your object to attain it. It all depends upon your efforts. In Lucknow and Kanpur you will find better men very soon addressing you on this subject, and if I can prepare the ground for the noble workers that are to come hereafter, I shall not have spoken in vain to day. It is a thing which you must look to now. 'Give up apathy. You are as good men as members of any other community in the world. You have hands and feet and you know what has been said in one of Shakespear's dramas.

We are certainly better than Japanese and yet Japan has attained what you seem hopeless to attain and are indifferent to aspire to get. Your fault lies not in the want of the will. You have not cultivated that will which you ought to have one. Will-power makes it as strong as you can and the material world round you cannot drive you from attaining the object which you will attain. You must make up that will and if that is made up by every community there is a proverb in my part that the divine power resides in five persons. Instead of 5 let me now change that 5 into 500 million; and if you realise the fact that you have a certain, object to get that, you must attain to a particular stage to which you are entitled as birth-right. You must say that this will so strengthened, can resist the forces that are arrayed against you. It is the will you have not been thinking over. You do not devote to it one moment of your life, one moment during the day. A Brahmin is, for instance, enjoined in the Shastras to perform his prayers once in the morning and once in the evening. What is that prayer ? It is the cultivation of the will. Now let your prayer be, 'I will try to have my birth-right'. 'Have that prayer every morning and evening. Do not forget it during all the work or business that you do during the day.

If there are temptations in your way repeat that prayer in the morning and evening. Prayer has such a power as to surmount all obstacles; that is the effect of prayer. It is no use praying merely for nothing. God does not want prayer for himself, God does not need it. God does not want any praise from you-it is all useless.

Realise that fact. What is the good of praying without any object. God has created you, God knows how to conduct his own creation. Do you mean to say that by your praying you cannot change the course of events of Karma ? Do pray morning and evening for Home Rule and I dare say that within a year or two you can attain your object. 'Thanking you for your reception I close my remarks on the Subject; and if any of you have not understood me because I have spoken in English, then some one of the gentlemen on the platform will undertake to repeat that for you, and I ask your pardon not to have been able to address you in your own words.' At Yeotmal, Tilak clarified a few significant points about Home Rule Movement. 'We tell the Government that we are no longer minors, nor are we lunatics, and we are able and competent to look after our affairs, our "home" and we will rule the "home"; we have got a right to say that we want this agent or that and we will guide the "Home policy".

This demand for "Home Rule" is not a new one; Congress and the other older and younger institutions in the country have been demanding it. 'Our opponents say we are not fit; but that is not true, Every one who is an adult and not a lunatic is fit to manage his house. We may commit mistakes in the beginning; but who is so perfect as to be beyond human feelings ? Even great men err. We want the right to commit mistakes also; we will commit mistakes and ourselves rectify them even the great Avatars commit mistakes. The Government does not Jay down any standard of fitness; if they will Jay down any, we will try to attain that standard. Government are not at all definite; those who ask us to be first fit and then demand Swaraj have no mind to give it to us at all. It is as good as to ask a boy to learn swimming and then to go into the river. You cannot separate Home Rule from us, as you cannot separate the quality of "heat" from fire; both are inseparably bound up, let your ideas be clear; let your motives be honest; let your efforts be strictly constitutional, and I am sure your efforts are bound to be crowned with success; never despair, be held and fearless and be sure that God is with you. Remember "God helps those who help themselves." In a largely attended public meeting at Akola in January 1917, Tilak expressed his feelings about the Home Rule for India thus. 'The ideal of Home Rule has passed through trials and ordeals, and stands today perfectly vindicated as both loyal and practical. It is now conclusively proved that the gain of the one is the gain of both, and in India's Self-government lies the future stability and safety of the British Empire. Since Home Rule became an ideal vindicated in courts of law as legal and loyal, it had to proved by arguments that India stood in immediate need of it, that India should demand it,, that the demand was justified by defects in the method of the working of the existing mode of Government which could not be remedied except by Self-Government and that it was also proved that we were fit for receiving and handling the rights of Swaraj when they came to us. "Self-Government as I told you, means Representative Government in which the wishes of the people will be respected and acted upon and not disregarded, as now, in the interests of a small minority of civil servants.

Let there be a Viceroy and let him be an Englishman if you like, but let him act according to the advice of the representatives of the people. Let our money be spent upon us and with our consent. Let public servants be really servants of the public and not their masters as they at present are. 'None will be more unlucky and unfortunate than yourselves if you lag behind at this critical moment. You have the ideal of Swaraj, you have the legal methods to work for it, and you know what the ideal means. The Almighty helps you in His inscrutable Divine ways by offering a unique opportunity. Now it is for you to say whether you will answer by vigorous efforts or sit silent and let the opportunity slip through your fingers. By allowing this golden opportunity escape, you are incurring the just blame of those that will be borne hereafter. Your daughters and sons will be ashamed of you and future generations will curse you. Take courage, therefore, and work now. Strike the iron whilst it is hot and yours shall be glory of success.' The following is the text of the speech delivered by Bal Gangadhar Tilak on 7th October 1917 in the compound of the Home Rule League, Allahabad under the presidentship of Mrs. Annie Besant. 'Every one knew what Home Rule meant. Home Rule was nothing but to have the management of their home in their own hands. That was simplest definition that, could be given of the word. There was absolutely nothing to, say why they wanted Home Rule. It was their birthright. Some people had been managing their affairs for them now, and they wanted that management should be transferred to their hands. They were entitled to that right and the burden of proving that they were not entitled to it lay on the other party. Home Rule was not a new expression. It was an expression that had a definite meaning and we should not misunderstand it. All that they asked for was not a change in their rulers of this country and the administrators who had been appointed or selected under the Government of India Act. His view was entirely different. Those were not the rulers in the strict sense of the word. They represented the King but they were not the King. The Indians also represented the King because they were his subjects just as much as those officers. So in the matter of representing the King the Indians and those officials stood on equal basis. What then was there more in the position of there officers which made them say that they were the real rulers ? That was that certain powers had been given to them-they had not usurped those powers-under a Statute of Parliament. If another Statute of Parliament repealing that Statute and giving the Indians those powers was passed the Indians would be what those officers were at present. That was Home Rule and nothing more. There would be no change in the Emperor, absolutely no change in the relations of India with England or in the relations of India with the Empire as a whole. What was there to complain of in this except that some men would lose their trade ? If the power was transferred from one man to another the man to whom it was transferred would gain and the other would lose and if that other man be angry it was natural.

He did not think that any English politician would be deterred by such things for a moment from doing his duties. 'Ten or fifteen years ago to talk of Home Rule was sedition and people were afraid, he himself was afraid, of talking about Home Rule. But now it was contended both by the judiciary and the executive that Home Rule was a proper ambition for a dependency to entertain. Ten years of fighting was thus required to remove this prejudice against Home Rule, and now they could talk about it as a legitimate aspiration. The Viceroy,)he Premier, the British nation and even the bureaucracy 'now agreed with them. Now what remained ? They said that it was a very good ambition for a dependency; but there was time for it. They said that it would take centuries to attain it, and instances were cited of a number of colonies which attained self-government in 50 or 60 years. His reply to it was this. The colonies, it was true, had attained selfgovernment in 50 or 60 years, but Indians were being ruled for 100 years, and they had not yet attained self-government. There must be a ,time limit fixed by the bureaucracy. The bureaucracy said that it was not in sight at present; he would say that this was an entirely selfish argument. What was it that was far from attaining the goal within a few years after the war when the empire would be reconstructed ? At present India was nothing but a stone in the neck of the empire. They knew on what principle the bureaucracy governed India for the last 100 years. They were a self-governing nation before. They knew how to organise an army, they knew how to dispense justice, they had laws, regulations, etc. All those have been swept away and now the bureaucracy said that they knew nothing about them. Who was responsible for that ? Not the Indians. When they came here their first care was-he gave credit to them for it-to reduce the disorders prevailing then. How was it done ? Firstly, by disarming them. Next all the principal posts in the administration were monopolised by them. Next there was a check to scientific progress, and industries gradually disappeared. But, they said, they restored peace. That was true, but peace was not everything. It was an introductory condition to further development. They had restored peace, they had given railways, telegraphs and other things. All credit to the bureaucrats for these things, but he could not give credit to them for doing anything which would develop their national instinct. They had not done anything which would enable them to stand on their legs. The result was when in the name of the empire they were asked to taken up arms and fight the enemy they found that so few men volunteered. What was it that made them incapable of assisting the Empire to the extent that they wished to do ? It was the system of administration followed by the bureaucracy. They bad governed them in such a way that unless radical improvement was made in the system of administration, the Empire would gain no material strength from this country. It was this thought that had actuated the best English statesmen to come forward and say that the system of administration in India must be revised after the war. 'From the time of Mr. Dadabhai Naoroji up to now they had been crying that they had been deprived of the powers of administration and they should be restored to them. Now the British democracy had clearly seen that there was much force in their cry of reform and they were willing to hear their cry. Now the question was whether the bureaucracy should have a say. There was a judge and he had given notice that he was coming here and would hear what the Indians would have to say. Therefore they must press their demand more strongly than their opponents. That was their duty at present. They had to convince him that all arguments used against them were due to prejudice. The great work before them at present was to educate the people to realize what Home Rule was, He would impress on them the supreme necessity of doing their best for getting Home Rule. They must wake up. If they made strenuous efforts then within a year or two they would realize, if not all, at least a part of their wishes. They did not want Home Rule at once; but they wanted a real beginning, and not a shadow beginning. When Mr. Montagu came here he would speak to their leaders about their demand and he wanted that they should have the solid support of the country behind them. If that was done Mr. Montagu would carry their message to the British people and effectively support it with the authority of his office.

It is quite clear from Tilak's ideology that he was determined to take full advantage of the government's involvement and helplessness in the war. He was not to wait the conclusion of the war. So far so he sent Joseph Baptista to London on 14 July 1987 with the advice to propagate the ideal of Home Rule on the basis of the Congress-League Scheme. Tilak travelled over two thousand miles and collected about fifty thousand rupees. With his weak ailing physique, he delivered as many as thirty-two speeches which were largely attended. He once remarked, 'People cannot possibly realise that I feel so weak. When the moment comes I make a speech. But the body is all the while under the strain. The speech over, I return from the crowds and sleep over my fatigue. Only my will to live sustains me.' 'Home Rule is my birthright ... There are higher powers that rule the destiny of things and it may be the will of Providence that the cause I represent may prosper more by my suffering than by my remaining free.' For the success of his Home Rule Movement, Tilak was fairly mobile. His movements tinged with propaganda work for the movement covered a huge area in north India. The terrible unrest in the Punjab engendered by the anti-government activities by the workers of the Ghadar party had made the whole administrative machinery much engaged in establishing law and order. At this point of time Tilak intended to enter the Punjab for the political propaganda work amongst the people, and when the government got the information that Tilak had planned to inaugurate a branch of the Home Rule League in the Punjab, it at once issued a notice to him under the Defence of India Consolidation Rules 1916 prohibiting his entry in the Punjab. Similarly the police chief of Delhi prohibited the entry of Tilak in the city. The personnel sufferings of Tilak during the long drawn political battle against the Raj were phenomena].

He had to face prosecution and hardships in the jail. 'He made life in jail for the political leaders in subject India an honourable and unavoidable service. His sufferings made blunt the edge of the hardships of jail life of political prisoners in India, and he served as the leader of mappers and miners in the life of the national army of Swaraj. By his ceaseless actions, his fearlessness, his selflessness, he infused courage into a generation that came forward to follow him, to support him, and to die for the cause of the motherland. Undoubtedly Tilak was a born rebel and his impatience with the prevailing structure of foreign rule made him raise the banner of revolt during his life. His relations with the revolutionaries was cordial although he did not participate in their violent activities. He opined that an armed revolt was also constitutional provided it was result-oriented. He had much sympathy with Senapati Bapat, Wasudeo Chapekar and other leaders engaged in revolutionary activities. He in fact strove hard to galvanise the Congress into a militant constitutional movement. By his incessant linkage with the hectic political activities, Tilak had endeared himself so much amongst the people that he was called by them Lokmanya i.e. adored by the people.

Whereas Valentine Chirol described him as the 'Father of Indian Unrest', C. Vijayaraghavachariar called him, 'a great son of India whose manhood was a life of selfless suffering in our country's cause in a spirit of dedication rarely surpassed in the annals of national struggle for freedom.' Tilak used his paper, the Kesari as the best organ for the propaganda of his political creed. Through his writings in it, he could influence a major portion of the population in the ,western region. He apprised the people of their fundamental rights and enjoined on them to prepare themselves for the grim battle of freedom. He wrote that the only way to settle the Indian problem was a proclamation by the King of England declaring that the ultimate object of the British government was to grant swaraj to the people of India and that the first fundamental step by the government should be to grant it after the war. Time and again, Tilak told the British bureaucracy that his countrymen were trying in India as the Irish Home rulers have been doing in Ireland, for a reform of the system of administration. His main argument centred round the idea that if Ireland could put a fight for their demand of Home Rule, why could a similar demand be not put forward by Indians. In this regard he wished to get a parliamentary bill moved so that Indians could manage their domestic affairs in a better shape. By doing so, he did not wish to severe ties with the British Empire, but he propagated swaraj within the Empire. The government watched the political propaganda made by Tilak amongst the masses with doubt and suspicion. Plans were made to muzzle his Home Rule propaganda. So in July 1916 a case was instituted against Tilak for certain seditious speeches which he had delivered during his tour of various regions. On 22 July 1916, an order was passed by the District Magistrate, Poona under sections 108 and 112 Criminal Procedure Code requiring Tilak to show cause why he should not be ordered to execute a bond for the sum of Rs. 20,000/- with two sureties each in a sum of Its 10,000/- to be of good behaviour for a period of one year.

In pursuance of this order, Tilak was bound down on 12 August 1916 for a period of one year and was to enter into a bond in a sum of Rs. 20,000/- with two securities, each in a sum of Rs. 10,000/- in consequence of certain speeches delivered by him on the Ist, 21st May and Ist Junc 1916. On appeal by Tilak, the High Court Bombay reversed the order of the District Magistrate, Poona ordering Tilak to execute a bond to be of good behaviour. These pinpricks did not cripple the political activities of Tilak, rather he continued his work with great-enthusiasm and patriotic fervour.

Tilak's Home Rule

Belgaum Speech

(The lecture below was delivered immediately after the meeting held under the auspices of the Historical Research Society, on the Ist May, 1916. Rajamanya Rajushri Dada Sahib Khaparde presided.) When I was requested to deliver a lecture here today, I did not know what to lecture. I do not stand before you today in any way prepared for any particular subject. I had come for the Conference. Thinking that it would not be out of place if I were to say a few words to you about those subjects which were discussed during the past few days and about the objects with which a Home Rule League was established here before Congress, I have selected that subject for today's lecture. What is Swarajaya ? Many have a misconception about this. Some understanding it, misrepresent it. Some do not want it.

Thus there are many kinds of people. I am not Prepared today to enter into any particular discussion of any sort beyond saying a few general words on the following among other points : What is Swarajya ? Why do we ask for it ? Are we fit for it or not ? In what manner must we make this demand for Swarajya of those of whom we have to make it ? In what direction and on what lines are we to carry on the work which we have to I carry on? It is not the case that these general words which I am going to say are the outcome of my effort and exertion alone. The idea of Swarajya is an old one. Of course when Swarajya is spoken of it shows that there is some kind of rule opposed to Swarajya, i.e. ours and that this idea originates at that time. This is plain. When such a condition arrives it begins to be thought that there should be Swarajya, and man make exertions for that purpose. You are at present in that sort of condition, Those who are ruling over you do not belong to your religion race or even country. The question whether this rule of the English Government is good or bad is one thing. The question of One's own and alien is quite another. Do not confuse the two at the outset. When the question 'alien', or 'once's own ?' comes, we must say 'alien'. When the question 'good or bad' comes, we may say 'good, or we may say 'bad'. If you say 'bad', then what is the improvement that must be made in it ? this question is different. If you say 'good' it must be seen what good there is under it which was not under the former rule. These are different points of view... Formerly there was Rajput rule, in some places there was Hindu rule and in some places there was Maratha rule-were these Swarajya good or bad ? I again remind you that this is a question different from our theme. We shall consider it afterwards. All other rules being broken up, the universal sovereignity of the English Government has been established in India. Today we have not to consider the history of other's downfall. We have also not to consider how they fell. Nor am I going to speak about that. Let us turn to the present system of administration. Some able men who have been educated in

English and have received college education there come to India and the State administration of India is carried on through them. 'Emperor' is a word. When you give a visible form to the sentiment which arises in your mind at the mention of the word Raja i.e., King, there is the present Emperor. This sentiment itself is invisible something there is the King-the Emperor. But the Emperor does not carry on the administration. The question of Swarajya is not about the Emperor, nor about this invisible sentiment. This must be remembered at the outset. Let there be any country, it must have a King, it must have some men to carry on its management and there must be exercised some sort of rule in it. The case of anarchical nations is different. These nations can never rise. As in a house an outsider is brought in as a trustee-just so is the case also with a kingdom. In every country there is a certain body for carrying on its administration and there is some sort of arrangement, An analysis must be made of both these things, viz., of this arrangement and this body and, as stated yesterday by the President (the President of the Provincial Conference), of the sentiment of 'King'? There must be a king, there must be state administration. Both these propositions are true from the historical point of view. Of a country where there is no supervising body, the Mahabharat says : A wise man should not live even for a moment at that place. There is no knowing when at that place, our lives may be destroyed, when our wealth may be stolen, when our house may be dacoited, may, set on fire. There must be a government. I will not say at length what there was in the Kritayuga in ancient times. The people of-that time did not require a King. Every one used to carry on business looking only to mutual good. Our Puranas say that there was once a condition when there was no king. But if we consider whether such a condition existed in historical times it will appear that such a condition did not exist. There must by some control or other. Control cannot be exercised always by all people assembling together at one place. Hence, sovereign authority is always divided into two parts : one the Advisory body, and the other executive body. The question about swarajya which has now arisen in India is not about the said invisible sentiment. The question is not about those who are to rule over us, (and) according to whose leadership, by whose order and under whose guidance, that rule is to be exercised. It is an undisputed fact that we should secure our own good under the supervision of the English nation, with the help of the English nation, through their sympathy, through their anxious care and through those high sentiments which they possess. And I have to say nothing about this (cheers). Note this first. Do not create confusion in your minds by confounding both the aspects. These two aspects are quite distinct. What we have to do we must do with the help of some one or another, since today we are in such a helpless condition. It is an undoubted fact that we must secure our, good under protection. Had it not been for that, your independence could would never have gone. If we take for granted that we have to bring about the drawn of good with the help of the English Government and the British Empire, then one more strange thing which some people see in this, will altogether disappear. To speak in other words there it no sedition in this. If then with the English Government-if the words "invisible English Government" be used for the words "English Government," there would be no mistake-if with the help of this invisible, English Government, with the aid of this invisible English Government, you are to bring about the dawn of your good fortune, then, what is it that you ask ? This second question arises. The answer to it, again, lies in the very distinction of which I spoke to you. Though a Government may be invisible, still when it begins to become visible, the management of that kingdom is carried on by its hands and by its action. This state of being visible is different from invisible Government, If you ask how, I say in the same manner as the great Brahma is different from Maya. I have taken the word visible and invisible from Vedanta (Philosophy). The great Brahma which is without attributes and form is different and the visible form which it assumes when it begins to come under the temptation of Maya is different. Hence these dealings which are due to Maya are sure to change. What is the characteristic of Maya ? It changes every moment. One Government will remain permanent (viz.) invisible Government; and the visible Government changes every moment. The word Swarajya which has now arisen relates to visible Government. Maintaining the invisible Government as one, what change, if effected in the momentarily changing visible Government, would be beneficial to our nation ? This is the question of Swarajya. And this being the question of Swarajya, there arises the further question : In whose hands should be the administration carried on in our India ? We do not wish to change the invisible Government-English Government. We say that the administration should not be in the hands of a visible entity by whose hands this invisible Government is getting work done, but should pass into some other's hands. The Swarajya agitation which is now carried on is carried on in the belief that this administration if carried on by some other hands or with the help of some one else, or some other visible form would be more beneficial to the people than when carried on by those whose hands it is now carried on. Let us take a parallel. There is an Emperor in England. An English Act contains the rule that the king commits no wrong. The king never commits a wrong (offence). His authority is limited in such a manner that he has always to be advised by a minister. The Prime Minister acts on his own responsibility. There may be a good many people here who have studied English history. This is the British constitution. When this principle was established in English History, the number of sedition cases began to fall. Here in India, we have the administrators instituting cases of sedition. Those who carry on the administration are different and the king is different. The king is one and the same. But the minister changes every five years. It would not be sedition if any were to start a discussion advocating a change of ministry. It happens every day before the eyes of the English people. The king's ministers go out of office after five years, go out of office after two years : they may quarrel among themselves as they like. What is that to the king ? He is the great Brahma Without attributes ? He is not affected by this. The Swarajya agitation now existing in India is then about change in such a ministry. Who rules in India ? Does the Emperor come and do it ? He is to be taken in procession like a god on a great occasion, we are to manifest our loyalty towards him. This is our duty. Through whom, then, is the administration carried on. It is carried on through those who are now servants (viz.) the State Secretary, Viceroy, Governor, and below him the Collector, the Patel and lastly the police sepoy. If it be said that one Police sepoy should be appointed would that constitute sedition ? If it be said that the Collector who has come is not wanted and that another is wanted, would that constitute sedition ? If it be said that one Governor is not wanted, another Governor should be appointed, would that constitute sedition ? If it be said 'This State Secretary is not wanted, bring another' would that constitute sedition ? Nobody has called this sedition. The same principle which is applicable to a Police sepoy is also applicable to the State Secretary. We are the subjects of the same king whose minister the State Secretary is and whose servant he is. This then being so, if any one were to say, "this State Secretary is not wanted, this Viceroy is not wanted. Fuller Sahab is not wanted in Bengal-such resolutions have often been passed in the case of Governors, not in the present but in the past time and were to give reasons for that, you may say about him that his head must have been turned and that the reasons he gives are not good or sufficient. But from the historical point of view, it does not follow that when he says so, that constitutes sedition (cheers). Our demand belongs to the second class. It is concerned with swarajya. Consider well what I say. If you think that the present administration is carried on well, then I have nothing to say. In the Congress and Conferences that are now held you come and say : "Our Kulkarni Vastan has been taken away, solum has been exercised upon us in connection with the Forest Department, liquor has spread more in connection with the Abkari Department, also we do not receive that sort of education which we ought to get." What is at the root of all this ? What is the benefit of merely saying this ? Why do you not get education ? Why are shops of the Abkari Department opened where we do not want them ? In the Forest Department, laws about reserved forests and about forest of this sort or of that sort are made. Why there they made ? At present, lists upon lists of grievances come before the Congress. Why was jury abolished against your will ? Why was no college opened in the Karnatic up to this time ? All these questions are of such a kind that there is but one answer to them. At present what do we do ? Is there no College ?—petition to the Collector or to the Governor, because he has power in his hands. If this power had come into your hands, if you bad been the officials in their place, or if their authority had been responsible to the public opinion, these things would not have happened. No other answer than this can be given to the above. These things happen because there is no authority in your hands. The authority to decide these matters is not given to you for whose good this whole arrangement is to be made. Hence we have to ask like children.

quite a third thing. The villager threw away the sheep. The men took it away. Our condition is like that. The story relates to human nature. There are among us people who are just like them. Why are we not fit ? Because fitness has not been created in us. We have not done it, our parents have not done it. We have not got such powers. But the Government has given you some powers in the Council. Sinha and Chaubal are in the Council. In the Executive Councils of other places also there are selected people. When these people were selected for appointment, did any one ever say, "We are not fit, do not give us the post." No one said it, (Cheers). What then is the use of saying so to our meeting ? I should concede these people were speaking true, if when the bureaucracy actually confers some great powers on them, they stand up and say "We do not want them, we are not fit for them-the Brahmins alone must some and perform Shraddha at our house, we cannot perform it." I think that those men who say things because such and such a person would like or would not like and bring forward excuses for that purpose, exhibit their own nature (cheers) 'Why are we not fit ? Have we no nose, no eyes, no ears, no intellects ? Can we not write ? Have we not read books ? Can we not ride a horse ? Why are we not fit ? As a Jew in one of Shakespeare's dramas asked, I ask you what have we not ? You have not discharged your work. If it is not given at all, when are you to discharge it ? (Cheers) Has it ever happened that we did not do work when it was given ? No one did say, we are unfit, do not appoint us. You appoint them. 'You get work done by them' and afterwards it is also announced in a Government Resolution. 'He has done his duty and so on.' If go further we may as 'You bring from England quite a new man of 21 years. What can he do ? Has he any experience at all ? He Comes all at once and straightaway becomes Assistant Collector, and becomes the superior of a mamlatdar though the latter be 60 years old. What is the comparison ? (cheers) Is 60 years' experience of no value ? A man of 21 years comes and begins to teach you. Generally be makes this

Mamlatdar of 60 years stand before him. He does not give him even a chair for sitting, and this poor man stands before him with joined hands because he has to get Rs. 150, 200 or 400 (cheers). How then is the Saheb to acquire experience, how is he to become fit, and how is the work to go on ? Has any one thought about this ? Had it been true that the people of India are not fit for swarajya and that they would not be able to keep kingdom in good order, then Hindus and Mohammedans should never have governed kingdoms in this country in ancient times. Formerly there were our kingdoms in this country. There were administrators. The proof of this is that before the advent of the English Government, in this county there was at least such order, the was no disorder everywhere and man did not kill another. Since there existed such order, how can it be said that the people are not fit for self-rule., Today science has made progress, knowledge has increased, and experience has accumulated in one place. We must have more liberty than before, and we must have become fitter. On the contrary it is said we are not fit. Whatever might have been the case in former times, this allegation is utterly false now. Better say, we shall not give you. What I say is, don't' apply the words 'not fit' to us. At least we shall know that we are not really to be given. We shall get it. But why do we do not get it ? It is indirectly said that we are not fit. They say it is teach us that they have come here. This is admitted. But how long will you teach us ? We ask (laughter). For one generation, two generation or three generations.' Is there any end to this ? Set some limit. You come to teach us. When we appoint a teacher at home for a boy we ask him within how many days he would teach him-whether in 10, 20 or 25 days, within two months, within four months. But if the study which should take six months for the boy to finish, would, he were to say contrary to our expectation, take one year, we tell him you are useless, go, we shall appoint another teacher (cheers). This applies to all people alike. Our officers have control over the people's education and it is their duty to improve them : this duty points one way, their attempts points another way. They say that whatever attempts they make it is impossible for the people to become fit for work. We say our people are men like you, as wise as you. You take them in service, get work done by them. Your strictness is proverbial. What is going on in the Khalsa territory ? There is no obstruction in the management. It is obstructed in Mysore ? Who are doing the work. The king of Mysore is a Hindu, the minister is a Hindu, the subjects are Hindus, the lower officers are Hindus. They carry on the administration of such a large kingdom as Mysore, but it-is said that the people of the two districts beyond Mysore cannot carry it on in that manner. (Laughter, cheers). There are six districts in Mysore, but it is said that the people of the two districts beyond Mysore cannot carry it on in that manner. (Laughter, cheers). There are six districts in the Mysore territory, hence, it is like saying that six are fit and eight are not fit. There is fitness in us beyond any doubt (cheers). You may then, we say, for some reason admit it or not. Well. What authority is there for thinking that we possess fitness ? I pointed to a Native State. I tell you another thing. Keep yourself aloof for 10 years and see whether it can be done or under your control after ten years (cheers). You are free to do so. This too, is not to be done. There is no Swarajya. There is no Swarajya. What does it mean ? What do we ask for ? Do we say Drive away the English Government ? But I ask what is it to the Emperor ? Does the Emperor lose anything whether the administration is carried on by a civil servant or by our Belvi Saheb ? (Cheers). The rule still remains. The Emperor still remains. The difference would be that the white servant who was with him would be replaced by a black servant (cheers). From whom then does this opposition comes? This opposition come from those peoples who are in power. It does not come from the Emperor. From the Emperor's point of view there is neither anarchy nor want of loyalty, nor sedition in this. What does rajadroha (sedition) mean ? Hatred of the king. Does 'King' mean a police sepoy 7

(Laughter) I said some time back that this distinction must first be made. Otherwise, if tomorrow you say 'remove the police sepoy' it would constitute sedition. Such is the belief of police sepoys (Laughter). In the same manner, go a little further and you will see that the demand made by us is right, proper, just and in conformity with human nature. Other nations have done what we are doing. It has not been done only in our country. Swarajya, Swarajya—what does it mean ? Not that you do not want the English rule. There is the mistake at the root. Some one has some object in perpetuating it. It is served out by men whose interest lies in deceiving you. Do not care for it at all. "If you think that you are men like other men, that is enough. When our objectors go to England their intellect and they are put to the test there. Therein we stand higher. What then is trotted out ? They say your intellect may be good, but you do not possess character, courage and other qualities. Their character, I admit for a ghatka (24 minutes) the absence of that particular character. But is does not follow that we cannot acquire it (laughter). How can such character be spent in service and in service alone ? Can it be said of any person-He worked as a clerk for 25 years, wrote on the cover the Saheb's orders, obtained the Saheb's signature thereon and thus he acquired'the necessary character after 25 years-Even if some truth is presumed in such a statement yet he will at first find it difficult to do responsible work. This-is not denied. But when the system under which such men are, has disappeared, it cannot be said that men would not become fit in the next generation. Hence in my opinion we are fit for Swarajya. I shall now briefly tell you what we wish to obtain and what we should demand and then concluded my speech. 'You know what Indian administration is. It must be noted that it is carried on in accordance with a particular law.

Its rules are fixed. What are the powers of the Secretary of State ? What are the powers of the Governor General ? They define. There are great parts of the system. The Secretary of State is in

England. The Governor-General is at Delhi in India. Under him there is a Governor for every Presidency. For the present let us omit those under him. But the main system is of the above triple character. Let us began to consider each. Who appoints the Secretary of State ? Not we. This is a heritage from the Company's Government. When there was the East India Company's rule in this country, all matters were carried on in the interests of trade. The whole attention was directed towards the question how might the Company's shareholders obtain considerable profit; the Company's, Directors were in the place of the present Secretary of State. You might say that it was a contract given for governing thee entire kingdom, You know for instance under the Peshwa's rule Mamlatdar's office were given away under a contract. The Indian administration was, as it were, according to the then law Government, a trade carried on by the East India Company. They were to derive from it as much profit as possible. The Company's Directors were to be in England. The attention of the administration was directed to the fact that profit was to be given to the Directors, i.e. shareholders. A letter used to come "to the Governor-General here to this effect : 'So much profit must be pain to us this year. Realise it and send it to us.' This was the administration. The people's good was not considered under it. It was the story of the milk-man and his cows. If the cows did not yield sufficient milk, he says fill the post with water. The administration of India was carried on like that subsequently it appeared after the discussion that the administration was not good. And when Queen Victoria-you may say the Parliament-took the administration into their own hands, the did not approve of this trading system. Therefore they took it into their bands. This was alright. However the system of administration was modelled on the policy which was in existence when the administration was assumed (by the Parliament) and under which the Directors were masters in English and their servants were masters here. The State Secretary has come in the place of the Directors, The Governor General has come in the place of their Governor. Thus what was done? The Sovereign-the Parliament-took the administration into their hands, but the establishment of employees which then existed has remained just as before. This happened in 1858 after the Mutiny. From that time to this the administration of India has been carried on in accordance with rules and arrangements formed as a heritage of the Company's policy. If the power had really to go to the sovereign this modelling after the policy of the Company should have disappeared. He is the King and we are his subjects. It is his duty to rule for the good of the subjects. And an arrangement should have been made in accordance with the rules-lawful-that may be included in that duty. But the arrangement was made thus the Directors disappeared, the Secretary of the State stepped into their shoes as the final authority. Who is to decide how much money is to be spent in India and what taxes are to be imposed ? The State Secretary. Such powers are not placed in the Governor-General's hands. He is the chief officer. The 'Governors are under him. They are servants. There are other servants under them. And the entire administration must be carried on with the consent of and in consultation with and with the advice of this State Secretary ? Such is the present policy. What has happened gradually ? It has continued but a commercial policy. Though the rule went into the hands of the Queen's Government, and though they issued a great proclamation, the policy of the administration is not on the lines of that proclamation, It is in accordance with the trading Company's policy, the administration of the Kingdom is in accordance with the Company's policy. So the proclamation has had no effect. (Laughter, cheers). Such was the arrangement. At the time our people did not know it. I believe, that if education had spread as much as it is now, the people would have contended that since the Queen had taken the reins of Government into her own hands, the administration of the kingdom should, as regards the sovereign and the subjects, be for the good of the subjects. Our people would then have told that the arrangement made by the Company was simply for its own benefit, and that a change must be made in that policy in that arrangement. Such contention did come. The people have now contended for many years. To put the matter very briefly, Mr. Dadabhai Naoroji (cheers), who is one of those living persons who clearly saw and pointed out the defects, began this work. How did he begin '! He said, What is the difference between the Company's system and this system ? We do not see any in it. The rules, are all made in accordance with the Company's policy. Are the people likely to derive any benefit from them ? Then came the Legislative councils. They were such that the Governor General was to appoint them. Originally the members were not to be elected by the people. Gradually you men became members of the Municipality and of the Legislative Council. Still the final keys are in the bands of the authorities. Discussion may be held in the Legislative Council. They say 'You have full liberty to hold a discussion. You may hold a discussion about spending the money in this country. But we shall decide whether it should be as spend or not. Exert yourself mentally and vocally as much as you can, we have no objection to it. Be awake throughout the night, prepare your speeches. Instead of printing them in a newspaper, we shall publish them in the Bombay (Government) Gazette. This is the result. Nothing is hereby gained. Hope is held out no doubt. There is a slokh (stanza) in the Mahabharat which says hope 'should be made dependent upon time.' Our friends say 'Rights are to be given to you when you become fit. We do not wish to remain in India. When you become fit, we shall give the bundle into your possession and go to England by the next English steamer.' (cheers) very well. A time limit should be laid down. 'We shall give in two years. We shall give in ten years.' It did come afterwards. Time should be coupled with obstacles. Ten years were mentioned. These years passed and were very wearisome. We are obliged to make them fifteen' was the next. Hope and time should be coupled with an obstacle.

The obstacle came, 'You yourselves must have brought it' was the retort. We did not bring it. We were awaiting good time. Excuse should be coupled with it. The excuse came. Now did it come ? It is an excuse, only nothing can be said about it. Some cause should be shown. This is a sort of policy. When you do not mean to give, you cannot do otherwise. This policy does not find a place in the modern works on morality and policies. Only, the old tradition has continued. Thus this bureaucracy has been cajoling us. For the last 5 or 50 years the State Secretary and the Governor-General too have been cajoling us in this manner, have kept us afloat. As soon as you proceed to make some noise, it is said there were five members, tomorrow we shall make them six.

What do we benefit by raising the number from five to six ? One of our men has merely to waste his time there for nothing for a while (Cheers). There is no more advantage Than that If you object to six they say we make them eight We raise 10 to 12, if necessary. The people are already convinced that this matter cannot be disposed of in this manner. Whatever rights you may give, give them to us-absolutely, however great you may keep your own powers. Take for instance, the management of the Educational Department. Most of the subordinate servants are from among us only. There is a Saheb at the head. Why is he kept there ? With a view to restrain their mouths and the scope of their intellect. Even if 20 years' service be put in by the next subordinate, work cannot be done without the Saheb. That poor man actually begins to say so. It is such men that are prepared. I shall present to you two points of view. When a gardener is asked to prepare a garden just here, beyond this place, be wants flower pots. When big forests are to be prepared under the Forest Department, pots are not required. Bags of seeds are brought and emptied. Trees grow everywhere to any extent. Some of them grow small, some big. The present arrangement is that of the gardener. Owing to this arrangement the trees amongst us do not grow. Nay, care is taken that are planted in pots look pretty, as that flowers can be reached and plucked by the hand. We are educated in such a way that such pretty plants may grow. In such a manner is our man treated and made to work. And then after 25 or 30 years are past, he begins to say 'I am really not fit for this work.' We do not want-this system. We want the English Government. We want to remain under the sway of this rule. But we do not want the State Secretary who has been created a son-in-law (cheers). We want at least our men, elected by us, in his council. This is the first reform that must be made. In like manner the decision as to who is to expend India's revenues, how much money is to be collected and how many taxes are to be imposed should rest in our hands. (Cheers). We say, there must not be those taxes. They saw how can the expenditure be met ? That, we will see afterwards. We know this much. Expenditure is to be proportionate to the money we have and that again has to be raised according to the expenditure undergone. We understand this. We will later see what arrangement should be made. The second principle of Home Rule is that these powers should be in the people's hands, in the hands of good man viz., in the hands of men elected by the people. At present a great war is going on in Europe. The Emperor does not decide how much money has to be spent on the war. Mr. Asquith decides it. If there is a complaint against the work done by Mr. Asquith, it goes before Parliament, and if Mr. Asquith was committed a mistake, he has to tender his resignation. Will it be sedition if he has to tender his resignation ? There is the difference in the arrangement, there is the difference in the organization, there is the difference in the system. And we are asking for a change to such a system. 'The rule will fall, the rule will go away'- these thoughts are utterly foreign to us, they do not come within our limits, our reach, our view. And we did not also wish it. I again say, if the nation is to get happiness, if the thousands of complaints that have arisen today are to be removed, then first of all, change this system of administration. There is saying in Marathi, "Why did the horse become restive ? Why did the betel-leaves rot ? Why did the breed get burnt ? There is one answer, 'For want of turning', the leaves ought to have been turned, the bread ought to have been turned. Had the horse been turned, it would not have become restive.' The root cause is here. Complaints about forests, complaints about Akbar, complaints about Kulkarni vatans, have arisen because authority is not in our hands. To state it in slightly changed words because we have not swarajya (cheers). That we should have swarajya for us is at the root of our demand, we need not then dance to anybody's tune. However, this thing may happen even in swarajya. I do not deny it. When we have deficiency of money, and powers are placed in our hands, we may increase the tax; we increase it altogether voluntarily. Otherwise whence is the expenditure to be met ? But as it will be increased voluntarily, it will not oppress our minds. Here is the right door. We are passing through it. When we are passing through it learned aliens may tell us that we should not pass through it but take another door. We cannot change. If others come and obstruct we must give them a push and make our way. The very same is the case with Swarajya. The obstruction comes from the Bureaucracy. We do not want such obstruction. The demand for Swarajya is such that it has nothing to do with sedition. It has nothing to say against the invisible Government. All domestic concerns should be managed by yourselves and by doing so what will happen is that in the first place your minds will remain peace. Whatever you have to do you will do with the thought that you are doing it for your good. May, you will also reduce the expenditure. I do not think that in any Native State a Collector does get a pay of twenty five hundred rupees. If there is any place in the world in which a man doing the work of a Collector gets the highest pay, it is India (cheers). To give 2,500 rupees as pay to a Collector, would, in terms of the former rule, have been like giving an annual Jahagir of Rs. 30,000. Have we ever given in our Swarajya such a Jahagir of Rs. 30,000 ? Rs. 30,000 is not a small amount. There are reasons however now for it. What reason is given ? Some reason or either can always be given. This man has to send Rs. 2,500 to England for his children, etc. For your welfare he has come from a cold climate to a hot climate risking his health. Must he no I then be paid ? The I.C.S. have laboured as so much, made such self-sacrifice, and suffered so many hardships, and you would not pay them money ? It appears to be right at first sight. But now the principal question is, who asked them to come here from there ? (Cheers). We did not call them. They do such work as they may be fit to do. We do possess as much fitness as they have, but we shall be able to do the work on less pay. Men can be had. Then why gives so much pay to them ? We don't need it. We feel that we do not get today money for education. The excuse of 'no funds' which is brought forward in connection with the execution of works of public utility will then disappear. Business will go on unobstructed just as at present. In the beginning it may not be so efficient. Perhaps it may be less by an anna in the rupee. Still the satisfactory thought that the business has been carried on by the people, is of greater value. In this direction good management is to be asked for in administration. The present law must be amended. It is to be brought about through Parliament. We will not ask for it from others. We have not to get this demand complied with by petitioning France. The Allies may be there, we have not to petition them. The petition is to be made to the English people, to the English Parliament. The present state of things is to be placed before them. We have to do whatever may be required for this. If you carry on such an effort for 5 or 25 years, you will never fail to obtain the fruit. Moreover, such a time has now arrived. On account of the war effort must be made as will increase the value of India. India's bravery, India's courage, and India's stability. If the facts that the nation itself is making this effort comes to the notice of the Government, then there is hope of our demand soon proving fruitful. I have, therefore, purposely brought this subject before you. The subject is being discussed elsewhere also. The League which we have established for this purpose is such that I myself or someone else will have occasion to place the subject before the people at every place, if not today some days afterwards, for carrying on this work. Let this subject be always be discussed by you. Always think about it, get its usefulness explained, and carefully consider how much of loyalty and how much of disloyalty is in it. This is all I have to tell you on the present occasion. Though what I have to say be much more than this, still I have told you its substance in a brief manner. If the consideration of this be begun among you, be begun in Maharashtra, be begun in India, then some day or other this work will succeed, and even if the matter lies in God's hands still this is necessary. I admit that it does not lie in our hands. But the effect of action (karma) cannot fail to take its place in this world. The effect of action may not be obtained as soon as I say, may not be obtained before my eyes, perhaps I may not be benefited by it. But this action must have its fruit (cheers). According to the law of action, when a certain action is done, another results from it, and a third one results out of that. Such succession goes on. Time will be required, there will be delay. But do we ask at all that we should have moksha before our eyes ? Again do we ask for it with the thought that we should have it in the hands of a certain person ? Only just a little age a Resolution was passed in our conference that the parties of Moderates and Nationalists are not wanted. That is to say, it is the same to us to whenever Swarajya is given. There is no objection even if powers be given to your sepoy tomorrow. You may say, how will the sepoy exercise such a great power ? The sepoy is to die some day or other and then we will see (cheers). We want rights. We want a certain sort of arrangement giving happiness. We will get it. Our children will get it. Make the effort that is to be made. Be ready to do this work with the thought that it belongs to you. I am sure that by the grace of God your next generation will riot fail to obtain the fruit of this work, though it may not be obtained in your life-time.

(The members of the Mahajan Sabha, the Madras Provincial Congress Committee, the Home Rule League, the Madras Presidency Association and the Andhra People's Association presented a joint address of welcome to Lok. Bal Gangadhar Tilak—a hearty and sincere welcome on his arrival at Madras. Mr. Tilak, in reply, said) : I thank you cordially for the honour you have done me and the other members of the Deputation in welcoming us here and in presenting an address which has been signed by almost all the representative bodies in this city. (A friend here suggests "all" representative bodies.) My knowledge of the place is so scanty that I saved myself by introducing the qualification "almost all" but I am prepared to accept the amendment moved by my friend, and I thank you all the more because all the representative bodies of this Presidency have given us their blessing and good wishes for the cause which is the cause of us all, the success of which we have all at heart. As observed by the venerable Chairman, there is one thing' which I wish to communicate to you at this moment. No one now requires to be told what Home means. I can safely drop that question. The only question is how Home Rule is to be fought out. The Government of India and the Secretary of State have both declared from their respective places, the one in Parliament and the other through the Gazette of India, that Responsible Government or Home Rule shall be the goal of British administration in India. The King, the Cabinet, the Governor-General and the Secretary of State are all agreed that it is proper and legal for you to ask for Responsible Government, and, secondly, that it ought to be the goal of the British administration in India, but the statement is not as complete as we want it to be. We are told that the Responsible Government will be granted to you by steps which will be decided by the Bureaucracy and not by us. That is not the doctrine of self-determination of which they talk so much in Great Britain. The steps are to be determined by us and not by the present bureaucratic administrators. Self-determination means that one must fix upon these steps, that we must fix upon the time limit and that the matter should not be left to the sweet discretion of bureaucracy which after 150 years of rule have now just come to see what the goal of their administration should be. They worked in utter darkness till now groping in the way, and when the war broke out, and when it was found that the Empire was in a danger they began to see what the goal of their administration ought to be. We do not want to quarrel with them for that. The goal is there and it is no longer seditious to say that we want Home Rule and that Home Rule is our birthright. We are going to England to tell the British Democracy plainly that the question as to what the first step should be and what the time of granting full Responsible Government should be is no longer a question on which bureaucratic opinion can be tolerated for a moment. We do not want the British Democracy to decide how they should act as an umpire between the Bureaucracy and ourselves. We are going to England for the purpose of convincing the British Democracy that the grant of Responsible Government is the necessity of the hour. It is no longer a question of benevolent generosity or favour. That was the position ten years ago. Now the position is entirely changed. Responsible Government has now become the necessity of the hour, the necessity of the Empire, and, I say, the safety of the Empire. We are going to England for the purpose of convincing the British Democracy that if Home Rule is not granted to India this Empire is in danger of being one day crippled. You all know what the situation is in Asia. India stands alone. Russian influence in Asia is dominated by German influence. Turkey is under the influence of Germany. Japan has the goal of self-aggrandisement. India cannot hereafter be defended by the naval and military forces of Great Britain; Naval Forces for reasons you all know; military forces, simply because there are none. If India is to be defended in the interests of the Empire, India must be trained to defend herself. Lock at the world map-India surrounded by China and Japan on one side, with Siberia on one side, with two Asiatic Turkeys under German influence, with Russia broken up into rival parties. Supposing you have to defend India against a combination inspired from Germany, what will you do ? (A cry "we will fight") I will tell you what my answer is. They say that they will not trust India. They will trust Japan and any other people on the surface of the earth but India. The work of the Deputation is to convince the British Democracy that the gravity of the situation-as the Chairman remarked, the centre of gravity-lies in India and not in England. It is here that the solution is to be found and not in America and Japan. The map of the world is changed and if we do not take the advantage of these circumstances which are providential, we do not deserve to be called citizens, we do not deserve to be called men. Times do not change for you. Time and tide wait for no man and you have to run with them. If you fail to take advantage of the time and circumstances. You fail in the Providence is favourable to important duties of citizenship, you. Why? Because the whole world is changed and it is impossible that there could not be a change. When the world is changed, if you propose to remain stationary, probably you will be wiped of speedily. You must move along with the times. What is necessary at present is to make the British people realise the position. We are not going to appeal to their generosity, and nothing could be gained by that procedure. We must make them realise that unless they are prepared to raise India, they must be prepared to lose India. If India remains stationary, she will be a dead weight round the neck of the Empire and there is a danger of both India and the Empire going to the bottom. That is the situation which I wish to point out to the British public. It is not a situation of our making. Providence has brought it about and, as Mr. Pal has said, Providence has been working for us all over the whole world. Providence is working in your own interest. If you have not the ears to hear or the hands to work in consonance with the spirit that is running abroad, I dare say every independent and civilised nation in the world will pass their judgment upon you and that judgment will be against you. Are you prepared to face it ? (Cries of No.) After all I am but one individual. Whatever I may hold or whatever I may think will count as the judgment of one man. I appeal to you to think of the situation. I am going to say in England that Home Rule for India is a question of necessity of the hour and that it must be realised. That is the decisive attitude which must be taken, which must be utilised, which be exploited to its utmost. We want your full support in that work. We are going to represent the cause of Home Rule through the British Democracy as a matter of necessity. We have fixed our demand. You know what happened in the case of Ireland. The British ministers and Cabinet asked the Irish people to meet in a Convention and to settle their demands. We are a bit shrewd people. We thought that such a demand would be made. We anticipated it and met in the Congress and Muslim League and we have fixed upon the minimum which ought to be conceded to us at once. All that remains is if the British Ministry wishes to treat us on the same footing as they treated the Irish, what we say is, here is our demand, settled at a Convention of the Congress and the Muslim League and no more Convention is necessary, therefore, extend to us the same liberty that you have given to Ireland and carry it through the Parliament. No second reference is necessary. We have our demand readymade. What is that demand ? We ask for complete Home Rule within a measurable time. Both of us have agreed happily on that, though the words "within a measurable time" are susceptible of being interpreted in different ways according to the interests of each party. We have fixed upon the first stage or the first step towards Home Rule and that step is that we want financial control. Let me enumerate the principles involved in that. We must have the control of the purse. We must have control over the Executive, The Executive must be prepared to carry out what the Legislature resolves. The Executive must be the servants of the Legislature. Our second demand is that there should be substantial majority of elected members in the Legislative Council. There are minor demands with regard to administration in the Provinces and so on. An attempt will be made—I say it from the knowledge of Bureaucracy-to tempt you to give up a part of your demands. There is no other alternative for the Bureaucracy. They have to accept the goal which has been published all over through the Gazette of India. We know where we are. Between Minto-Morley Reforms and complete Responsible Government the Bureaucracy wants small installments to be fixed at their discretion. That would not do. We say that we are even prepared to accept reforms in instalments but we say that then first instalment should be substantial and should be what we have asked for in the Congress-League Scheme, and that after the payment of the first instalment, the instalments that are to follow should be distributed over as small a number of years as possible. We ask for the control of the purse, control over the Executive and a substantial majority in the Legislative Councils. Without these reforms no improvement in the state of the country will be brought about. We do not want Home Rule so that we may get a few more Government posts, nor is it that we should associate with the Bureaucracy in their costly administrations. We say that the Empire is in danger and that we are willing to save the Empire. We want Home Rule in order that we may be better qualified to render-that assistance to the Empire within ten or fifteen years to come. We are anxious to serve the Empire, we are anxious to be a living member, a self-dependent member of the Empire like the other parts of the Empire. Let us have sufficient power that would enable us to achieve this goal within as short a time as possible. Japan became a nation within a comparatively short period. We hope that if we are granted the power and the right that we ask for, the first instalment that we ask for will convert India from a dead-weight into a self-dependent unit of the Empire. Our object is imperial and with that object in view, we press that the Congress demand is the minimum demand that we make. Mind that we are not extravagant. The caution that was necessary to be used and perhaps more than necessary to be-used has been set aside and this demand has been fixed with the consent of Hindus and Mohammedans of all shades of political opinion. That is a compromise that we have arrived at. If after bidding farewell to us after allowing us to work in England for some time, you change your mind, imagine what the consequences would be. It will be a great error, also a disaster, to send us to England and then; change your mind behind our back. You had better not send us to England at all if you are likely to change your mind. I wish to take the verdict from you before we are going to England. If you will be content with less when temptations are put before you and when Bureaucracy say that you will ruin your path unless you accept less-they will try to throw the responsibility of the failure on you-it is a very spacious argument, an argument that is likely to appeal to people who have something else in view, be firm at that time. If you really want us to go to England and plead the cause of the country, we expect full and unstinted support from you all. (Cheers) If you have no mind to stick to the programme you have made, please let us know about it and we shall know how to act. Otherwise we are going to take the Congress Scheme as the basis of our demand. The Congress Scheme excludes the military and foreign affairs but in the case of military matters the Congress Scheme demands that the Government of India should make a declaration as regards its future policy. We do not ask for control over military affairs because the bureaucracy would suspect that we have some ulterior motive. We still want a definite declaration as to future military policy. We want volunteering to be allowed and military colleges to be opened. In the military matter, it is impossible to utilise the manpower of India without the full consent of the people of India and their full consent to support the Empire. Who can expect any people on the surface of the earth to fight for a country unless the fighter hopes that he will improve his material position in this world ? The Bhagvad Gets has beautifully expressed that if you die on a battle-field there are gates of heaven open to you. The bureaucracy has refused encouragement to volunteering. There are thousands in this meeting who would declare their willingness to volunteer, who are prepared to defend their country as the Colonies have done. I see a number of young people before me who would come forward with the greatest satisfaction if the Government of India declares their military policy tomorrow. I do not know from what portion of the Empire they can find manpower as much as from India. You will be told that the Government of India is very liberal and that if we accept Responsible Government as the goal of British administration in India everything else will follow. I say, No. I say that the first instalment ought to be such as would make us qualify within 10 or 15 years to take part in the defence of our Empire. The Anglo-Indian Association and Lord Sydenham are saying that India is unfit for Home Rule that Indian women are not yet liberated, that the caste system is widely prevalent, the Indians have not changed their colour and that therefore Home Rule should not be granted. I do not think that there is any chance of this argument being heard by the democracy. We must be there on their spot. We must be able to say what are the essential conditions necessary to grant Home Rule to India. Have we prevented Government from introducing free and compulsory education among the masses ? If the masses are uneducated it is not our fault.

There are said to be difficulties in the way of finding funds for educational purposes but funds are easily found for other purposes such as the grant of Exchange Compensation to Civilians and others. We want authority to abolish the bureaucratic policy of administration, and we want the whole policy to be changed and the character of the administration to be converted from bureaucratic to responsible power. Let us have your full support, your full sympathy and let us have a continued agitation even more than desirable, for in such a matter excess is not to be condemned. Even more than now keep on your agitation. Let us hear the echoes of your agitation in England, Nothing can be more cheering to us than those echoes. I promise on behalf of the deputation that we shall do our best to carry out the object upon which we go there, not for ourselves but for the country. We are going there in obedience to a call from Providence, from a higher power-an inspiration which we cannot resist. We go in spite of bad health and other circumstances. It is a mission from God, a mission from above, and if we are determined to follow it up with all your power and sympathy, there will be enough energy given to us to carry it out. We feel that times are changed, we feel that it is the will of God to grant Home Rule to India. We possess confidence, that Providence which inspired us in the past, will give us the necessary strength to carry that impulse safely through. I again thank you for the honour you have done to us.

Tilak's Home Rule League's Second Conference

The second Conference of the Indian (Mr. Tilak's) Home Rule League was held at night on Tuesday, in a specially erected 'Shamiana' at the Chaupati end foot of the French Bridge under the presidency of Mr. B.G. Tilak. The proceedings commenced a little after ten o'clock and lasted up to 2-30 a.m. The 'Shamiana' was filled 'to the brim' with an enthusiastic audience consisting of not small number of ladies. Members of different Class Volunteers' Corps were drawn of in an attractive manner in different parts of the hall, the most noticeable among them being the tiny 'soldiers' bailing from the Depressed Class Volunteer Corps. 'Distinguished gentlemen' began to pour in from 9-450 the first of the gentry to arrive being Mr. S.R. Bomanji accompanied by Mr. Jamnadas Dwarkadas. Then came the Hon. Mr. Belvi (Belgaum), the Hon. Mr. Manmohandas Ramji (Bombay), Messrs. N.C. Kelkar (Poona) and R.P. Karandikar (Satara) arriving at five minutes past ten.

At 10-15 the air was suddenly rent with cries of Vande Mataram by the thousands of people that had ensconced themselves on the French Bridgeroadway and the parapet wall-announcing the arrival of Messers. K.P. Khadilkar, followed a few seconds afterwards by Mr. Tilak. Cheers after cheers rang in the 'Shamiana', the enthusiasm of the audience being further kindled by the encouraging words emanating from the lips of some of the more energetic members of the audience. As soon as Mr. Tilak's turban was seed through the crevices of people's necks, the whole assembly rose to its feet and gave him a very cordial welcome. Bowing and bowing and bowing, he ascended the 'dais', and that was the signal for Mr. Paluskar, proprietor of the Gandharva Mahavidyalaya, to strike up the note of 'Bharat amara desh hai, The singing over, Mr. Tilak asked the Hon. Mr. Manmohandas Ramji, Chairman of the Reception Committee of the Conference, to deliver his opening speech. Mr. Manmohandas rose amid cheers and said as follows :

Speech of Chairman

I have great pleasure in welcoming you all on behalf of the second Indian Home Rule League Conference. The first Conference, as you know, met at Nasik last year and was presided over by Mr. Joseph Baptista, Bar-at-law, who is now have to undergo a great deal of expense and so wherever he has gone he has been given something and so we, the millhands of Bombay also intend to give him something that lies in our power. Every one of us has given something willingly. No one has been forced to give anything. Mr. Tilak who was received with cries of Bande Mataram and Tilak Maharaj ki Jaya, said : Mr. Chairman and gentlemen, a representation is going to England on behalf of the Home Rule League and I am one of that representation. I will first of all tell you why this representation is going to England, what is their duty, what is the relationship between you and that representation, how we all will be benefited by home rule and what this representation is going to do there.

Some people who are not our friends but who are our enemies and your enemies also say that we are cheating the marwaries and tradesmen and millhands. They say that the people of India and especially the masses should hear what Government tells them and that they should not hear what the Khatpati Brahmins like us tell them. They say that we should all obey without any complaint the Collector and the Police Commissioner and all other Government officials. They say that we should not even dispute their unjust actions and that we should not criticise their actions. We have no right to say whether their actions are just or unjust. They say that we should allow the Government officials to manage the people just as a shepherd manages his flock of sheep. They say that we are not fit for home rule and that we are only fit to be ruled by them. Lord Sydenham (cries of shame, shame) the late Governor of Bombay is saying all these things in England at present. His regime is well known to all of you. He used to do anything he liked when he was here. He was at that time called the wise Governor of Bombay and he is now using his wisdom in England and telling the English people that we are not fit for home rule, that the masses of India do not want home rule and that if home rule is given to India the masses will be trodden down by Brahmins. Now when that is the case is it not better that there should, be some one there in England to refute all his arguments. Last time when I spoke to you I told you what is home rule. Our opponents say that the millhands and the masses of India do not want home rule. And the object of today's meeting is that when we go to England we must be able to tell the English labour class that the millhands of Bombay are on our side, that such a vast gathering of millhands is behind us, that they are helping us and that we are not only the representatives of the educated India but of the masses of India. (Applause). Today's gathering is the vivid proof of the fact that so many people know what is home rule and that they know why we the representatives of the home rule league are going to England. I am very glad to find that you also participate with us in this great cause. You have not gathered together here today for me and I have not come here for you. But we all have gathered together here today to help in the cause of home rule.

You must not think that you have come here for me. I have come here for some work sacred to my heart and I am going to England for the work which is as much yours as mine. The first essential thing that you ought to remember is that home rule is not the rule of Brahmins as our opponents, the bureaucracy, is telling you. When we have home rule whoever are elected will be the members of the cabinet. What we want is that we must have the power of electing the officers who are to administer the law. Now some of us say there ought to be community election. I do not agree with them ; that is a wrong idea. We have now got the bureaucracy, namely the collectors and the Commissioners etc. who are appointed by the Governors, and the Governors and Governor-Generals who are appointed by the King. There is one Act called the Government of India Act and that Act says that the Secretary of State is the minister of the King and that he ought to appoint the other officers of the bureaucracy and that they should administer the laws in this country. At present the people of India have no right to say that such and a man should be the Collector or the Police Commissioner of Bombay. It is the bureaucracy who makes the laws and it is the bureaucracy who administers them according to their discretion. We have got legislative Councils but they are in name only. Suppose a certain community says "We do not want a liquor shop in our vicinity" they have got no power to dictate to the officers. If the officers desire that the shop should be there the community are helpless. What kind of administration is this ? Under the present administration even time may come tomorrow when the bureaucracy may tell us that we must eat only a circular or a triangular bread and if such things happen we are nothing better than beasts. That is the way how India is being administered at present. We are not heard at all. We have to .abide by the wishes of the bureaucracy, The will of the bureaucracy is the law. And this is the state of affairs not only of Brahmins but of all creeds and classes in India at present. This morning we had a depressed classes mission Conference. It is not only the Antayjas who are depressed but the whole of India is at present depressed. All the classes and creeds in India are being treated by the bureaucracy as depressed (Antyajas). The present state of affairs is troubling not only Brahmins but it is troublesome to all castes and creeds in India. And to remedy this evil we went home rule. Now if they do not give us home rule we are not going to have a revolt against them. We are not going to break railways or burn mills. Railways and mills are the means of increasing our wealth and we do want them. We only want that the administration of the country should be carried on in such a way that it should be beneficial to us, the people of India, Suppose tomorrow the bureaucracy want to tax the mills. It is not in your power or even in the hands of your mill-owners to prohibit them from doing that. No doubt there are our legislative councils where there are our representatives. But these legislative councils, as I told you, are a mere farce. I say they are a farce because not withstanding our representatives being there, when the time of voting for a measure which we disapprove comes, we find that the white hands outnumber the black hands. Even if our elected members raise both their bands they cannot outnumber the white hands (Laughter). The Acts under which India is administered at present are passed in the legislative council in this manner and we all have to suffer from the effects of those Acts. No doubt the bureaucracy is opening its eyes only now-a-days.

Of course the King does not know all these things. And we do not blame him and we are not against the King and the King is not against us. It is the bureaucracy who is against us and it is the bureaucracy against whom we are complaining. It is the bureaucratic administration from the Secretary of State down to the police that we are complaining against. Formerly there was the East India Company who was administering India and under the administration of the East India Company we were not being treated properly and so the present bureaucratic administration was created. Now if we show to the Parliament and the Kings that this bureaucracy is not administrating India properly, the King and the Parliament will appoint some other body to administer India. Once we prove that the present bureaucratic administration is bad we can ask the Parliament for whatever kind of administration we want. Take the example of your mills. If your mill-owner finds that his officers do not carry on the management of the mill properly he dismisses them and appoints other officers. In the same manner if the King and the Parliament find out that under the present bureaucratic administration India is not being governed properly they will give us some other administration. When the administration of the East India Company was taken over by the pre 'sent bureaucratic administration it was declared that this present administration was appointed for the comelioration of the condition of the Indian people. And we must therefore see whether the present administration has in any way benefited us and is benefiting us. Now workmen in England know all these things about administration which knowledge you all lack. Mr. LLoyd George once asked a workman in England whether be was satisfied with his administration and the workman told him of course he was but that if he had not been satisfied he would have through his representative outvoted him from the cabinet. Now is there any chance of any one of you and the Governor to speak like this ? Can any one of you say to the Governor that if you did not like his administration you would outvote him and ask for another Governor ? Hardly any one of you know that the bureaucracy that is administering India is being paid by us. Some years ago there was one Viceroy by name Lord Curzon who was ruling over us and he then said that it was impossible to administer India according to the Queen's Proclamation. Why ? Because it did not suit his way of administering India. Now by having home rule we do not want this bureaucracy to go away from India. We do want collectors and commissioners but we want collectors and commissioners who we will hear us to the way in which they should work and not there who will tell us that it is they who will impose their will upon us. We want our own laws made by our own legislative councils of our own representatives who should be in majority therein. We shall only be in good condition on the day on which we shall have our own legislative councils with a majority of our own elected representatives. Now as regards representation the question of communities has nothing to do with it.

If you want communal representation, tomorrow even our Bhikshuks (Brahmin priests) will ask for having their own representative in the legislative councils. This is the question of administration. You all must remember that communal representation is destructive to ourselves. The question of caste should not come in home rule. Every one who has the good of his country at heart should have the right to vote.

Once we are given the Tight of voting we shall elect the men of our own choice. That should be the spirit. You must not fight for such things as communal representation at such a time. It is nothing but treason to think of such things at such a time. Now I turn to the question as to why our representation is going to England. As I said before the bureaucracy has opened its eyes. The British Parliament is also now of opinion that the present bureaucratic administration is not administering India properly, and they are thinking of effecting some change in that administration. But there are some self-styled well-wishers of India like Lord Sydenham (cries of shame, shame) who have eaten the slat of India, who are misrepresenting facts in England. From there he is also fostering trouble among the various classes here. This Lord Sydenham and Co. are telling the British people that the masses of India are quite satisfied with the present administration and that it is only the Brahmins who want home rule. Now this Lord Sydenham and Lord Harris were the cruelest Governors of Bombay as you all well know. While here they tried to tyranise over us as much as they could when they were Governors of Bombay, and now in England in their-, old age, they are trying their best against us. I will tell you the story of a magistrate. There was once a gentleman who during all his service was a magistrate and was accustomed to pass sentences of imprisonment and fine. After be retired be was unable to pass his time as he had no opportunity to pass sentences of imprisonment and fine. He then tried through some of his friends to get himself appointed an honorary magistrate and when as such he began to pass sentences upon people be felt at ease. The same is the case with these two gentlemen, Lord Sydenham and Lord Harris. While in India as Governors they were accustomed to tyranise over us and now in their retirement they are unable to pass their time without doing some tyrannical act to India and therefore they are 'trying to put their spokes in the wheel of Indians getting something better in the form of home rule.

And so at such a time it is necessary that our representation should go to England and should counteract their efforts. Owing to this great war the English people have opened their eyes. They now sympathise with you. The time has now come when they have lost their faith in the bureaucracy. We have been complaining against the administration of the bureaucracy for the last forty years in our journals but upto now the British people did not believe us. Upto now they believed in the bureaucracy. But now owing to this great war they are feeling the want of man-power. Germany has got 50 lakhs of army while the English people have got only 5 lakhs. So now they want to increase their army. Upto now they did not take us into their confidence. Had they done that their army would have been double of that of Germany. Now although their eyes are opened they are not opened fully. There is still want of confidence in us. Some months ago I gave a lecture in Bombay on recruiting and 8000 people came forward to enlist themselves. But none of them were taken. Some of them were not taken because they were home rulers. Some did not get replies to their applications at all. Some were given some other reasons and in fact none were taken. We ate ready to fight for the empire, Hindus, Musalmans, Parsis, Brahmins and all castes and creeds. But they would not take us, the people of India, into their confidence. They do not want that we should rise higher. They want to keep us pressed. But now the times are changed. The eyes of the British administrators are opening. They are finding out that we are not being treated properly. They now feel that they have committed a mistake in not allowing the Indian people that place in the empire which would have made them think themselves as a part and parcel of the empire.

They are feeling now that bad they taken these thirty crores of people into their confidence they would have been able to defy Germany in point of the numerical strength of their army. They now feel why they are not getting recruits readily of course no one would like to endanger his life for Rs. 11. You millhands get more than Rs. 11 in your mills. Had the Indian people been accustomed to think that they were being treated as part and parcel of the empire they would certainly have thought it their duty to endanger their life for the empire. But they say, why should they fight, and for whom they should fight. They say that if we are to remain depressed-as we are' it is better to die of plague than to die in war. When people will have confidence in the administration and when people will get home rule they will surely feel that they are a part and parcel of the empire and then they will certainly fight for the empire and will be ready to die for the empire. The British

Parliament and ministers have now recognized this. Ten years ago the state of affairs in England was such that even an author and a minister like Lord Morley had expressed his opinion that India will not get home rule any time. He said to in the face of the late Mr. Gokhale. But now see how times are changed. The thing which Lord Morley ,even never dreamt of has now found expansion in the speech of Mr. Montagu. Mr. Montagu wants to give us something. In the days gone by these British Ministers were deaf to our cry but the shots of German guns have opened their ears-now. Guns generally make people deaf but the German guns have opened the ears of the British ministers. Now even Lloyd George is for home rule for India. The Country like America-who has fought for its liberty is also saying that India must have home rule. We say that not only that we are fit for home rule but that if we are given home rule we are fit to kill the German Imperialism. Such is the time. The King and his ministers and the British people are thinking of giving us home rule. If Lord-Sydenham and his party have thought there was no possibility of our getting home rule now, they would never have commenced their campaign against home rule in England. But now they are sure that India is about to get home rule and so they are working against us. I would ask you to imagine that our suit is before the Court of the British people. We Indians are the plaintiffs, and Lord Sydenham and his party are the defendants. Tradesmen in England are helping Lord Sydenham's party. But the working class which is styled as labour party is with us. The labour party is not helping Lord Sydenham and his party in their campaign. This is the state of affairs at present in England.

The labour party is full of hope that the labour ministry which is likely to come into power hereafter will surely give us home rule. Home rule will not only do good to the educated people but it will do good to all and when we get home rule your own status, that is the status of the millhands and the working people will also be changed. In England on the election day even a labourer thinks that he himself is the king that day because he has the right to vote and the different candidates come to him seeking his vote. When we get home rule you will also have such a day when you will think yourself to be the king that day. When you get the power of voting these big people will send their carriages for you to come and vote for them. This is how your status will be changed if we get home rule. When the whole of the working class will get the right of vote it will create inspiration in you. And when you get the right of voting on the election day you will consider yourself to be the king. There is the benefit of home rule. Perhaps instead of working in the mills some of you will get places in the army. Owing to having been depressed by the bureaucracy we have lost our Kshatra Tej (warrior's spirit) and we have become of feminate. When we get home rule there will be no depression by the bureaucracy and with the inspiration that homer rule will instill in us our Kshatra Tej will return among us.

You must remember that you are the meant of the riches of Bombay. It is by means of your labour that your mill-owners become rich. And it is in your hands to settle what rights you should have and what is for your own good. When we are given home rule you must try to elect good men. So our representation is now going to England to tell the, British people the real state of affairs, and it is with the greatest glory that I will describe to them the occasion of today's gathering. We will prove to the British people that what Lord Sydenham is telling them is not true about India. I can tell them many things against him now because I know that now he cannot imprison me although I am sure that had he been the Governor of Bombay now he would surely have imprisoned me. (Laughter). At present Lord Sydenham is like a bird without feathers. He had feathers when he was Governor of Bombay but those borrowed feathers have been removed and he is now a bird without feathers. Now I am telling you in plain words that this work for which we are going to England is the work of all of you. If we get home rule each one of you will get the right of voting so each one of you will be king at least on the day of voting. Do you prefer that or do you prefer to remain labourers for the whole of your life ? I do not think that there is any one amongst you who would like to remain a labourer the whole of his life. If we are asked in England whether the working classes of India are on our side we must be able to says yes, I have seen them, thousands and thousands of workmen attended a meeting to wish me god-speed and that they have expressed their consent to our demand of home rule for India. I must be able to reply like that and that is the reason why this monster meeting is called today. I do not wish to have any money from you, The rich are giving money.

This is the question-of demanding our birthright and all castes and creeds in India', Hindus, Musalmans, Parsis all are unanimous in thinking that we must try and do away with the yoke of the bureaucratic administration under which we are bending down. Justice is on our side, the time has arrived when the British people are willing to hear us. It is only the party of Lord Sydenham (cries of shame, shame) that is trying to spoil our pot of home rule which we have boiled and made ready for us. Now some people say Tilak is going to England in his old days. Well I am sorry it is so. Now that the time has come for work I must go. I must not take back because I am old. God is always willing to help us.

There are signs which are showing that the time has come for our good days. Even astrologers of this nation are telling us that time has come when India will see good days. This is not the question of caste or creed. The whole nation will be benefited if it gets home rule. Try therefore to help those who are trying and exerting for home rule and help in the evolution of the Indian Nation. With these word I beg your leave. (Deafening cries of Bande Mataram and Tilak Maharaj ki Jaya and Tilak Rai ki jaya). Representatives of about ten mills then presented purses and garlands to Mr. Tilak. Mr. Gangadharrao Deshpande, the chairman said : I need not remind you all what happened to Lokmanya in the regime of Lord Sydenham and how you showed your disapproval of his action that time. Lord Sydenham has still some feathers and with them he is working against us in England and it is to counteract that work that we are sending Lokmanya and others to England.

Now there is every likelihood of Lord Sydenham and his party creating difficulties in the way of the work that Lokmanya is going to do in England and it is to be. On Sunday the 24th March 1918 in the morning Mr. Tilak, immediately after his arrival in Bombay, was present at the Depressed Classes Mission Conference held in the Mandap near the French Bridge. In moving the resolution about allowing the representatives of the depressed classes to be present at the meetings of the national congress, industrial conference, social conference etc. Mr. Tilak said : Mr. President and gentlemen, the question of the depressed classes and of the untouchables is very important and from the political and social point of view it must be solved sooner or later and it is quite possible to do so. What are the depressed classes and the untouchables ? Is there any authority in the shastras to call any class of the community depressed or untouchable ? There is none.

The question whether the depressed classes and the untouchables should have the right of communal representation is, in my opinion, a different one. The question of communal representation has nothing to do with the question of the untouchables.

The untouchables must mix with all of us. Political and social work is the work of the whole country and the question of untouchables does not come in there. We do want the untouchables to join us in our national work. During the times of the Peshwas Brahmin sepoys in the army used to drink water from the Pakhals brought by untouchables. You find instances in the Peshwa's Daftar that the Peshwas themselves used to drink water from the Pakhals. The very fact that socially we are treating the depressed classes as untouchables and are keeping them apart from us shows that we are losing our nationality. Only consider what is happening at present. In India in the eyes of a white man a black man is untouchable. But what is happening on the front at present ?

There as well as in Mesopotamia while fighting the whites and the blacks have to fight shoulder to shoulder and they forget there the difference between the white and the black. It is stated in the Shastras that before the king, in great Darbars and at the time of fighting the question. Let me tell you how I myself treat these untouchables. I do not observe this difference between touchables and untouchables at my place. (Loud applause). Some Mahars of the Chokhamela creed had come to me for some business once. I did not make them stand outside my house but I allowed them to come and sit with me in my sitting room. So what I want to tell you is this that although I have not taken this work in my hand I fully sympathise with it. If the main work which I have taken in hand is done I will consider that I have fulfilled my mission of life. When that main work is done the question of touchables and untouchables will be solved by itself. As we sympathise with the question of the untouchables, they must also sympathise with the work that we have taken in hand. Let me tell you plainly that I am not at all against the untouchables. I am strongly of opinion that the word untouchable must disappear from amongst us. It is only a custom or traditional usage which must disappear. Just as the bureaucracy has at present created the untouchableness of a sort, the Brahmins had done the same many years ago. This question of untouchableness is a kind of disease which is eating away the society, And is the bounden duty of every one of us to do away with this disease. And I am full of hope that this disease will soon disappear. A public meeting of the Marwari merchants of Bombay was held in the hall of the Marwari Vidyalaya on Sunday the 24th March 1918 at 3 p.m. in honour of Mr. Tilak. The hall was tastefully decorated. Most of the leading members of the Marwari community and some Brahmins were present. The hall was overcrowded and a large number of people were standing in the compound. Mr. Tilak, Khaparde and Belvi arrived at three o'clock when all got up. Mr. Govindlal Shivlal Motilal who presided on the occasion explained the object of that day's gathering. He said Tilak and other members of the deputation were going to England to place before the British Democracy their case for home rule for India and that it was their duty to honour them and to help them. Another Marwari gentleman declared that they intended that day to present Rs. 15000 to Mr. Tilak. They had already collected Rs. 12000 and he hoped they would be able to collect Rs. 3000 more there on the spot. There was some commotion among the audience for some time and after about twenty five minutes the Chairman declared that he was glad to announce that they were able to complete the sum of Rs. 15000. A purse of Rs. 15000 was then presented to Mr. Tilak by the Chairman on behalf of the Marwari community of Bombay for being used in the cause of home rule. Mr. Tilak then rose to speak and he spoke in Hindustani for about ten minutes. He said : Mr. President and gentlemen, it is really a matter of great delight to find so many merchants coming together to help us in the cause of home rule.

Why have all of you gathered together in this ball on this occasion ? Why have I come here today ? Our chairman said just now that you have been called here today to do me honour. I disagree with him. You have come here today not do me or the deputation honour. You have come here to show your appreciation of the work that some of us are doing in connection with the cause of home rule. I have not come here to do you any honour. I have also come here to show my appreciation for the very keen interest you all, business men, take in the cause of home rule. What does this home rule mean ? It does not mean, as our opponents have been telling you, the rule of Brahmins. The question of caste or creed or profession does not come in home rule. Suppose tomorrow Government want to impose a certain tax on a certain kind of commodity in which some of you are trading. It is not in your power to prevent Government from imposing that tax. No doubt we have got our legislative councils in which all such measures are discussed. But at present our representatives there are in minority and the resolutions of the legislative councils are not binding upon Government. By the congress-league scheme we have asked for a substantial instalment of home rule, and if we are granted that substantial instalment of home rule, it is not the Brahmins and educated people only who will be benefited but even you businessmen will also derive a benefit. Our opponents, Lord Sydenham and his party, have collected Rs. 30,00000 from British merchants to fight against us in the cause of home rule. It is therefore in the fitness of things that you, Indian merchants, should also show your willingness to help us in the cause of home rule. When in England if I am asked whether the merchants of India are with us and whether they want home rule with us, I will proudly say that the merchant class of India is also behind us and that at such and such a gathering I have been presented with this valuable course for being used in the cause of home rule. (Loud applause). Mr. Khaparde, Sheth Madhavprasad, Mr. Fatechand Rula and two other Marwari gentlemen then addressed the meeting in Hindustani. In their speeches they enlogised Mr. Tilak's services to the country and expressed a sincere hope that the deputation would return to India with success in the cause of home rule. The meeting was then dissolved amidst cries of bande mataram. On behalf of the Lokmanya Swagat Mandal citizens of Bombay gave an At Home in honour of Mr. Tilak at the China Bagh on Monday the 25th March 1918 at 5-30. Many of Mr. Tilak's upcountry friends who had come to Bombay specially for the occasion were present. Messrs. Tilak, Khaparde and others were Photographed. After light refreshments Mr. S.R. Bomanji thanked the distinguished guests for gracing the occasion and requested Mr. Jinnah to speak.

Mr. Jinnah enumerated the singular services Mr. Tilak had rendered to the country and said that since their opponents were misrepresenting facts to the British public it was but meet that some of them ought to go there to counteract that misrepresentation. Mr. Tilak thanked all present and said : We are going to England to clear the way for the congress representation that is following us. We are going now because we are convinced that this is the proper time to place our grievances before the British Parliament and the British public. You all are fully aware of what our opponents are doing there. Just imagine what will happen when Mr. Montagu goes to England and places his views before the Parliament. If we are not there to represent our grievances, do not you think that the verdict of the Parliament will be one sided ? No doubt my first object in going there is in connection with my own appeal. Mr. Bomanji : That is also our work. Mr. Tilak (continuing) : After my work in connection with the appeal is over, I shall be devoting my attention towards ventilating our grievances before the British public. I am going to tell them in plain language that if India is not given home rule the empire will be in very great danger (Hear, hear). Our demand is cut and dried in the draft of the congress-league scheme. You all must remember that we are, not going there to beg something of them but that we are going there to demand what is our birth right. God is on our side. By His grace time will soon come when all of us will assemble here to thank England for having given us home rule. Mr. Bipin Chandra Pal was then requested to speak. He said : Why are we going to England? Is it because our countrymen want us to go? No, we are going to England because the empire's call has dinned into our ears. (Cheers). The empire at present is in great danger.

And we are going to England to show to the British public how they can escape from that danger. (Applause). The manpower of England is now growing feeble and now they cannot do without taking the help of the manpower of India. Such is the state of affairs now. Unless the people of India are satisfied, unless their ,expectations in the matter of home rule are fulfilled, they will never be ready to fight for the empire.

We are going to say so in plain language to the British public. (Applause). Messrs. Khaparde and Kelkar then thanked the organisers of the At Home. The audience then urged on Mr. Horniman to speak and he said: Gentlemen, as a loyal Englishman I am of opinion that the grant of home rule is absolutely necessary for the safety and protection of the British Empire. I am one of those who maintain that home rule must be granted to India not only for the safety of the Empire but for the principles of human liberty and justice. As a loyal Englishman and one devoted to the British Empire I would like to see the British Empire, to go to rack and ruin rather than to be working against its great principles in any part of the Empire. (Applause). Mr. Jamnadas Dwarkadas then said : I am glad to offer our best wishes to Mr. Tilak and his colleagues on behalf of the younger generation. Mr. Tilak has for the whole of his life been fighting. A mass meeting attended by about 5000 people was held ,on Tuesday the 26th March 1918 at 6.30 p.m. to give a hearty send off to Mr. Tilak and other members of the Home Rule-deputation in the compound of Shantaram's Chawl, Kandewadi. Members of the deputation, Messrs. Tilak, Khaparde, Bipin Chandra Pal, Karandikar and N.C. Kelkar, and other home rulers like Messrs. P.K. Telang, Horniman, Jamnadas, Ratansi Dharamsi, Dr. Munje, Hon. Mr. Upasani and others were among those sitting on the platform. Dr. M.D. Welkar said: Gentlemen, we have met here this evening to bid bon voyage and safe and speedy return to Lokmanya Tilak and the other members of the Home Rule Deputation that is going to England shortly, and you will all agree with me, I am sure, when I propose that the President of our Home Rule League, the Hon'ble Mr. Jinnah should preside on this occasion. Mr. Tuljapurkar in seconding the motion said : Gentlemen, I will not take much of your time in seconding the motion. Mr. Jinnah is the President of our Home Rule league and he is the real jina (ladder) of Swarajya. Had it not been for such a ladder it would not have been possible for the home rule league to attain that amount of success that it had attained in such a very short time and it is therefore but meet and proper that he should preside on this memorable occasion. The Hon'ble Mr. Jinnah then rose to speak amidst loud cheers and said : Gentlemen, I feel sure that I am voicing the feelings of all assembled here this evening when I say that we all wish the members of our deputation most heartily bon voyage safe and speedy return and every success in their mission. I feel sure also that you will all agree with me when I say that no man is more fitted to voice the views of India to the English Democracy than Mr. Tilak who has devoted the whole of his life for the national cause and whose words would surely carry a great weight in England. Before Mr. Montague arrived in India we were asked to maintain a calm atmosphere and we are maintaining a calm atmosphere because Mr. Montague is at present here and he is investigating the case for home rule for India. And we desire that there should be no bungling. We say so in plain words that let it be clearly understood that the demand for the immediate step towards the transfer into our hands of the control of the Government of this country and for the marking of a clear road to establish self-Government is the united demand of the whole of India and not a demand of a particular class or creed. Home rule is the birth of every man and in demanding home rule we are simply claiming our birth right and it is laying down of the principle of self-determination for India. And we feel sure that Mr. Tilak is the man who will be able to place our case in the best possible manner not only before the English Democracy but before the English Nation. Mr. Tilak on rising to speak was received with deafening cries of Bande Mataram and Tilak Maharaj ki jaya and Tilak Raja ki jaya. He said : Mr. Jinnah and gentlemen, I thank you all very sincerely for the honour you have done me and my party and for the good wishes for our success.

The principle of self-determination lays down that every nation, every country, has the right to choose the sort of Government they should have and it should precede self-government. We are determined to have selfgovernment in the near future-at an early date-and to have a substantial instalment to begin with. While the question of self-determination for the European Nations and the African colonies was discussed India was excluded. President Wilson said that Ireland should have self-determination and our Prime Minister convened the Irish Convention to draft a scheme of their own, but India without any such declaration, formulated a scheme of its own. Mr. Montague came to India and he studied on the spot in consultation with the members of the bureaucracy who were primarily opposed to any sort of self-government in this country. He was to formulate a scheme and act as an umpire and arrive at a settlement, a compromise between the two parties-the people and the bureaucracy. We want responsible government which has been agreed to by the bureaucracy except in connection with the steps and the time for establishing the same. The chances or Mr. Montague's scheme, I think, though I am an optimist, are not so bright as many of our people imagine them to be. Our opponents are trying to impress upon the British people that if selfgovernment were granted to India the empire would go to ruins and that in the interest of the empire India must be continued to be Government in a despotic manner. A very keen campaign has been undertaken by determined people to defeat our object. We have now to fight two parties, the Cabinet who would have to be convinced and the Sydenhamites (cries of shame, shame) who would have to be The Hon'ble Mr. Jinnah : Suppressed. Mr. Tilak (continuing) : And the Sydenhamites who would have to be "suppressed" as our President suggests. The way is not so smooth as some of us believe. The question to be determined is whether if Mr. Montague's scheme fell short, our leaders would accept the temptation held out and would be prepared to receive something shadowy but apparently substantial. Some of our leaders might advise it. Surely our Anglo-Indian friends and newspapers might do that. We are going to plead before the British Democracy the cause of self-government for India taking our stand upon the Congress League Scheme. I therefore earnestly urge upon you to stand by us not only now but two months hence like men, like resolute men, and insist upon having nothing less than the Congress League Scheme. There ought to be no compromise in this matter (Applause). Remember, if you accept any compromise, we shall be left in the lurch in all humiliation and we shall be laughed at by the whole world. (Cries of no, no). The bureaucracy whose interest is sure to suffer if we get home rule, might try to create a split amongst us. The bureaucracy, might say that they have done enough by giving us something and that we ought to be satisfied with that something. But I warn you, you will ruin your country if you accept any such compromise. You must remember that America did not enter the war simply because of German Kaiserdom being substituted by bureaucratic Kaiserdom. America did not go to help England simply because England was her mother country or simply to, protect England, but America joined the war to put an end to, despotism in any and every part of the world. I earnestly appeal to you to be careful, attentive and to act as men, resolute men, and to stand by the resolution of the Congress and the Muslim League. The Hon'ble Mr. Khaparde then addressed the audience, He said : Gentlemen, we must remain firm in our demand and must guard against temptation. The bureaucracy will surely try their utmost to put temptations in our way because it is, the interest of the bureaucracy which will suffer if we get all that we ask for. The bureaucracy will therefore try to put temptations in our way under any guise and we must be careful not to fall a prey to any compromising, attitude, because you must remember that if you fall a prey to any compromise you are sure to lose everything. Mr.

Bipin Chandra Pal said: Gentlemen, there is no doubt that we owe a great deal to Mr. Montague for his visit although I am not sure as to what would be the practical result of Mr. Montague's visit. But, gentlemen I know this much that the sun of Mr. Montague who had risen on the political horizon of India freed us from the mosquitoes and fleas of the C.I.D. (cries of shame, shame) who were following us everywhere. Last year when I came here I was not allowed to deliver any speech. I was even threatened with internment under the Defence of India Act (cries of shame, shame). Do not cry shame, shame, my friends. Police is all powerful at present and we want to deprive them of this power and we want to put that power into the bands of the people and that is why we are crying for home rule. The whole question before us at present is how to transfer that power from the bureaucracy to ourselves. If you had asked to go to England as one of the deputation years ago I would never have agreed to go. I did not like to go to England to beg alms of the English people. But I see that now the times are changed. We now are going to England not as mendicants to beg for the gift of home rule but we are going to tell the British Democracy that if Home Rule is not granted to India it would be done so at the risk not of the future of India but of the Empire and of the whole civilized world. (Applause), No doubt the hands of India are weak at present but the future of England and of the Empire is at present in the hands of India. At present there is one nation in the world, in Asia, whose army and navy is invincible.

That nation is not affected by the present war but it has enriched itself by furnishing ammunitions to the warring nations. And that nation is Japan. No doubt at present Japan is one of the allies. But sometimes we feel doubtful when we think of her movements in Siberia. If Japan turns into a belligerent nation who will save India from her. It is not possible unless they raise a national army in India. England at present is lacking in manpower. If England wants to use the manpower of India she must at first remove the dissatisfaction among the people and must satisfy the political ambition of the Indian people. If England takes the Indian people into its confidence the national army of the thirty crores of Indians will be on her side. We are claiming home rule from the British Democracy by placing all these things before them. I thank you all for your good wishes and I hope and trust that day and night you all would be ready to strive and work and suffer for the realization of our aspirations. I implore you all to work without flinching, without violence and without fear. I appeal to you to hold on to the cause and the banner of home rule and thus proceed to victory. Mr. R.P. Karandikar then addressed the meeting in Marathi. He said : Gentlemen, in the Bible there is a sentence "knock and it will open", and that is the characteristic of the English people. Unless we knock at the door of the British people for Swarajya, they will open the door of home rule for us. We are going to knock at their door and we are sure that with our knocking at their door in England and with your continuing the agitation in India we are sure to reach our goal., (Applause). Mr. N.C. Kelkar then addressed the meeting in Marathi. He said : Gentlemen, I will say what I have to say in three minutes. Wherever we go we are asked. "Why do you go to England ?" Well, I answer we to England for asking for Swarajya. Well, they say, "Why do you go to England for asking Swarajya ?" Well, I tell them if we are not to go to England for asking for Swarajya, are we to go to Japan ? If our present rulers do not give us Swarajya, perhaps time may come when we may have to go to Japan to ask for Swarajya. But at present we must ask for Swarajya from England and that is the reason why we are going to England. Well, then some people ask, "Why do you go to England ?" I say if some one else wants to go we do not want to go. Because others do not want to go we are going. Then others ask "Are you going to England ?" I tell them we are not going there for good but we are going there and coming back. Mr. Tilak and other members of the deputation were then garlanded amidst cheers. Mr. S.R. Bomanji in proposing a hearty vote of thanks to the chairman said : Gentlemen, I need not say anything more about our Chairman. He accepted the Presidentship of the Home Rule League at a time when some people used to laugh at our movement. And under his presidentship the Home Rule-League has attained the status which is well known to you all. Mr. Jamnadas Dwarkadas seconded the proposal which was carried unanimously. The Hon'ble Mr. Jinnah in replying to the vote of thanks said : Mr. Tilak and gentlemen, I assure you all that I feel it a very great honour to be asked to preside over a meeting like this and express our feelings to Mr. Tilak and other members of the deputation. Let me assure you, Mr. Tilak, that the Congress would stand by the principles it advocated for the last 32 years and as clearly embodied in the Congress League Scheme and that the leaders of the Indian National Congress were not likely to be taken into the trap laid by the bureaucracy and that they would not serve from their resolution by one inch or iota. The meeting was then dissolved amidst the deafening cries of Bande Mataram and Tilak Maharaj ki Jaya). (A great mass meeting was held on Sunday (15-11-17) in the Conference Randall at Godhra, when Mr. Tilak delivered a striking address on Indian Home Rule. Mr. Gandhi presided). Mr. Tilak, who was accorded a tremendous ovation on rising to speak, apologised to them for the unavoidable necessity of his having to speak to 'them in Marathi. He then delivered his address on "Swarajya" and why they wanted it. He referred at the outset to the forces of opposition and reaction that had recently been brought into active play. An attempt was being made by these forces to create misunderstanding in the minds of ignorant Englishmen as to what they wanted in India. It was unfortunate that some of their own men should have allowed themselves to be led away by the campaign of calumny against the Home Rulers. Of course, it was explicable why the authorities were up in arms against the agitation for constitutional reform in India. They feared very naturally that, if the Indian demand were conceded, it would seriously interfere with the unfettered exercise of their power and authority to which they had been long used.

Laterly, a body of retired Englishmen who had lost all touch with the rate of progress in India and who had otherwise done little or nothing to acquaint themselves about the real India had begun to pose themselves as the great "friends" of the Indian people and had been giving the world to understand that they were out for helping Indian to attain Nationhood. It was indeed very kind of them to be taking so much trouble for their sake. But it was somewhat curious that the Harrises and Sydenhams who in their day never did a good work to the Indian people should have now come forward, especially on the eve of Mr. Montague's visit to this country. He next referred to the internment of Mrs. Besant and the great humiliation that was in store for the Madras bureaucrats led by Lord Pentland. It had irritated them considerably no doubt, and they lost their perspective in consequence. It had been forgotten that they did not want Lord Pentland to be removed but they wanted that Lord Pentland should act in consonance with their will. The Civil Servants too were afraid that if "Swarajya" were given to the people, their power and authority (Izzat and Ibradat) would be gone, and the Civil Servants were, therefore opposed to it. "Swarajya" meant only one thing, continued Mr. Tilak, and that thing was that the power should be vested in them (the people). It meant that, under it, the Sovereign Power would be strengthened and not Authority. The great claim of the bureaucracy was that it had made India "prosperous." He would concede it, but the facts were against it. During their 100 years' work in India, he wanted to know what the bureaucracy had done to train the people industrially and otherwise and make them self-helping and self-reliant. It was an open secret that the cotton duties, which had happily been done away with now, had been hitherto maintained in the interests of Lancashire cotton spinners.

The authorities were naturally anxious to maintain power in their own hands and they had no quarrel with them for that. But that desire was unjustifiable the moment the lawful claimants demanded it back. It had been said that the English Government had given India peace and order; but that was all. The peace and order had been accompanied by no tangible results. During the time of the Peshwas, there were no elaborate commissariat arrangements and yet at a moment's notice hundreds of people were ready to render service to the State and it was not said that the Peshwas, had not maintained peace and order. As he had already remarked, it was the great secret of political Government by England that a so-called peace and order bad been given without any tangible results. In this connection, he referred to Dadabhai's famous indictment of British Rule and paid a warm tribute of praise to the great work of the deceased patriot. Referring to the Queen's Proclamation of 1858, he pointed out now it had been treated by many of the bureaucrats, responsible as well as irresponsible, as no better than of anti-quarian interest.

To the ruler, colour made no difference in the treatment of his subjects, but men in authority were swayed by their own passions and prejudices and had nullified the great pledges given to them in the past. Dealing with the Morley-Minto Reforms, he observed that while there was some improvement over the past state of affairs, the progress was by no means satisfactory or even consistent with their actual needs. In the Legislative Councils, they were like witnesses in a Court of Law : they were mere lookers-on of the great drama of Government. They did not certainly want that kind of farce any more. What they wanted was real, effective control over the administration both Legislative and Executive. Mr. Tilak also referred to the recent Italian reverses and regretted that India was not in a position to support the Allied cause as well as they might have wished. India's military power had remained unexploited, and he doubted very much if it would have been so if the Government were "popular".

As Mr. Lloyd George had said in his message to Lord Willingdon, what was wanted was that India's heart should be "touched". Until that was done, it was not possible to expect great help from India. After all, the Government had to remember that with this War, all the trouble would not automatically cease. As Mr. Bonar Law once remarked, "there might be a second Punic war yet. The future was full of perils and grave portents and it was statesmanship to be ready to face any eventualities." The Anglo-Indians' hue and cry was not only ill-timed and-ill advised but was positively harmful to the lasting interests of the Empire. The people wanted Self-Government not only for their own benefit but for the sake of the Empire. In any struggle or crisis a contented Self-governing India was the greatest and surest asset of the Empire, and those who overlooked it were doing the greatest mischief to the Imperial cause. Apart from it the case for Self-Government was invincible.

A strong wave of democracy was passing all the world over and even the British Government had hailed the Russian Revolution as the "first great triumph of the present War." Lord Sydenham's contention that they in India take advantage of Britain's troubles to agitate for Self-Government was false. They had already been agitating for Self-Government for over 30 years. All over the world Self-Government was on the anvil, and India alone could not be expected to sit still. People were no longer prepared to put up with "stone laying" governors and a civil service that spent public money as it pleased. They wanted to see that, after the War, the Government was thoroughly responsible to the people and carried on the administration according to their needs. Before resuming his seat, Mr. Tilak exhorted the audience to be hold and courageous and frankly tell the officials, if they were asked, that they wanted Home Rule. It was no crime to say that. The demand had been admitted to be fair, legitimate and constitutional by the highest judicial and executive authorities in the land, and lately His Majesty's Government had accepted it as the goal of British rule in India. Mr. Tilak resumed his seat amidst a fresh outburst of cheering after he had spoken for fully an hour.

5

Tilak : His Contribution to Education

Practice of Education in India

To understand Lokmanya Tilak's contribution to philosophy and practice of Education in India it is necessary to acquaint ourselves with the situation that existed in India during the 19th century.

The Education System in India before the Advent of the British

The Peshwas did not pay any special attention to education, nor did they have any systematic plan for education of the people. Generally, according to the requirements of the villagers, at least one school was run in every village. Reading, Writing and Arithmetic useful for keeping accounts, were the subjects taught. Education necessary for meeting the requirements of day to day life was given. Teachers did not get a fixed regular salary. At many places they had to depend upon gifts and offerings by students or patronage of wealthy people. At some places monthly fees were charged, which ranged from 5 to 50 paise. The number of students varied from place to place. At some places it would be less than ten, at others it would be close to a hundred. Students from all castes except the Dalits (the downtrodden) were given admissions. Girls were not allowed to take education. School timings, the duration of teaching, holidays and fees were decided according to the conveniences of teachers and students. The emphasis was on rote-learning. Dust boards were used for writing. There were no independent buildings for schools. Schools were held in public places like temples and choultries or in some villages, in the house of a wealthy man. In those days such rural schools were known as 'Tatya Pantoji's Schools'.

"In Pantoji's School, the curriculum comprised of modi script, reading, writing, tables, and practising alphabets. Learning meant practising the writing of alphabets, writing and reciting tables, doing sums of addition, subtraction, multiplication and division and some mental calculations. Same things were repeated again and again. There were no qualifications required for teaching. Anybody who had the will could get a few children and open a school. Reading and writing Devnagri script was the privilege of priests. Householders learnt modi".

The above description written around 1838-39 by Ravsaheb Bhawalkar can be accepted as a representative depiction of rural schools.

Studies of Vedas and Shastras enjoyed high social esteem. There were schools run by learned teachers and Brahmins took advantage of them. A large number of people were in family business or occupation. They used to get the necessary training in the house itself, starting from their early childhood. Mostly women and those belonging to the lowest castes were prohibited from acquiring even the basic skills of reading.

In mosques, mullahs and moulavis used to teach religious and practical matters in Urdu or Persian. At some places Muslim boys went to a Hindu teacher's school. These schools were private and were not controlled by any authority. They were totally autonomous. On the whole this type of education did cater to the needs of the contemporary society.

The Advent of the Company Government in the Field of Education

The English came to India for trade on behalf the East India Company, and then taking advantage of the situation obtained here, became the rulers. In keeping with their changed role, their educational policy was modified.

In 1793, while granting licence to the Company, Wilber Force made a suggestion.

"The court of Directors of the company shall be empowered and commissioned to nominate and send out from time to time a sufficient number of skilled and suitable persons who shall attain the aforesaid object by serving as school-masters, missionaries or otherwise". These objectives were the advancement of the natives in useful knowledge, and also their religious and moral improvement.

But this suggestion was turned down for social and political motives. "In the debate held at that time someone plainly said that the British had lost America by opening schools and colleges there, and that mistake should not be repeated in the case of India." Some people were opposed to taking the responsibility of educating the natives.

In 1813 again, while renewing the Company's licence the question of imparting education to the natives came up for discussion again. Due to the insistence of some progressive liberals, it was included in the licence that "it shall be the duty of the Governor General in Council to set apart every year a lakh of rupees and to spend the same for the revival and improvement of literature and encouragement of the learned native of India and for the introduction and production of knowledge of sciences to away the inhabitants of the British territories in India".

But there was a lot of controversy about the content and medium of education whether to impart their traditional oriental education or the modern western education; whether the medium of instruction should be a distinguished ancient language such as Sanskrit or Pharsee, a regional language in use in those days, or English. These discussions were necessary, because the decisions taken were going to be of great importance for the British rule in India. The future of the British rule depended on the kind of education that would be given to the natives. The long term consequence of the new education would be the end of the British rule. At the same time this process of education, if followed step by step, would strengthen its foundations.

Spread of Education by the Missionaries

Soon Christian missionaries arrived in India, following the footsteps of the traders. In the early days the Company officers co-operated with them. Even in England religious institutions were asked to take the responsibility of education. In India, too, missionaries opened schools to serve the cause of education. Among them were schools for girls and the downtrodden people too. Education was free. Only sometimes a small fee was charged. Scholarships were given for encouragement.

In the Bombay province, missionaries had started promoting education even before the Company arrived on the scene. "Mr. Hall and Mr. Nut were the first ones to start a school. They made a rule by which children of all castes and classes were eligible for admission. By the end of 1817, there were six missionary schools altogether, and they had admitted around eight hundred children. There was not even one government school at that time. The government had not even thought of educating the natives by opening schools". This quotation is from the 16th May 1853 issue of 'Jnanoday'.

The main motive of the missionaries behind promoting education was religious propaganda and conversions to Christianity. That was the reason why the upper caste Hindus were not willing to send their children to missionary schools. Janardanpant Kirtane and Govindrao Ranade (Father of Justice M. G. Ranadé) preferred to send their children to the Elphinstone college, surpassing the political agent Col. Reeves advice to put them in the Wilson College.

An article entitled 'Bombay Brahmins Boycott Christian Missionary Schools' says-

> "The Christian missionaries, alias Fathers distribute books in this country in order to spread Christianity. With this intention they have opened many schools here. The Hindu children who go to these schools, many times, do not know their own religion well. They hear the Fathers praising Christianity and criticizing Hinduism all the time. As a result, many Hindus have got converted so far, and there will be many more conversions in the years to come. Therefore, for protection of our religion, the following resolution is passed Brahmins shall not attend missionary schools nor they hear sermons on Christianity. They shall also stop their children and the people belonging to lower castes from doing so".

The above letter published in the 24th Sep. 1842 issue of 'Prabhakar' is also noteworthy.

In this context the missionaries themselves had the following opinion. "Western India proved to be a much harder ground for missionary work than among other part of India. Prejudice against the foreigners and foreign faith were stronger here than in Calcutta or Madras. In Western India the loss of political independence of the Marathas coincided with the commencement of missionary work".

Religious education was unavoidable in missionary schools. That was why the Company authorities were against giving the responsibilities of education in India to the missionaries. They understood the importance of religious neutrality for strengthening the newly acquired political power. Elphinstone, the Governor of the Bombay Province did not take objection to the Scottish missionaries activities in Hernai or Bankot. He even gave them donations in personal capacity. But he never openly supported them as a part of his political and administrative policy.

Elphinstone's Educational Policy

Elphinstone was the Resident in the court of Peshwas from 1811 to 1818. In 1819 he was appointed the Governor of Bombay, and retired from the same post in 1827. He had keen interest in the education of the natives. He was of the opinion that teaching and learning in the mother tongue saved time and toil, and so if the mother-tongue was used as the medium of instruction, education could reach the power centres at different levels. He firmly believed that the vicious customs in this country would be uprooted only through education. He also maintained that the education of the poor and the funds required for it was the Government's responsibility.

In the licence issued in 1813, though the general objectives of Indian education were mentioned, the details had yet to be worked out. Elphinstone recommended new western education through regional languages- Marathi or Gujrathi.

In 1815 the "Bombay Education Society" was established for the education of the English and the Anglo-Indian children. In August 1820, a meeting of the Society was held under the chairmanship of Elphinstone. Jagannath Shankarseth, Jamshethji Jijibhai, Framji Kawasji, Mohammed Ibrahim Makwa and some respectable businessmen of Bombay were present at this meeting. Resolutions were passed regarding writing of text-books in English, Marathi and Gujrathi, giving grants to the native schools working at that time, and establishment of new schools. Another very important resolution was passed by which the medium of instruction in those schools would be regional languages.

For the execution of this new policy 'The Native School and School Book Committee' was constituted. But the scope of this committee was more extensive than the original policy of the society, so the Bombay Education Society restricted its own activities to European and Anglo-Indian students. As the Bombay Education

Society thus changed its policy, in 1822 a new society called 'The Bombay Native School Book and School Society' was formed.

This Society started new type of schools in native languages on the Island of Bombay. In 1824, an English school was also opened. Many parents hesitated to send their children to English medium schools for the fear of conversion.

"In order to remove their misconceptions and make modern education acceptable to them, along with Capt. Jervis, Kashinath alias Bapu Chhatre was appointed Native Secretary on Rs. 100/- per month".12 In 1830 Balshastri Jambhekar was appointed as Deputy Native Secretary, and in 1832, he who was in his twenties (born in 1812) was promoted to the post of Deputy Secretary. This was really a great honor to the achievement of a native scholar.

The secretary of the 'Bombay Native' used to be a government servant and the members used to be private citizens. This institution used to get a government grant to the tune of Pounds 5000 per annum. They also collected donations from private sources. From that fund they used to run schools in Bombay and else where. There were thirteen Europeans and eleven Indians on the Managing Committee. The European persons were names like Candy, Jervis etc. Elphinstone was the first chairman followed by Malcom.

The job of spreading education in the Bombay Province was entrusted to this society. Elphinstone has many times expressed his views on education for the natives. While recommending the Institutions for financial aid, he made the following suggestions.

"(i)to improve the mode of teaching at the native schools and to increase the member of schools, (ii) to supply them with books, (iii) to hold out some encouragement to the lower orders of natives to avail themselves of the means of instructions thus offered to them, (iv) to establish schools for teaching the European Sciences and improvements in the higher branches of Education, (v) to provide for the preparation and publication of books and moral and physical science in native languages, (vi) to establish schools for the purpose of teaching English to those disposed to pursue it as a classical language and as a means of acquiring knowledge of the European discoveries, and (vii) to hold forth encouragement to the natives in the pursuit of those lost branches of knowledge".

If the medium of instruction was to be a vernacular, it was necessary to write books in that language. Elphinstone appointed a committee for this purpose. That committee produced some really good text books.

During the years 1818 to 1827 three books were published in Marathi and all the three books were translations of English books on mathematics. During the period 1827 to 1838, ten books were published - two on medical science, two of Jambhekar's on Mathematics and Geometry, two Readers by Major Candy, Dadoba Pandurang's Grammar, and Hari Keshavji Pathare's book on Physics. From 1837 to 1847, thirty books were published, and from 1847-1857 the number rose to hundred and two. During the course of eight years from 1857 to 1864, five hundred and fifty books were published.

Till the year 1850, a Marathi dictionary with grants from the Government, Moulsworth's Marathi-English dictionary, Major Candy's dictionary, Shrikrishna Shastri's concise dictionary were published. A dictionary and Grammar were new to Marathi and was encouraging for the language.

Among the books written during this period, text-books written for schools had a large share. But it was a welcome trend that books in Astronomy, Geography, Physics, Chemistry, Mechanics etc., albeit through translations, were brought in to Marathi. On the whole the number of books translated from Sanskrit and English was very large. But as time passed the number of original works increased. In the beginning the authors were mostly from Bombay and so their diction had an influence of Konkani, but later, authors who had studied in grammar schools in Pune, had their prose style influenced by Sanskrit.

Bombay was a business centre, bustling with followers of different religions. It had been under the British rule since 1665, So the Bombayites were conversant with the English culture. No wonder their mode of thinking was influenced by it. Puneites hated the English whom they considered responsible for the loss of their Kingdom.

"Robertson was appointed the Collector of Pune. One day his Secretary received an application saying, "Let us know in your reply when the British rule will come to an end". However the applicant had concealed his identity. The collector said, "Write at the bottom of the application that our Kingdom will fall only when either we get divided, or the natives get united. Not till then". Writing their remarks on the application, he gave orders to stick it like a decree near the gate of Tulsibag if the applicant did not come forth; accordingly, it was stuck there".

The city of Pune was orthodox and conservative. "A man by name Gangadhar Dikshit Phadke was a teacher in Bombay from 1820 to 1825, where he taught the English people. When he later came to Pune, he was ostracized because the Puneites thought that he could not have escaped eating or doing things not permitted in the Hindu community. In the end he had to leave Pune and lead a life of renunciation".

At the same time there was a large number of Brahmins who had once enjoyed power, but now had no patronage. "A few days back, the Brahmins were most honoured, they were the religious and political leaders. But all of a sudden they lost their prosperity and progress. Their 'mantra' became powerless and they themselves helpless".

The sting of fall was still fresh in their minds. "This class of Brahmins was not only strong in numbers, but had in them the seeds of systematic governance, a good social order and ancient culture. It was on the strength of these qualities the Hindu Society stayed stable and integrated for centuries. In this class of Brahmins there was no dearth of scholars, soldiers, learned people or civilized householders. Who else was required for administration?"

Elphinstone knew that the British rulers could not afford to keep this class discontented or neglected. It was absolutely necessary to pacify their anger and win their sympathy, if the British rule was to stabilize. That was why, Elphinstone who advocated modern education through regional languages, opened a college for Sanskrit studies in Pune, on the auspicious day of Dasshera.

Shastris and Vedics were appointed as teachers in this College. Subjects like the Vedas, Grammar, medicine, figures of speech, were taught there. "At Diwali time, besides a good bath in the early morning, students were served special Diwali sweets like Ladu, Karanjya, Anarase and so on. It was all Peshwa style in that College. The British Principal was not allowed to enter the College building. It is said that on one occasion when he did, 'Udakshanti' was performed".

The Managing Committee was opposed to spending money on this Sanskrit College. But Elphinstone convinced them that the expenditure was permissible because the money was spent from the amount which had already been sanctioned for Shravanmas charity. The establishment of the Sanskrit College was a part of Elphinstone's policy of the appeasement of the people and the Brahmins. It was mainly for the sake of stability for the English rule.

Later on, the nature of this Pathashala underwent a lot of change. English classes were incorporated, and ultimately it got transformed, first as the Poona College, and later as the Deccan College.

Lokmanya Tilak says, "The task of destroying self rule and establishing foreign rule is an extremely difficult task because the natives keep smarting under the insult. In such circumstances the ruler needs great tact", and Elphinstone did possess it.

The fact that he adopted two different policies for Bombay and Pune proves his cleverness.

1827 to 1840 : The Bombay Native Education Society

In 1827, 'The Bombay Native School Book and School Society' was renamed as the 'Bombay Native Education Society', in keeping with the changed objectives. This Society enjoyed Elphinstone's support and guidance. He invited some highly respectable contemporary Indian personalities, and introduced them to the working of the Society.

In 1827, Elphinstone retired. In commemoration of his excellent services the Bombay Native Education Society decided to collect Rs. 1,20,500 for creation of a professorship in his name. In this context the following resolution was passed.

To enable the Society to erect an educational memorial to Elphinstone, people voluntarily collected a fund of Rupees 2,00,000/-. The Board of Directors contributed sumptuously. In 1834 the Elphinstone Institute was founded, which started the Elphinstone College. The English medium school in Bombay was renamed as the Elphinstone School.

Upto 1840, the Bombay Native Education Society did substantial work in the field of education in the Bombay Province. The Society used to run schools in Bombay, Thane, Panvel, and Pune. The principals of these schools used be Europeans. Though these schools were called primary schools, their nature was just like that of our middle schools. Subjects like Reading, Writing, Arithmetic, Euclidean Geometry, History of England, History of India, Astronomy, Philosophy, Algebra etc. were taught there.

Due to this attitude, the Society gave priority to opening more and more primary schools of the above type. In 1840 the society ran as many as 115 schools. Inadequate funds and scarcity of trained teachers, were the two factors which brought the Society's standard down.

During 1825 to 1832, the society spent more than Rs. 2,00,000/- on book- writing, publications and encouragement awards. In the history of a native language this was the first event when rulers and thinkers made such a concerned effort.

However, later on, when the supporters of English as the medium of instruction became more powerful, the Regulatory Body of the Company Government sent a letter in 1832 expressing displeasure at the way the Bombay Province was squandering money on the native languages. Gradually the pace of the Society's work slowed down.

In those days the Bombay Government used to manage the colleges in Bombay and Pune, and also the 63 primary schools in the Purandar Taluka in Pune District. These Purandar primary schools were unique in the sense they were different from the primary schools mentioned above. Their curriculum was similar to that of 'Tatya Pantoji Schools', but the teachers were government employees. These schools were established in 1837 on the suggestion of the Assistant Collector of that region Capt. Shortrede. They were under the control of the Revenue Department till 1840. These schools were used for promotion of education of the masses.

1840 to 1854 : The Board of Education

In 1840, the Bombay Government constituted the 'Board of Education' to look after the management of all the institutions. That was the end of the Bombay Native Education Society. There were seven members on the Board, out of which three were recommended by the Bombay Native Education Society. All the three were natives. All the schools managed by the Society and the Government as well as the colleges in Bombay and Pune, were handed over to the Board for management. In 1842 the Bombay Province was divided into three sectors for administrative convenience, each of which was supervised by a European inspector. The Board opened primary schools in the villages having a population of two thousand and above, if the villagers gave land for the school and were ready to pay one anna as the monthly fee. Generally speaking, the Board continued the policies of the Bombay Native Society. In 1845 a training class for primary teachers was started in Elphinstone Institute in Bombay. In 1854 the report on the Board's performance, the following statement is found, "Considerable attention has also been paid in Bombay to education through the medium of vernacular languages It appears that 215 vernacular schools are under management of the Board of Education — the schools are reported to be improving and masters trained in the Government College have been recently appointed —. These results are very creditable to the residency of Bombay".

The question of the medium of instruction was controversial and especially in Bengal, Raja Ram Mohan Roy also insisted on English. There it was Arabi, Sanskrit or English. In 1934 Macaulay came to India. He was the Chairman of the 'General Committee of Public Instruction' and the law Member of the Executive Committee of the Governor General. In his opinion "A single shelf of a good European library was worth the whole native literatures of India and Arabia".

Such was his ignorance of the oriental culture. He did not know Sanskrit or Arabic languages and had no interest in them either. His opinion of the native languages was that they were backward. He propagated English emphatically. The Governor General Bentinck was also of the same opinion. In 1835 he gave orders. "The great object of the British Government ought to be the promotion of European literature and science among the natives of India and that all the funds appropriated for the purpose of education would be best employed on English education alone"

In the Bombay Province the choice was not between English and Sanskrit, it was between a regional language and English. This policy of the Governor General had its impact in Bombay too.

In 1843, Eraskin Perry became the chairman of the Board of Education. He was a supporter of English as the medium of instruction. He did not agree with the policy of the Bombay National Education Society, of using an Indian language to impart higher education as far as possible. He put forth a proposal that like Bengal, Bombay also should adopt English as the medium of instruction. But Jagannath Shankarseth, Framji Kawasji and Mohammed Ibrahim Makwas opposed it vehemently. They supported the use of Indian languages. In the end the question was referred to the Government and in 1848 the Government took the decision, "When examinations in Marathi, Gujrathi and

English were conducted, it was doubtlessly proved that those who study in the mother tongue learn quickly. So, the Government's opinion is that learning should be in one's own language".

Taking into consideration the differences between the situations in Bengal and Bombay, it was decided that the vernacular would be used in primary schools, where-as in colleges English would be the medium of instruction.

By that time English was granted the status of the official language. Knowledge of English was obligatory for the Government service. The demand for English went up because of the financial benefits of knowing it. The inevitable consequence was that, schools using Indian languages began to be considered inferior, and even in the Bombay Province English got an entry everywhere except the lowest standards.

Students' Literary and Scientific Society

Another noteworthy event of this period is the foundation of the 'Students' Literary And Scientific Society' in 1848, by Prof. Paton of the Elphinstone College. In the same year, two branches-one for Marathi and one for Gujrathi and Parsi were opened. The Marathi branch was named 'Upayukta Jnanprasarak Sabha'. Dadoba Pandurang was the chairman. 'Upayukta' means useful in practical life, 'Jnan' means knowledge, and 'Prasarak' means one who spreads it. So, to popularize knowledge, skills, arts and other things desirable to learn, was the principal objective of this Association.

In 1850 this Association started a magazine called 'Marathi Jnanaprasarak'. Its contents included articles on various subjects like Biology, Chemistry, Physics, Politics, Economics, Sociology, Stories, Poetry, drama, fiction etc.

Great leaders in Bombay like Dr. Atmaram Pandurang, Dr. Sakharam Arjun, Bhau Daji, Kero Laxman, Chhatre, Vishwanath Narayan Mandlik, Govind Narayan, Hari Keshavji, K. T. Telang, and also students who later became famous, such as Justice Ranade, R. G. Bhandarkar, M.M. Kunte, Mama Parmanand, B. D. Palande, V. A. Modak, Vishnushstri Pandit, were members of this Society.

For some time this Society managed schools for girls. Till 1854, the number of girls schools went up to nine. About six hundred girls were studying in them.33

1855 to 1880 The Department of Education

In 1854, Wood's despatch about Education put an end to the Board of Education. A new Department of Education was established. Under the Director of Public Education for the four sectors Presidency, Deccan, Sindh and Gujrat - four Inspectors were appointed and they were given Deputy Inspectors to assist them. The function of the Department was to work as consultant on educational matters, manage the funds kept aside for education by the central or provincial Governments, manage a particular institute, supervise the working of Government aided or registered schools, and look after the development of education in general. A separate Department of Education was put on the right track.

With this notification issued in 1854, The University of Bombay was founded in 1857. The main function of the University was to hold examinations and issue certificates. Teaching was done in respective colleges.

Teaching of regional languages like Marathi was a controversial topic in the University too. In the beginning Marathi was one of the subjects in the University of Bombay. But in 1866-67, it was declared that, 'Persons who matriculated before the close of 1863 may be examined in Portuguese, Marathi, Gujrathi, Canarese, Hindustani, Persian or Sindhi in the Bombay University Calendar.

It meant that in the course of three years, step by step, Marathi would be eliminated from colleges. So, in 1867 teaching of Marathi was completely stopped being taught in colleges.

In this circular of 1854, the place of Marathi as a medium was not denied. It has maintained that regional languages should be promoted. Yet, in reality, mother tongue medium schools were considered less important. The Department, too, did not take much cognizance of them. It is clear from the nature of the plan for primary and middle school education. The primary school which had a six year curriculum, did not teach English. But a student passing the fourth standard was allowed admission to a secondary school. The duration of secondary school curriculum was seven years. In the first three years English was taught as one of the subject, but it was the medium of instruction for the next four years.

During this period there were less controversies about the nature and medium of education. There was an integrated policy.

A graded course from standard first to graduation, came into force, and it lasted for a long time.

Till this time, though the rulers showed some interest in education in general, they do not seem to have done anything for women and the Dalits. In this context, it is worth noting that in 1851-52, Mahatma Phule opened schools for women and the downtrodden i.e. Dalits in Pune. The rulers decided to give the western education to the natives, but did not bother much about the vocational or technical education, or if at all they gave any thought to it, it was not put into practice.

In 1824, the Bombay Native Education Society had started a course in Engineering. In 1844, Elphinstone school opened one too, but Pune had to wait till 1854, for a course in Engineering.

In 1845 Grant Medical College was opened in Bombay. In 1855 two professorships, one for Law and one for Justice, were created in Bombay. The part-time evening courses in Law were also run in the Government Law College.

From the generous donation of one lakh of rupees by Jamsethji Jijibhai, J. J. School of Art was opened in Bombay in 1856.

In the Director's report of the Department of Education of the Bombay province, 1855-56 there is a reference to a photography class started in the previous September which is said to have taken advantage of by many young people from Government and private offices.

In the same report it is said that in Purandar area many classes were run in the evening and their progress was satisfactory. But such facilities were limited and inadequate, and for years there was no addition to the number of these classes.

The University of Bombay was founded in 1857 and the first matriculation Examination was held in 1859. Twenty nine students passed in that examination. Ten years later, in 1869, thirty students graduated from the University. Out of them nineteen got their B. A. degree, two got the M.A. degree, and nine students were from other branches of knowledge. Such was the rate of progress in education.

In opening engineering and medical colleges the Government thought more of its own advantage than that of the people. Construction of roads, buildings and waterways, and treatment of soldiers or diseases would become easier due to the availability of trained people and side by side the public also would profit by it.

In 1882, the 'Indian Education Commission' was constituted. It was supposed to take an up to date review of the state of education and give guidance for future policies.By this time the native thinkers had started understanding the nature of western education and its positive and negative sides.

Nature and Objectives of Education

While taking decisions about the education to be given to the natives and its medium of instruction, there were lots of agreements, for and against, put forth by the British thinkers, missionaries, Company officials, and the members of the Board of Directors. Preservation of the oriental knowledge, encouragement to study and research moral and religious reformation of Indians, sifting the good in the native culture and coupling it with the good in the western culture, these were some of the points debated. They also discussed whether education of the natives was the responsibility of the rulers for the atonement, for the acquisition of their land, and how to win the confidence of the upper strata of society which had lost its importance under the British rule.

Out of these the most powerful decisions which proved fruitful were -

(a) The English rulers need a large number of class II officers to sustain their rule in the subcontinent. If these officers were to discharge their duties promptly and efficiently, they needed to be educated. In the new regime, the traditional knowledge acquired in old-fashioned schools was not going to help. So the rulers had to get a well-educated or atleast just educated class of servants. It was not only expensive and impracticable but literally impossible to bring such people from England.

At the foundation ceremony of the Elphinstone Institute some of the Directors expressed hope that "a class of persons qualified by their intelligence and morality for high employment in the civil administration of India would be producted by the Institute".

This makes clear with what purpose they were running the Institute.

(b) A class of people would be produced, who took English education and therefore got to know the English culture and so would be in favour of the English regime "we must do our best to form a class who may be interpreters between us and the millions whom we govern, a class of persons Indian in blood and colour but English in taste, in opinion, words and intellect".37 Without education there was no other means of realising the dream of Macaulay.

(c) The main objective of imparting education was spread of Christianity."Western light and knowledge should take the place of eastern culture and religion"38 was the expectation of Charles Grant.

(d) The Anglicised class would also be helpful for trade and spread of Christianity. Though the policy of religious neutrality was adopted for the sake of political stability, it was but natural that the Christian rulers, would have, in their minds sympathy for the missionaries.

(e) Since English was made the official language, the top British Officers would not need to learn the native languages in this country of many dialects, nor would they have to depend on their subordinates for the purpose of governance. On the contrary an English knowledge servant class was going to be easily available. "It is neither our aim nor desire to substitute the English language for the vernacular dialects of the country. The vernacular languages must be employed to teach the far large classes." Despatch of the honerable court of Directors no 49. 19 July 1854.

Although such assurance was given, it was obvious that whenever principles came in conflict with practical convenience, the rulers always gave priority to the latter.

Though the Government adopted the policy of giving western education in English medium, they had never intended to train the natives for highest posts like Generals, Diplomats or legal experts.

By making education accessible to a small group of people, the Government thought its responsibility was over. They thought that education given at the top would automatically percolate to the lower strata of the society. There was no need of any special efforts; this was the Government's role in taking education to the masses. The Government which expressed a desire to reform the natives had no intention of making primary education free or compulsory for the poor people.

The British Government also did not bother to promote vocational education. In this context it must be noted that after taking the responsibility of the native education, only one engineering class was opened in Bombay over a period of twelve years, and that too was meant to meet the requirements of the Government.

The Government policy was to be frugal in expenses on education.

In the 1870-71 report of the Department of Education, the disparity between the salaries of employees in other departments and the Department of Education is highlighted.

In the Department of education nobody's salaries were like Rs. 800, Rs. 700 or Rs. 600 per month. Monthly salary of Rs. 500 per month was given only to two native professors, whereas even a class III subordinate or Deputy Collector got the same salary.

Three Headmasters got Rs. 200/- per month, which is the salary of class V Judge or a Deputy Collector.

A Deputy Inspector gets Rs. 100/- per month, which is also the salary a small size school headmaster. This is the minimum scale for mamlatdars.

The Director of Education complains that because of the lower grades of salary bright or really well-educated people do not like to work in this field, and even if a few come they take the first opportunity to move out for a better paid job.

On the whole, education that will help the British regime, its administration and stability, was the objective of education.

Consequences of this kind of Education

(1) **Dominance of English** - As English was the medium of education, it also became the language of communication of the educated class. Book writing and even private correspondence was done in English. Vishnushastri Chiplunkar and Lokmanya Tilak also were no exceptions to this rule. The prefaces and covers of Marathi books were written in English. "From this, we can see how the influence of the foreign language of a foreign government spreads in all walks of life. Marathi is banished", says V. K. Rajwade.

(2) The Government wanted the people who had acquired knowledge in English to take it to their countrymen through Marathi medium. But these people had no love for Marathi. Already a note of anger was being heard. In September 1860 issue of 'Marathi Jnanaprasarak' Vinayak Janardan Kirtane writies -

> "Many of us have got to taste the sweet diet of modern European sciences and Literature, and some others have got the unparalleled juice of Sanskrit language to taste, so both classes of people are neglecting their own language. Those who have studied English say "sheer

> nonsense. What is there in Marathi? What we have to do with it"- and those who have studied Sanskrit say - "There is nothing interesting in Marathi. Why Should we bother to study it ?"

In the end, Kirtane earnestly requests the English and Sanskrit scholars, "There are millions of your country men around you, who look up to you as their saviours from the whirlpool of ignorance. Take them out of it. Take them out of the darkness and show them a ray of light. This will give you the great satisfaction of fulfilment of your duties".

In the very first year of 'Vijvidh jnana Vistar' in the November 1867 issue, the same note is struck at a higher pitch. In an article entitled 'Marathi Bhasha' the writer says,

> "In the first Convocation ceremony the chairman had said, 'The purpose of these degrees and honours conferred on you is that you should make a good use of them. You must try hard to pass on the knowledge we have given you with so much effort, cost, to your countrymen who speak your language'. But has anyone followed this suggestion in practice ? Some people make an excuse saying that there are no corresponding words in Marathi. This is only a hollow excuse. The Government has appointed teachers on big salaries for the education of their people. But if they cannot pass on what they have received from others, then what is so great about taking those degrees?"

In the 1870-71 report of the Education Department, J. B. Paile has expressed the same kind of disapproval in the following words "Even if it be granted that there neither is nor even will be an original vernacular literature worthy to take its place with the literature of the west, — but it is no reason why the educated Indian should not learn to use with force and correctness the language to which he was born, and in which alone the mass of his fellow-country men can be addressed".

(3) **Stunted Growth of Regional Languages** - In the Bombay Province, Regional languages were used as mediums of instruction, for some years in the beginning. Some book writing - may be just translated text books of physical sciences was stimulated. As these branches of knowledge were new to Marathi, new terminology was created. If this policy had continued, after

some time Marathi would have given up dependence on the walker of translations, and would have become not only the carrier of knowledge, but would have also undertaken original and varied book-writing. In time to come Marathi would have become a source of knowledge. Marathi, as well as other regional languages would have developed, but because of the universal dominance of English, the regional languages were suppressed and their growth was stunted.

(4) **A New Awakening to History** - The history of India was included in the curriculum of those days. The early writers were English men. The history books studied in schools and colleges were written by foreigners, especially foreign rulers. Prejudice, inadequacy, misinterpretation, one sidedness, and contempt for the natives appeared at many places.

"Shivaji was a Whimsical Person. Many of his deeds were evil conquering a fort or land by fighting Guerilla wars. He liked deceitful ways more than the straight forward ones. This was one of the defects of his character. He has proved his cruelty and harmfulness on many occasions".

This is a quotation from Capt. Dough. He says, "Shivaji's behaviour was just like what we find everywhere in Asia or backward countries. He showed his bad qualities on various occasions just like a king, a plunderer, or a head of dacoits tribe, in those countries. He dealt with situation as they arose. For success in his undertaking, he did not hesitate to do anything. It is difficult to call this man a man of principles. It was his principle to hate all those who opposed his religion and towards the end he, like Aurangzeb, had started persecuting people belonging to other religions".

Even Elphinstone wrote on the same lines. He writes, "Shivaji was a son of a great General. He started his career like an adventurous and treacherous dacoit, but in the end he became an independent, sagacious ruler".

This example is significant enough. Of course there were many reactions to it. In the April 1860 issue of 'Marathi Jnanaprasarak', there was a series of articles entitled 'Shivaji Maharajancha Vrittanta'. In the final article the writer says, "The foreign historians take Shivaji for a dacoit and plunderer, and many learned men amongst us have accepted this improper view. The historians who would clap for Wallace, Bruce or Tell, who worked for the betterment of their countries, would shamelessly use word of abuse for Shivaji. We wouldn't have thought it worthwhile to refute the opinions of these partial historians. But when so many Hindu Scholars do not hesitate to support this view, we feel it necessary to refute it" The articles end as follows.

> "Shivaji did not have a desire to wipe out other kingdoms by fighting crooked and unfair battles. Shivaji rose against people who were making life difficult for his countrymen, and hurt the interest of those who did not belong to their religion. He rose to protect his country, his religion and his people against these onslaughts. Is it right to call him a dacoit, only because there were a few lapses on his part while achieving his goal. There is no doubt that if they bother to take notice of his praiseworthy cause, they will be convinced that Shivaji was one like Wallace, Bruce and Tell who loved their country".

In a paper read by Nilkantha Janardan Kirtane in 'Poona Young Men's Association' it is said, "Grantsahib has made one mistake. While writing of Shivaji's biography he did not trust the works of a Maratha. He himself has said that the parts which defile Shivaji were taken from the writings of the Muslims".44

Around the same time, Mahadeo Govind Ranade, who was still a student, wrote harsh articles of the true Marathi nature of Nana Phadnavis. Vitthalrao Pathak told the essence of Maratha history in 'Jnaprasarak'. V. J. Kirtane read a play on the senior Mahadevrao Peshwe, in a meeting held by 'Marathi Janaprasarak'.

Thus there was at least a little, just a seed's, consciousness of self-respect and their ego began to wake up. Seeds of inclination for independent thinking were sown. That the need for putting forth such a view was felt, was itself great. Even the British would not have expected this to happen so soon.

The history of England was included in the curriculum. The concepts of control of the king's power by public opinion, participation of the people in governance, individual freedom, establishment of Democracy etc., became familiar to the newly educated natives, who in the beginning thought that the rulers who enforced the rules in their country would be true to their sense of fairness and enforce them in India too.

Although they showered praise on the British regime, the thought that the British would have to leave this country one day, kept on recurring to their minds.

"The British Government is making efforts to educate the natives through the local Government and the English people. If they educate the natives, the latter will acquire the capability for self-rule. The historical annals show that no nation which can have self-rule has ever allowed others to rule them. So it should happen in this country, and it will be for the good of both the countries India and England". This was what Balashastri Jambhekar has written in the May 1840 issue of "Digdarshan".

Lokhitwadi too, who often praised the British rule, and mercilessly hammered the defects on the natives, is seen expressing the hope that "when people become enlightened they will gently tell the British, "We are educated just like you, why not have powers? "Then, probably, they will get the posts of Governors also. When they get powers, they will become independent like Americans, and ask the British to go back to their country. "Now we can govern our country very well. We don't want your advice and we don't want your domination". This will be the condition of our country".

This awakening is a consequence of English education.

(5) **Loyal Government Servants** - The British changed the traditional subjects and the mediums of education, but the change was not limited to these factors. With education the mode of thinking also changed. After some time this educated class adopted even the clothing of the British. A new class of loyal government servants came into existence. This class was self-satisfied and totally cut off from the society.

(6) **Lack of Religious Education** - In the government run or government aided schools, there was no place either for Christianity or for any of the native religions. The moral education was given through translated books like 'Balmitra', or 'Isapneeti'. Students were not introduced to the religious and cultural traditions of this country. Getting it impressed on the mind or taking pride in it was far away dream.

(7) **Inferiority Complex** - The English medium, the western content of education, teachers indebted to the fixed British curriculum and text-books. There were few teachers who would go beyond this and enkindle a flame of nationalism, mothertongue, own religion and culture in the minds of students. Most of the student's aim was to get a government job. Very few took education

for the sake of knowledge. In this condition everything English - Their language their material progress, their achievements, their ettiquettes and thoughts, their culture, in short, everything of theirs was superior, great, for most of the students. As a result, we natives are backward and can never be their equals', such inferiority complex took hold of their minds.

In short the class of people who had the capacity for independent thinking and forms the very backbone of a nation, was a slave of the British. This was most unfortunate for this Country.

If the Hindu subjects would be allowed to use native languages for practical purposes, they would not follow the English, and would desire to re-establish their rule of their own religion. So Lord Bentinck insisted on English medium and his expectations were fulfilled, because, in fact, most of the people were Pro-English. Those who aimed only at a government job, were influenced by the British rule, Still, the Indian patriots should be grateful to the British diplomats who though for selfish reasons, imparted education to the natives and allowed their gradual participation in politics".

The above remark by Acharya Javdekar is quite apt. Because of the English education, intelligent students who were not contented just with the curriculum and text-books, had a new vista of knowledge opened to them. They became conscious of their identify. They started comparative studies of occidental and oriental cultures. They began to think it necessary to preserve the immortal in our culture and couple it with the useful in the western culture. In order to fulfil this purpose, though in government services, without crossing its limits, and avoiding sychophancy, Balshastri Jambhekar, Lokhitwadi, Krishnashastri Chiplunkar, Kerunana Chhachtre, Mahadev Moreshwar Kunte, Justice Ranade and some others preserved their self-respect and began their movement of mass-education through meeting, institutions, newspapers, writings etc. Their objectives were progress and prosperity of their own nation, language, people and religion. They did imply total Independence in the time to come on the scene.

Soon after this Vishnushastri Chiplunkar spurned the bondage of the government services and founded the "New English School" on 1st Jan., 1880. After him Tilak and Agarkar took a vow of patriotism and service to the country, without even thinking of joining government service.

When Tilak established educational institutions he set a pattern of management of such institutions. The conflict, political versus social reforms is presented next. Lokmanya Tilak as a propounder of nationalistic and political education has been amply described in the next four essays. Tilak was a political leader, a researcher and a scholar too. His work on Indology and Maratha History finds place in the next two essays. Tilak's views on women's education and the medium of instruction are presented in the last two essays.

Personality and Philosophy of Lokmanya B.G. Tilak

Lokmanya B.G. Tilak realised that the loss of freedom was not merely a loss of political power but a total destruction of the indigeneous culture, religion and language.

Therefore, to awaken the people towards the goal of freedom became his lifetime pursuit. He was associated with Vishnushastri Chiplunkar in establishing the New English School (1880) to impart National Education in place of British imperialist education to students.

According to him the content of education was an urge for freedom and to prepare the people to fight for the same.

With the help of educational institutions, religious platforms (e.g. Ganeshotsav) and newspapers (Kesari and Maratha) which is quite significant he put an end to mere propagation of knowledge and started an era of actual activities.

His mission of national education and social organisation which he carried with unflinching faith and spiritual strength was the outcome of the life-foundations he secured from the 'Bhagvadgita'. One can know his personality and life philosophy best through his classical book 'Gita-Rahasya'. His views on life and duty rested on the Eternal Law and theistic faith. While propagating, in practical life, the 'Desireless Life of Action' he believed in final emancipationas the ultimate aim of man's action. As his was an integrated personality, this philosophy of life was reflected in his social life which became the philosophy of nationalism which Mahatma Gandhi further strengthened.

Education in India During the Period 1800 AD to 1880 AD

To understand Lokmanya Tilak's contribution to philosophy and practice of Education in India, it is necessary to acquaint ourselves with the situation that existed in India during the 19th century.

In the early years of 19th century Tatya Pantoji (one teacher) schools existed in most villages. Reading, writing, arithmetic were the subjects taught. This education was enough to meet everyday needs. Fees were also meagre. However, this education was not open to women and to the scheduled castes. 'Modi' a script similar to Devnagari was also taught.

In 1793 while granting license to the East India Company, the Board of Directors told the company that they would send skilled and suitable persons to India to serve as school masters. Missionaries would also be encouraged. The Board of Directors wanted to educate the natives of India.

In 1813 the British Government asked the Governor General to reserve one lakh rupees every year for the revival and improvement of literature in India and for the introduction and promotion of knowledge of science among the people of India.

Missionaries came to India in the 18th century following the foot-steps of the traders and undertook the responsibility of educating Indians. However, their main aim was to convert the poor and the needy to Christianity. As this was quite clear to upper class Hindus they did not send their children to missionary schools.

In the then Bombay Province, Mount Stuart Elphinstone was appointed as Governor from 1819 to 1827. He had deep interest in the education of Indians. He was in favour of the mother tongue as the medium of instruction. He was of the view that it was the Government's responsibility to educate the people. Due to his encouragement many books were translated into Marathi. English-Marathi Dictionaries were also published.

Educational activity was quite prominent in Mumbai. In 1827 the Bombay Native Education Society was formed. In 1854 a Board of Education was constituted. In 1855, a separate department of Education was also established. During this time there was awakening among the Indians also. Mahatma Phule established his school in 1851-52.

With Wood's Despatch and Macaulay's minutes the upper strata of the society accepted the importance of Western Education with English as the medium. The conflict, Eastern (or Oriental) versus Western was buried and a New Era of Western Education was started by Govt. schools and colleges as also by missionary schools and colleges.

Payments to teachers were low and the percentage of girls and women in schools and colleges was also low.

Tilak, Agarkar and their colleagues started their work against this background.

Lokmanya Tilak on Nature and Management of Educational Institutions

Though education occupied only a few years of his public and social life, his contribution in this field is unique in the sense that the pattern of education he selected and the management style he professed was emulated in the 20th century.

Lokmanya Tilak's contribution to Education is reflected through four important events. They are (i) The establishment of the New English School, Pune, (ii) The formation of the Deccan Education Society, Pune, (iii) The establishment of the Fergusson College, Pune and (iv) Tilak's resignation of life-membership of the Deccan Education society.

The University of Bombay (Mumbai) was established in 1857. The middle class persons and those who had some influence in the Society had accepted Western Education with English as the medium. Tilak, Agarkar and their colleagues had no alternative but to start a school imparting that education. However, there was a vast difference between leaders like Tilak conducting schools and missionaries doing it. Opening of the school proved a new era in the educational and public life of Maharashtra. Following this example many people opened schools in their own towns. People were convinced that Education was a tool towards achieving freedom of the country.

The management style that Tilak and his colleagues formulated while writing the constitution of the Deccan Education Society must be considered unique. They introduced the concept of institutions managed by teachers themselves a new concept of Life-Members. This style spread all over western Maharashtra and inspite of all its weaknesses noticed while practicing, it stood the test of time. Life-Membership stood for Service, Sacrifice and Integrity. When there arose differences between Life-Members and particularly between Tilak and Agarkar on how to define sacrifice, Tilak resigned his Life-Membership of the Deccan Education Society.

Fergusson College, Pune, was started on 2nd January 1885. This college was granted affiliation by the University of Bombay. Reputation of this college spread all over the country in later years. Lala Lajpat Rai, Shrinivas Shastri, Pandit Madan Mohan Malviya and many others have recorded their appreciation of the work done by Tilak and his colleagues.

Educational Thoughts of Tilak's Contemporary : Gopal Ganesh Agarkar

Tilaks' contemporary, Gopal Ganesh Agarkar, was a great reformer of the 19th century. He was also the dearest friend of Tilak. He was one of those great personalities of the time who dedicated themselves to the field of education. These people were influenced by the new rationality of western thought. They believed in the social reforms and boldly advocated the same. Agarkar started his newspaper 'Sudharak' to propagate his new social reforms. His task was very difficult.

Taking into account the conditions then existing, which were mostly dominated by religious sanctions, one can imagine how difficult was the challenge before Agarkar to stand against the existing social order. He had to face humiliation, anger and short-sightedness of people. Many people threatened him with dire consequences but he withstood all such pressures.

As a contemporary social reformer of Tilak, Agarkar repeatedly stressed on people's education through 'Sudharak'. His educational outlook was different from others and was based on a strong belief on rational thinking, scientific approach, individual freedom and moral values.

His main priority was education for all without discrimination of caste, sex, economic strata, etc. He was a true visionary to envisage hundred years ago the difficulties of women's education.

We can summarise his views on education as follows :

1. All kinds of reforms though classified as social, political, behavioural and ranked as first, second, etc. for the sake of thinking, are all of equal importance and are interdependent.
2. Necessity of education for all the people in the society to eradicate ignorance and untouchability.
3. Compulsory and primary education should be the responsibility of the Government.

4. Girls' education should be given more importance and equal opportunities must be given to them to learn the same subjects with boys in co-educational system.

Lokmanya Tilak : The Pioneer of the Concept of National Education

Lokmanya Bal Gangadhar Tilak was one of the architects of our freedom. He taught people that Swarajya was their birth-right. His teachings had a great impact on the minds of the people because he practiced what he preached. Like many of our political leaders Tilak started his public life as a teacher because he regarded education as a powerful instrument for moulding the impressionable minds of students and for bringing about a change in our society's outlook on life.

Tilak and his colleague Agarkar were idealists who were restless owing to the degenerated conditions of our country. They were greatly impressed by the efforts made by Justice Mahadeo Govind Ranade for enlightening the society. They were also impressed by the writings of the young, powerful writer, Vishnu Shastri Chiplunkar. Agarkar and Tilak were not content with their work as teachers. They decided to undertake the work of educating the people and launched two news papers Kesari and Mahratta. They gave an institutional base to their educational effort by founding educational institutions.

Tilak and his colleagues came from families with a tradition of learning. They perhaps did not realise the aspirations of the masses and put forth the elitist point of view which unintentionally supported social inequality and gave special advantages to the so called higher caste communities.

After leaving the Deccan Education society and Fergusson College Tilak concentrated on Kesari and Mahratha. He mainly appealed to the intellect of the readers rather than striving to arouse their emotions. Tilak taught the people to be conscious of their rights. Through his writings Tilak reached a wide section of the society. As an editor he became an educator.

Tilak wanted to involve the generality of the people in social and political activities. He thought of starting public festivals which would become instruments of public education. He advocated that Ganapati Festival should be celebrated publicly. It should include lectures by eminent persons on different subjects followed by group discussions and group singing. Tilak also launched the Shivaji

Festival as Shivaji was a National Hero and a perennial source of inspiration for patriotism. Tilak felt that English education was responsible for destroying the essential bond of relationship between learning, ethics, religious faith and family life. However, he considered Education as an instrument of National Awakening.

Tilak had sown the seeds of the ideal of National Education. After Tilak's demise Gandhiji laid great emphasis on National Education. In Tilak Maharashtra Vidyapeeth in Pune teachers like Acharya Bhagwat, Acharya Jawadekar and others while delivering inspiring lectures on politics, history and literature inculcated in students a national outlook. Almost all of them participated in the Satyagraha movement in 1930. Thus the seed sown by Tilak had grown into a huge banyan tree. In the real sense of the term he was a pioneer of National Education.

Lokmanya Tilak : Propounder of Nationalistic Education

It is the purpose of Education to till the soil of the existing social order and to plant the seeds from which new farms and new social orders grow. When the soil is recalcitrant and unyielding, resistant to the natural forces for change, more radical forces emerge. This applies to the situation that existed in India prior to the Tilak Era. Lokmanya Tilak had to work hard to instil a new spirit in the Indian Society and make the masses understand the importance of freedom. He propounded Nationalistic Education as a path towards Independence or Swaraj.

Nationalism is defined as a state of the mind in which the individual feels that every one owes his supreme secular loyalty to the nation or the state. Nationalistic education instils among the masses the spirit of Nationalism. Tilak's work has to be viewed in the light of these assumptions.

India as a nation is not only a geographical concept or a political entity. It is supposed to be the collective soul of all Indians. In history though India was not geographically a nation there were strong feelings of Nationalism among the Indians even in historical times. As the entire country came under British power and as communication developed in the continent a new wave of Nationalism arose among the Indians.

When Tilak and his colleague Agarkar got their graduation they came to the conclusion that spread of Education was the only method for the country's uplift. Education of the rising generations by the Indians was according to them a sure way to inculcate a National feeling among the youngsters. Keeping this in mind Tilak and his colleagues established the New English School, the Deccan Education Society and the Fergusson College.

Tilak's educational thoughts, especially about nationalistic education evolved out of his own personality as a committed Indian. In his late life Tilak evolved as a public leader. However, it must be noted that the first chapter of his public career opened in the field of education. He had an indomitable spirit, tenacity of purpose and strong determination.

Tilak propounded his concept of Nationalistic Education through the institutions he opened, through his news papers Kesari and Mahratta to which he contributed extensively and through his public speeches.

He was so successful in his mission that he is known as the 'Father of the Indian unrest.'

Political Education by Lokmanya Tilak

Every political system operates in a given society which has its own political culture distinct from that of other countries. The political system, for its maintenance and growth, requires certain knowledge, skills and values on the part of the people. The process of political education gives knowledge, tries to create skills and inculcates values congenial for the working of the political system. As the society consists of divergent groups, the dissatisfied sections in the society can be given political education for the overthrow of the political system. If this attempt gets necessary support from the people there is change in the government and in the political system. The main objective of Lokmanya Tilak was to impart political education to Indian masses and to overthrow the British Rule by peaceful means.

Political Education needs knowledge of the existing society, of the new society that the nation desires to create, the existing government of the country and the basic problems of the country. Skills involve skills of understanding, problem solving, working in groups, skills to understand conflicts and skills to express oneself adequately. Political education also involves education of values some of which are fundamental and absolute.

The Britishers had evolved the policy of divide and rule in India. The British always argued that the Indians did not deserve self-government. Their objective of education was to create a class of people who would act as interpreters between the rulers and the ruled. The British preached superiority of the British over India. Tilak wanted to undo what had happened and therefore undertook a crusade of political education.

Tilak educated masses through social functions like Ganpati Festival and Shivaji Festival, through his writings in Kesari and Mahratta and through his lectures. He became a hero of the masses as he stood like a rock even when persecuted by the British for over two decades. Tilak attempted to promote the concepts of Swadeshi and boycott of foreign goods. He also introduced the concept of National Education. This 'Trisutri' or three devices along with festivals, writings and lectures were his tools of Political Education. Though the British tried to create a wedge between the Hindus and the Muslims, Tilak invited the Muslims to join him in his efforts to gain swaraj. He was mostly successful.

In this way Tilak became the first mass leader of India. He became popular among all castes and religions, equally among the educated and the uneducated as also among the rich and the poor. Tilak was thus the first political educator in India who also got international accredition for the cause for which he fought.

People's Education Through the Editorials of 'Kesari'

Lokmanya Tilak was a leader of the down-trodden. He was in a sense a mass-educator. Naturally he used 'Kesari' a newspaper in Marathi as a medium for educating the masses. His editorials in 'Kesari' had a lasting impact on the masses on the subjects like national-education, people's rights, unrest towards British Rule, inculcation of a new idea, i.e. 'Swaraj' as a birth right of every Indian, a mass movement for 'Swadeshi', pride for what is indigenous, etc.

His editorials are the testimony of his special style of writing. The titles of editorials were quite attractive e.g. 'Is the Govt. in its sense?' or 'It is dawn, but where is the sun?', 'The udders of the male buffalo', etc.

He made good use of Shlokas verses in Sanskrit in the beginning of some editorials. It was his speciality to use folk stories and simple illustrations from the practical day-to-day life which made his point clearer to the common people.

Tilak could establish a dialogue between the Editor and the readers at large through his editorials in his oratorial style.

He tried to supplement his views by facts and figures, sometimes in the form of statistical tables. This was very useful for the people to feel the exact pulse of any problem.

Originally being a teacher, Tilak had a strong urge to awaken the people and instigate them to rise against their subjugation, against the unjust and oppressive British Rule.

His 'Kesari' the lion was always kept roaring. From his editorials, one can feel that a newspaper is a good medium for mass-education.

Lokmanya Tilak : A Great Indologist

It is now well-known that Tilak was also a great scholar and his researches in Indology were widely recognised by his contemporaries all over the world. His main contributions to Indology consist of (1) The Orion Researches into the Antiquity of the Vedas (2) The Arctic home in Vedas (3) The Gita Rahasya (4) Vedic chronology and the Vedanga Jyotish. Mention may also be made of his editorials on the Mahabharata which testify his versatile genius.

The Orion Tilak had realised that western scholars were not prepared to accept a high antiquity for vedic literature. All this dating by Max Mullar and others was done on literacy evidence. Tilak was justified in arguing that this method was rather vague and uncertain. The entire gamut of vedic literature was thus hanging in a sort of chronological vacuum.

When Tilak came across a reference in the Bhagwad Gita that Krishna was 'the margasirsa of the months (masanam margasirsoham) it immediately struck him that astronomy may offer some clue to the dating of the vedas. To his great surprise he was proved right and he could therefore develop his chronology of the vedic literature. So Tilak's theory is based essentially on astronomical evidence. Tilak developed his chronology for vedic literature as follows :

(i) The oldest period or Aditi or pre-Orion period according to Tilak can be provided in the 6000-4000 B.C. time bracket.

(ii) The Orion period (4000-2500 B.C.). According to Tilak this was the most important period in the development of the Aryan civilization.

(iii) The Krittika period (2500-1400 B.C.). It was period of Taittriya Samhita. Tilak said, "The hymns of the

Rigveda had already become unique and unintelligible by this time and Brahmavadinis engaged in speculations about the real meaning of these hymns and legends".

(iv) Pre Buddist period (1400-500 B.C.) This was the period when the sutra literature was composed. "The astronomical method, I admit, is not adequate to determine the exact date of all the vedic hymns or works, but it is certainly superior to the linguistic method as it supplies us with certain, definite, undisputed facts, the position of equinoxes, which can safely be made the nuclei of the different periods of antiquity", said Tilak It will be interesting to examine Tilak's theory in the light of recent archaeological research as at his time the Indus civilization had not been discovered and no evidence for the Aryan invasion was found. Beginning of settled life in the Indian subcontinent dates back to ten thousand years from the excavation at Mehragh. Excavation evidence points to continuous habitations starting from 7500 B.C and ending around 3000 B.C.

The only noticeable cultural change in all four and a half millennia of continuous habitation is between 6000 B.C. to 4500 B.C. which indicates the arrival of a new group of people or new cultural influences. These are the precise dates that Tilak has assigned to his preorion period. This may be sheer coincidence and it will not be prudent to read too much into it at this stage but at the same time it cannot be dismissed as irrelevant.

The Arctic Home of the Vedas

The statement from Rigveda, "Suryodayat prak bahuni ahani asan" meaning many days have passed before sunrise, highly impressed him and led him to trace the original home of the Aryans in the Artic region. This phenomenon occurs only in polar regions. Arctic region in those days was characterised by cool summer and warm winters (inter glacial period) a sort of perpetual spring was good for habitation.

He has written 'Gita Rahasya' in the Mandalay prison. He wrote in Marathi for the common man to imbibe the karma-yoga as interpreted by him. When the book was first published in 1915,

6000 copies were sold like hot cake. The book was very popular. It teaches you about 'Niskam Karma-yoga'.

He also wrote other research papers, like The Chaldean and Indian Vedas or 'A missing verse' in the 'Sankhya Karikas'. There were 69 verses and one was missing so Tilak constructed the missing verse on the basis of the evidence of the commentary of Gaudapada. According to Dr. Radhakrishnan this is his most notable contribution. He also wrote some research papers in vedic chronology and vedang Jyotish. He also wrote eight articles on the Mahabharat. He was a great Indologist.

Lokmanya Tilak and Maratha History

Lokmanya Bal Gangadhar Tialk, the father of Indian unrest, belonged to the generation of the 19th century Maharashtra. The state had not yet forgotten that they were the rulers of this country in the immediate past. He must have thought of History as the most suitable and effective method to mobilize public opinion against the tyrannical rule of the British. He thought that the adventurous and brave career of Shivaji, was not yet forgotten by the people and would be the best tool which could be used to attract the masses towards the freedom struggle. This led him to indulge in deep research about the Marathas, particularly Shivaji. Tilak was not a professional historian. He entered into the field of research by sheer accident.

As a researcher he wrote 'Orion' and 'Arctic Home In The Vedas'. However the peculiar circumstances that were prevailing in the last decade of the 19th century made him plunge into the history of the immediate past of Maharashtra i.e. the 'Maratha History'.

A British visitor who visited Shivaji's tomb at Raigad published a book reporting about the dilapidated condition of Shivaji's tomb which resulted in immediate research on Shivaji. Native opinion of V.N. Mandlik (1895) kindled the imagination of Tilak and he wrote an article in Kesari (23rd April 1895). This article had a proper effect of the minds of the common people, and he could raise funds to maintain Shivaji's Samadhi at Raigad. This gave rise to a national movement known as 'Shivaji movement'.

He appealed to national leaders to celebrate Shivaji's birthday as a national festival. During the birthday celebrations of Shivaji, Tilak came to know about the controversy over the birth date of Shivaji and he made a deep research on the birth date of Shivaji. He finally accepted the date which was nearer to 'bakhas'. It was Shaka 1549, Pravhav Samvatsar, Vaishakh Shudha Pratipada Ashiwini Nakshatra equivalent to 6th April 1627. He confessed that there was a great deal of confusion regarding the birth date of Shivaji and he appealed for more research in this area. The Maharashtra Govt. appointed a committee to give a final decision over the long pending controversy of the birth date of Shivaji Maharaj. The Govt. declared officially Falgun Vadya Tritiya of Shaka 1551 (1630 AD) as an authentic date for celebration of Shiv Jayanti. Tilak must be given credit for this research.

His Indirect Contribution to History

He encouraged other historians to write in Kesari. He gave opportunities to many scholars to publish their researches on controversial issues, in Kesari or Mahratta.

Many people had raised objection against the Shivaji Movement. Tilak stressed that Shivaji is remembered for his nation-building activities and Shivaji gave us the idea that Swarajya was a fundamental right. Biographies of great leaders like Shivaji are sources of inspiration to the younger generation. The purpose of the Shivaji festival was promotion of patriotism and nationalism among the people of this country.

He said, "Research cannot be done by all. It is the privilage of a chosen few. Research should be done for the sake of research only and not for its results or effects. Every activity should not be motivated by material gains. Man works both for his maintenance as well as for satisfying his urge for pure knowledge. It depends on the nature of man, to which he should give priority." One can hardly explain to a common man the ecstasy one gets through research resulting in advancement of knowledge. Tilak knew how to reconcile historical research for political purpose as well as for the advancement of knowledge. His contribution to historical research deserves the attention of scholars and political leaders of modern times.

Lokmanya Bal Gangadhar Tilak's Views on Women's Education

As we enter the new century, it is an appropriate time to look back and take a review of the historical changes that this country has brought in the field of education and especially women's education. Women's education cannot be thought of without its relationship with the other social aspects of women's life such as child marriage, widow remarriage, women's position in the society. In Tilak's time his contemporaries like Gopal Ganesh Agarkar, Mahatma Phule, Vitthal Ramji Shinde, Maharshi Dhondo Keshav Karve, held a different view. It will be interesting to study the reasons for such a different view.

Tilak has written editorials in his newspapers Kesari and Mahratta. Firstly he objected to the curriculum of the girls school because it was just like that of British schools. The cultural and social background of Indian girls is totally different from that of British girls, and so should be the curricula. Secondly he objected the full day school timing i.e. six hours a day for the girls. If necessary they should attend the half-day school, after finishing their duties in the house which according to him was their first moral obligation. His third objection for women's education was that the education given to them would help them become clerks in the British offices. If they start working in these offices they will neglect their first duty which is household work. This is most disgusting and hence should be abandoned. His fourth objection was against hasty reforms. Educating few women would not help the society, but educating the common masses would only help. Spending money hastily on women's education would be a waste if very few women get education.

All these views of Tilak about women's education came as a reaction to the extreme views of the reformists of his time.

Lokmanya Bal Gangadhar Tilak's Thoughts on Language Teaching and Medium of Instruction

1st January 1880, the day of the establishment of the New English School at Pune is a landmark in the field of education. The school was established with a view to inculcate the spirit of National Education in the minds of the young generation.

Tilak in one of his speeches mentioned that English being a strange language one cannot learn it fast. The grammar of English is different than that of vernacular. Learning this language becomes a burden on the learner, and expressing thoughts in that language becomes more difficult. The time spent in learning English is a waste. If the knowledge is imparted through mother-tongue, it can be learnt faster. Thus time and energy can be saved. Therefore, vernacular should be the language of instruction. The knowledge, in other European languages was translated in English and so English became a rich language. We too, can enrich our own language. The educated people from our own land should not forget this and try to enrich vernacular. As saints contributed to enrich our language so should the learned people.

The education given to our children through English, will help them to become clerks in the British offices. This will be harmful to the progress of our society. When University will place vernacular at a higher place in the curricula and judiciary, administration markets start using vernacular for communication then only the society will progress.

6

Tilak : His National Education

Lokamanya Bal Gangadhar Tilak was one of the architects of our freedom. He taught people that Swarajya was their birth-right. His teachings had a great impact on the minds of the people because he practised what he preached. Like many of our political leaders Tilak started his public life as a teacher because he regarded education as a powerful instrument of moulding the impressionable minds of students and of bringing about a change in our society's outlook on life.

An Idealist

It is necessary to study how Tilak's mind was moulded and how and why later on he took this decision to become a teacher. During his childhood his father Gangadhar Shastri, made him recite Sanskrit and Marathi verses, which sharpened his memory. During his school days, he developed a special liking for Mathematics. His sharp intellect prompted him to study the basic principles of different subjects, instead of just preparing for examinations. After passing the Matriculation examination, Bal Gangadhar Tilak joined Deccan Collage in Pune. As he was staying in the college-hostel, he could take the advantage of the college library and read books by eminent writers and thinkers on different subjects. He was also greatly influenced by the teaching of Prof. Chhatre, who inspired him to study the fundamentals of Mathematics. He offered Mathematics as his principal subject for the B.A. examination. Tilak formed a close friendship with his classmate Gopal Ganesh Agarkar who was a student of philosophy. Tilak and Agarkar were idealist youths who were restless owing to the degenerate condition of their country. They were greatly impressed by the efforts made by Justice Mahadev Govind Ranade for enlightening the society through institutions like Vasant Vyakhyana Mala, and Sarvajanik Sabha. Tilak and Agarkar were also impressed by the writings of a young, powerful writer, Vishnu Shastri Chiplunkar, who appealed to people to develop a sense of self-respect, instead of imitating the British rulers. Tilak and Agarkar had heated discussions about the future course of action in life. Unlike most of their contemporaries, these two young idealists decided not to join Government service and instead work for the uplift of their country. Tilak argued that it was necessary to start political work first, while Agarkar argued that they should first strive to bring about reforms in society, and then start political work. After long and heated discussions, these two young idealists took the decision to work on the common platform of education. Both of them realized that it was necessary to educate the people in general and the youths in particular before working for either social reforms or the political movement. After taking this bold decision, Tilak and Agarkar along with Vishnu Shastri Chiplunkar decided to start a High School. Shri. Vaman Shivram Apte, an eminent Sanskrit Scholar, and V.B.Namjoshi - a young idealist who was also a realist, also joined the trio. Starting of the New English School was an event which shook the student world of Pune, and as the young teachers proved their ability, the response both of the students and their guardians became more and more enthusiastic.

The trio, Chiplunkar, Agarkar and Tilak were not content with just their work as teachers. They were searching fresh fields and new pastures. They decided to undertake the work of educating the people and launched two news-papers - 'Kesari' in Marathi and 'Mahratta' in English in January 1881. The editorials in Kesari were written in a direct and simple style and the editor never lost sight of the main purpose of educating public opinion. The profession of journalism has its trials. Tilak and Agarkar as editors championed the cause of the ruler of Kolhapur. They however wrote something which was challenged in the court and as the young editors could not produce evidence supporting their statements, they were sentenced to three months' imprisonment. Tilak and Agarkar boldly accepted the punishment and their prestige as editors rose, in society, During this period of imprisonment, Tilak and Agarkar picked up the thread of their discussions in college and realized that the gap between their views was widening. Tilak made a fervent plea for political activity while Agarkar was equally emphatic about the need for social reforms. After their release from prison, Tilak and Agarkar once again devoted themselves to educational work, while carrying out their responsibility as editors. The next step in the field of education was the founding of the Deccan Education Society in 1884. This gave an institutional base to the educational effort, the next step of which was the starting of Fergusson College in January, 1885. The statement made on the occasion of the establishment of the Deccan Education Society, throws light on the ideological position of Tilak, Agarkar, Apte and their colleagues. It reads as follows :

> "We have undertaken this work of popular education, with the firmest conviction and belief that of all agents of human civilization, Education is the only one that brings about material, moral and religious regeneration of fallen countries, and raises them up to the level of the most advanced nations by slow and peaceful revolutions."

Prin. Apte gave evidence before the Education Commission presided over by William Wilson Hunter on 9th September 1882. His views were representative of the point of view of his colleagues in the Deccan Education Society. There was a strong plea for an indigenous agency for educational effort. It was also stated that greater opportunities for collegiate and university education should be given to the students coming from those sections of society which had a tradition of learning. The ground for this demand was that through this enlightened class education would percolate to other strata of society. This view was in sharp contrast with the view expressed by Jyotirao Phule, the great social reformer, that it was the primary responsibility of the Government to give education for seven years to students from all sections of society. He argued that the more intelligent students would then take advantage of the facilities for higher education. Phule made a fervent plea for equal opportunities for learning to all and said that the level of enlightenment of the entire society must be raised and education should not become the monopoly of the chosen few. Phule showed a progressive vision but his plea was not accepted by the Government.

It was evident that Apte and Tilak, who came from families with a tradition of learning, did not understand the aspirations of the masses and putforth the elitist point of view which perpetuated social inequality and gave special advantages to the so-called higher communities.

Due to differences among the Life-Members of DE Society Tilak resigned from the Deccan Education Society and Fergusson College, but he continued his vocation as a teacher. He started conducting Law Classes for the High Court Pleader's examination. Tilak had passed the LL.B. exam. with merit and owing to his analytical mind, he developed a rare insight in different branches of Law and particularly in Hindu Law. He elucidated the different topics in such a manner that the students, besides getting the necessary guidance for the examination, were stimulated to think in a novel and original manner.

Editor as Educator

After the parting of ways in the Deccan Education Society, Tilak took over the 'Kesari' and the 'Mahratta'. Tilak regarded the work of an Editor as a sacred vocation where it was his responsibility to educate the people and enlighten them. He felt that his sphere of activity as a teacher had widened. Tilak never lost sight of the principle that a Teacher has to remain a student for life time and that a person gets the moral right to educate others only when he has studied the subject which he is teaching or on which he is writing. He read extensively and carefully and only when he was convinced that he had fully grasped all the implications of the topic which he wanted to elucidate, that he expressed his point of view through the editorial. He first gave the information about the concerned subject, then analysed it and out of such delineation of facts, emerged his editorial comment. It was no wonder, therefore, that the readers, on most occasions, were persuaded to accept his point of view. Tilak, who was a keen student of mathematics, was always logical in his argument and was very disciplined in his exposition of ideas. Tilak did not like stylistic flourishes and always avoided rhetoric. His style of writing was simple and direct. He explained the subject but avoided superfluous expression. His style of writing was compressed and had a masculine dignity.

He mainly appealed to the intellect of his readers rather than striving to arouse their emotions. In 1886, there was a famine in Maharashtra. Tilak first carefully studied The Famine Relief Code, published by the Government after the famine in 1872. He immediately understood the significance and the implications of the Government's Resolution. In the Famine Relief code, the Government had committed itself to certain relief measures such as distributing food grains at a cheap rate, a concession in land-revenue etc. Tilak first published in Kesari, the summary of the Famine Relief Code in Marathi. He then explained to the readers that it was the moral responsibility of the Government to implement their own decision and it was the moral right of the people to demand the relief measures, incorporated by the Government in their own Famine Relief Code. Tilak then printed a small booklet which contained the important provision of the code and, with the help of the volunteers, of the Sarvajanik Sabha, distributed the copies of the booklet in the famine affected parts of Bombay Presidency. In the then Colaba district, when the Government prosecuted the volunteers, Tilak rushed to the Tehsil town Pen and in a hugely attended meeting of peasants, condemned the prosecution. He challenged the Government to prosecute him, because he had printed the booklet which contained a part of the G. R. - The Famine Relief Code - and that as the Secretary of the Sarvajanik Sabha, he had asked the volunteers to distribute it. The collector of Colaba district was present and he then withdrew the prosecution. Tilak thus repudiated the saying that 'he who can does, he who cannot, teaches'. Tilak taught the people to become conscious of their rights; he also acted boldly and challenged the Government. He succeeded because his action was based on the knowledge of the contents and also the implications of the Famine Relief Code.

When Tilak was teaching in the New English School and later on in Pune, his students were not adults and the classrooms were enclosed with walls. When Tilak started his work as Editor and social-worker, he had undertaken the job of educating adult people. This was a public-school for grown up persons and this school had no walls. Through his writings he reached a wide section of society. Although Tilak did not appoint any deputies, many enthusiastic young people in different towns and villages in Maharashtra read out before a group of adult audience the Kesari and particularly the editorials of Tilak. Thus communication was established between Tilak and the people. The editor became educator.

Education through National Festivals

Tilak wanted to extend his sphere of education through other methods. He had read the History of Greece in which there was a description of different cultural festivals. The Greek, enthusiastically participated in them and were thus involved in the affairs of the state. Tilak wanted to involve the generality of the people in social and political activities in a similar manner. He therefore thought of starting public festivals which would become instruments of public education. He then started the Ganapati festival as a social event and got a very enthusiastic response from the people in Pune and also in some other places. Traditionally, the worship of the idol of Ganapati was a domestic celebration. Tilak gave a new orientation to this practice and widened its significance to educate the people. He advocated that the Ganapati festival be celebrated publicly and besides the ritual of worship and Aarati, it should include lectures by eminent persons on different subjects, group singing and other cultural programmes by groups of youths. Tilak thus created a new public platform for educating the people. Tilak also launched the Shivaji Festival. He was quite explicit about its object which was the celebration of the glory and achievements of Chhatrapati Shivaji Maharaj. Tilak told the people that Shivaji was a National Hero, and a perennial source of inspiration for patriotism. Tilak observed that in times when national qualities such as patriotism, sense of solidarity and brotherhood, and hatred of tyranny were absent, it was necessary to celebrate the achievements of the National Hero, Shivaji who was a symbol of all these noble national virtues. Tilak in his speech at Amravati said," On one day at least in a year, every person should think about his village or town, about his country. He should ask himself the question whether the condition of the country was in a flourishing state or had decayed. If it had decayed, he must try to find out the means for its improvement. It is with this end in view that the Shivaji festival is being celebrated." Tilak wrote that no other hero in Maratha History was so respected by all sections of the public as Shivaji Maharaj. Tilak drew the attention of the people to the fact that the forts standing in different parts of Sahyadri ranges in Maharashtra were a living testimony to Shivaji's prowess and a number of places were remembered for their association with the exploits of Shivaji Maharaj.

In an article in 'Mahratta' Tilak wrote, "Hero-worship is a feeling deeply implanted in human nature and our political aspirations need all the strength which the worship of a swadeshi hero is likely to inspire into our minds. For this purpose Shivaji is the only hero to be found in Indian history. He was born at a time when the whole nation required relief from mis-rule and by his self-sacrifice and courage, he proved to the world that India was not a country forsaken by providence".

While launching the Shivaji festival and Ganapati festival Tilak was using the revivalist method in order to awaken the sense of hope and self-confidence among the people. He regarded these festivals as a means to national awakening and also as a means to giving an ethical basis to the political aspirations. Tilak wanted to revive the creative spirit of the old times and not the form of the old institutions or religion. He regarded the traditional way of life like a tree and wanted to graft on it, the new ideas such as nationalism. Tilak's criticism of liberal leaders like Ranade was, that they were trying to implant alien ideas in Indian soil. Tilak said that it was necessary to utilise the vitality of the indigenous way of life and give it a new orientation. He once said, "Love for one's country is a natural instinct. We have to give a new orientation to it and make people accept the ideology of nationalism". Thus, through the Shivaji Festival and Ganapati Festival, Tilak was playing a significant role as a teacher who wanted to mould public opinion and inculcate in people the spirit of patriotism.

In spite of his editorial responsibilities and in spite of his continuous efforts to give a momentum to the Shivaji Festival and Ganpati Festival, Tilak still found time to pursue his research on the chronology of Vedas with the help of astronomy. Tilak submitted a Paper to the Ninth Oriental Congress held in London in 1882. The Paper which was based on his research on the "antiquity of the Vedas" by giving astronomical evidence with the help of Vedanga Jyotisha put forth the theory that the Vedas were written during the period 4000-2500 B.C. Though there were different opinions about the proposition put forth by Tilak, it was accepted as a serious effort by Oriental scholars.

During this period, Tilak also wrote in Kesari detailed reviews of the new editions of the Mahabharat and Ramayana and stated his own theories about their dates, origin and several important and textual interpretative problems connected with them.

Apart from these, Tilak wrote extensive reviews of two important books of a political nature Dadabhai Naoroji's "Poverty and Un-British rule in India" and Digby's "Prosperous British India." Tilak wrote the reviews under the caption 'Two Good Books'.

As a conscientious teacher of his readers, he first gave a detailed summary of these books, and after stating clearly the main proposition in these two serious works, analysed their contents and made his own detailed comments on them. Dadabhai Naoroji, the great sage "Maharshi" of Indian politics, showed in a convincing manner that the British Empire had carried on a relentless economic exploitation of India, destroyed its agro-industrial pattern of life and reduced India to beggary. Both Dadabhai Naoroji and Digby had thrown light on the growing poverty in India caused by the British rule. Tilak's reviews were models of educative journalism. Tilak's obituary articles on some of his great contemporaries like Justice Ranade, Prin. Agarkar, Vivekanand, Max Mueller and Herbert Spencer, were also written with the same educative approach. In these articles he did not just pay tributes to these great men. He evaluated the significant contribution of these eminent persons, in the context of the social and political situation prevailing in India. In his article on "Vishnu Shastri Chiplunkar", Tilak expressed his criticism of English education. He wrote :

"English education was responsible for destroying that essential bond of relationship between learning, ethics, religious faith and family life."

Tilak participated in the work of the Indian National Congress from its very inception and made a fervent plea that instead of following the moderate method of petition and prayer, the Congress should create a political sanction to support their demand for political rights. At the same time, Tilak always sought an opportunity to draw the attention of the people to the problems of education. In the seventeenth session of the Indian National Congress at Calucutta, Tilak seconded the resolution on the appointment of an Education Commission. In his speech Tilak made a comparison between the Japanese and Indian systems of education and said, "It was because of the independent system of education, with facilities for technical training that Japan had forged ahead. On the contrary, education in India had dwarfed the intellect of young men. You might point out a Jagadeesh Chandra Bose here or a Dr. R. P. Paranjpye there, but let me remind you that they are exceptions which prove the rule. Our ancient system of education cultivated a love for learning and produced men, whose intellectual attainments are still the wonder of the world. Education in India had been reduced to the position of a subordinate handmaid of administration and unless it is raised to a real position of the Goddess of learning, India could not be raised to the status of the civilised nations of the West."

Education—an Instrument of National Awakening

It is argued by some people that politics and education go ill together. This observation can be valid only if politics is regard as a game for grabbing power and money. If on the other hand, politics means an effort of the people to fight against injustice and to end tyranny, education forms a major part of political action. Tilak as the leader of the movement launched against the partition of Bengal by Lord Curzon, made national education a major part of the four point progamme which developed in to a nationwide movement. Tilak always regarded education as a powerful instrument of social transformation and used it as a weapon not only in the movement against Bengal Partition but in the struggle for Swaraj. I think it is necessary to describe in some details the political situation in which national education emerged as an important programme.

In 1905 Lord Curzon, the Viceroy of India, announced his decision of the 'partition' of the province of Bengal. The autocratic decision was an attack on the growing spirit of nationalism and the sense of solidarity among the people of Bengal. The sinister motives of Lord Curzon had become clear from his speeches in East Bengal wherein he made an effort to create enmity between the Hindus and the Muslims in pursuance of the imperialist policy of "Divide and Rule". However, Curzon's attempt to divide Bengal, made Bengal united. All sections in Bengal, rich and poor, landlords and tenants, young and old, moderates and extremists saw in the partition an insult to their honour and a threat to their solidarity. The Partition of Bengal and people's protest against it might have become only a local affair confined only to the people of Bengal. But the trio of India's political leaders - Lala Lajpat Rai, Bal Gangadhar Tilak and Bipin Chandra Pal - Lal, Bal and Pal - showed great political foresight and lifted the struggle of the people of Bengal to the national plane. These three leaders converted Curzon's onslaught into an opportunity for creating national solidarity. Protests against Bengal's partition were held all over India and the people of India demonstrated their solidarity against the tyranny of the British Empire. It is, however necessary to know the difference in the attitude of the leaders who represented three different trends of thought, three different currents in Indian politics, not merely at that juncture but through out India's freedom struggle. The first trend was that of moderate leaders like Gopal Krishna Gokhale and Pherozshah Mehta, who followed only constitutional methods. These liberal leaders rendered yeoman's service to the nation during the first phase by laying the foundation of our future political movement. But theirs was the politics of the elite, only of eminent personalities with a rare ability to represent the cause of India before the British Parliament.

At the other end, there were the revolutionaries, who believed that freedom could be won only through armed struggle. Some of them had become martyrs and their supreme sacrifice had kindled the flame of patriotism in the hearts of many Indian youths. However only extraordinarily brave persons who were prepared to lay down their lives at the altar of liberty could follow this path. The moderates and the revolutionaries were poles apart from each other in their methods. However, the common people could not follow either of these groups. There was the third group of leaders - the trio of Tilak, Lala Lajpat Rai, and Bipin Chandra Pal, who had realized that it was necessary to bring the common people of India in the freedom struggle. They therefore placed before the nation a constructive and combative programme which would develop into a mass movement. When Bengal was partitioned, moderate leaders like Gokhale expressed their protest only through circulars, memoranda, and speeches. Aurobindo Ghosh wanted to follow the path of armed revolution. But Tilak and his colleagues, Lajpat Rai and Pal, put forth the four point programme of Swadeshi, Boycott, National Education and Swaraj. This programme enabled these leaders to involve thousands of people in this apparently modest political action. Tilak firmly believed that such a constructive and combative programme alone would arouse the uncommon strength of the common man. It must be noted that national education formed an important part of the nation-wide agitation. Tilak expressed his views on National Education, through the editorials in Kesari and through many of his speeches. Tilak never did anything in a half-hearted manner. In the editorial on the programme of boycott of foreign goods Tilak described Boycott as "Yoga". He also regarded "National Education" as "Yoga" which implied highest level of concentration, resulting in rare skills -. He expected teachers to work with a missionary zeal. In one of his speeches Tilak said that he wanted "Graduate Ramdasis" (The followers of Saint Ramdas who aroused the sense of self-respect and patriotism in people) to carry on the movement for Swaraj. Tilak expected that teachers must have love for knowledge, love for students and the ability to develop the personalities of youth is by inculcating in them the spirit of patriotism. He expected the guardians to co-operate with this effort of moulding and sharpening the new generation by making their wards accept the discipline of the novel experiment in the field of education. Tilak expected the students to instil in themselves the virtues of courage, truthfulness, sacrifice and above all an attitude of self-reliance. He expected educationists like Prof. Vijapurkar to make bold experiments and evolve the pattern of National Education. Tilak, in one of his speeches said that learning and character must be blended so that instead of producing clerks required for the administration of British rule, National Education would train students in such a manner that in future life they would build India as a Nation.

Tilak wrote a number of editorials in Kesari on the subject of National Education and elucidated his ideas. Tilak made a fervent plea for making Marathi the medium of instruction in Maharashtra. He observed that education imparted through the mother-tongue stimulated the thought process of students. On the other hand, while learning through English, the students faltered because they were not familiar with that language and found it difficult to express whatever they know. As a result, many students were obsessed with the notion of fluency in English and their thinking process was dwarfed. In one of his editorials Tilak wrote, "If I had learnt through Marathi, the knowledge that I have accumulated at the age of fifty-two, would have easily been gained by me at the age of thirty."

In one of the editorials he developed the idea that knowledge was power, while in one of his speeches he developed the idea . That is knowledge which liberates the mind. Tilak said that because of the rule of the British many educated people had developed a sense of inferiority. If the right type of education i.e. national education was imparted to students, they would be mentally liberated and would boldly think in an independent manner. Tilak while elucidating his concept of National Education, always emphasised the need for removing the bifurcation of the life of the people and the education imparted to them. He said, "education must make people fearless, truthful and enable them to earn their livelihood with self-respect; but the purpose of the British rulers was to create a class which would help them carry on their administration by acting as a link between the rulers and the ruled. They expected from this class not just obedience but a servility of what was taught in schools and colleges was a means of conditioning the mind of students for promoting in them a slavish outlook. The purpose of national education is just the opposite. We want a new generation of youths who would respect our nation. our religion and language."

Communicating the Message of Bhagwad-Gita

At Mandalay, Tilak used his imprisonment for the pursuit of knowledge in right earnest. He learnt two foreign languages, viz. French and German, in order to read the works of philosophers like Comte in the original French language. One is amazed at the long list of books read by Tilak during his incarceration in the Mandalay prison. Tilak once again felt that he would be able to play the role of a teacher of the people only if he would explain to them the message of the 'Bhagwad Gita'. To Tilak, the Gita was a perennial source of inspiration. While passing through the trials and ordeals of his life, it intensified his faith. 'Gita-Rahasya' was the quintessence of this life's message. Tilak had not just read about Karma-Yoga in Bhagwad-Gita, he had lived as a Karma Yogi through out his life. He felt that the message of Bhagwad-Gita would inspire the people to lead a life of action in order to realize their dream of swarajya. Tilak, who because of his sacrifice and suffering, had become Lokamanya was confident that if he would communicate to them the message of the Bhagwad-Gita, they would try to follow it and strive for Swaraj. Tilak was conscious of the fact that his efforts would not bear fruit in his life-time; but the ideal of "action without any expectation" as stated in Bhagwad Gita enabled him to carry on his effort vigorously, throughout his life. Lokamanya Tilak wrote 'Gita Rahasya' and in doing this he was carrying on the tradition sages - Rishis - in ancient India, whose teachings transcended the limitations of time and distance. Through 'Gita Rahasya', Tilak emerged as a teacher of teachers, and also as a guide and philosopher to many of his countrymen.

After his release from Mandalay jail in 1914, Lokamanya Tilak, who was the accredited leader of the whole India, directed his energies to the task of consolidating the political forces. His efforts were successful in the Lucknow Session of the Indian National Congress held in 1916. The last five years of his life were full of hectic political activities and he hardly had any time to give impetus to the effort of national education. He taught people the lesson that Swarajya was their birth-right and that they should strive to get it. In his speeches on the political ideal of Swarajya, he time and again referred to education as a powerful means of instilling the spirit of patriotism in youth. On 17th April 1917, Lokamanya Tilak delivered a speech at Chikodi, near Belgaum and the subject of his speech was 'My ideal of Education'. In that speech he made a fervent plea for free and compulsory primary education. He told the people that through national education, they would become conscious of their right to get Swarajya and would also realize that it was their responsibility to strive for it.

Tilak made a fervent plea for the spread of education. However, owing to his traditional mental make-up, he did not advocate the cause of women's education. He was brought up in the society dominated by men and he, therefore, felt that the primary duty of women was to look after the family and bring up children. When a female High School was started in Pune, Tilak wrote against it. He was of the opinion that if at all education is to be given to girls in schools, it must be such as would make them good mothers and efficient house-wives. His views were diametrically opposite to those of Prin. Gopal Ganesh Agarkar who wrote in his journal 'Sudharak' that there should be co-education and that education imparted to girls should not be different from the education given to boys. When there was a growing demand for women's education, Tilak said that time was not ripe for such a reform. He did not want to oppose the prevalent conservatism in Hindu society so far as women's education was concerned. When Prof. Dhondo Keshav Karve started a residential school where widows were given admission, Tilak did not write anything in support of that effort. In 1916, owing to the efforts of Prof. Karve, the first women's University was started in Pune, Tilak did not welcome that event, which had a great social significance.

When Lokamanya Tilak went to England in 1917, with the help of Barrister Baptista, he brought out an excellent pamphlet 'Self Determination' which made a fervent plea for Home Rule in India. Tilak sent copies of this pamphlet to all the editors of newspapers in England and also to the members of British Parliament. When one of his followers asked him about this, Tilak said, "We have to educate the British people about the conditions in India and I am confident that owing to our pamphlet on self-determination, I would ensure the support of the Labour Party to our cause."

A Pioneer of National Education

Tilak had sown the seeds of the ideal of national education. After Tilak's demise when Gandhiji emerged as the leader of the freedom struggle, he gave great emphasis on national education. After the non-co-operation movement of 1920, Gandhiji asked many of his followers to dedicate themselves to the work of national education. The Gujrat Vidyapeeth at Ahmedabad, The Tilak Maharashtra Vidyapeeth in Pune and many Rashtriya Shalas were started in different parts of the India. In Tilak Maharashtra Vidyapeeth at Pune, teachers like Acharya Bhagwat, Acharya Jawadekar and others, while delivering inspiring lectures on politics, history and literature, inculcated in students a national outlook. Almost all these students participated in the Satyagraha movement in 1930. Thus the seed sown by Tilak had grown into a huge banyan tree. Tilak titled as 'Lokamanya' by the people of India, is regarded by all as one of the main architects of our freedom struggle. However, it is equally necessary for us to understand the significance of his efforts for giving a new orientation to education and developing it as an instrument of guarding our freedom.

7

Tilak : Management of Institution of Education

Education has been one small aspect of Lokmanya Tilak's contribution to Indian Social Life. There are different sides to Tilak's life of which the most prominent is his political contribution. However, he was not only a political leader but also a great scholar and a journalist. He illuminated every subject he took up. Though Education occupied only a few years of his public and social life, his contribution in this field is unique in the sense that during the entire 20th century the country followed the pattern of education he selected and emulated the management style he professed.

Four important events of Tilak's educational contribution which have been considered in this essay are (i) The foundation of the New English School at Pune, (ii) The formation of the Deccan Education Society, (iii) The establishment of the Fergusson College, and (iv) His resignation of Life Membership of the Deccan Education Society. Tilak voiced his ideas and opinions mainly through articles in Kesari and through letters written by him to his colleagues in the Deccan Education Society. Let us take up these events one by one.

Foundation of New English School, Pune

The closing of the East India Company's regime in India was the beginning of a new era in our country. The failure of the uprising of 1857 had signified that the emancipation of our land and people was to be achieved through peaceful and constitutional means. Raja Ram Mohan Roy in Bengal and Mahadeo Govind Ranade in Maharashtra were the heralds of this new orientation. A very important aspect of this Indian Renaissance was the recognition of the vital part that education had to play in the creation of modern India. The historic debate on the type of education to be imparted to our people had already been settled in favour of the modern West rather than of the ancient East. The verdict in favour of western rather than oriental education had not only meant the virtual suppression of the old by foreigners and christian missionaries. Such a transfer of educational power, though natural and inevitable under the circumstances, was neither necessary for all the time nor wholesome. Nation building education, national education, was what we wanted, and this could not be at the hands of foreigners and missionaries, for obvious reasons. National education, education of the entire nation to achieve national ends, education of the people, for the people and by the people, was the need of the hour.

The famous Wood's Education Despatch was released in 1854. It provided for establishing administrative machinery and colleges for training teachers. The despatch, no doubt, provided the essential framework for our educational system. It was highly appreciative of western education but it introduced a very tight bureaucratic control over the educational system in the country. The despatch appreciated the value of liberal education and education for women. Though the provisions in the despatch were good in character, in effect they proved useful to the Government and to missionaries than to the people. Govt. got an assured supply of servants. In addition as the despatch had provided for grants-in-aid to institutions the missionaries were mainly benefited because of this provision. They got grants without sacrificing their religious activities. The good intentions expressed in the despatch regarding popular education and encouragement to Indian vernaculars remained unrealised. The despatch did not refer to universal literacy although it expected education to spread over a wider field, through the grant-in-aid system. It did not recognize the obligation of the State to educate every child under a certain age; it did not declare that poverty shall be no bar to education of the deserving. The despatch did not visualise education for leadership, or for industrial regeneration nor for the defence of the motherland. As private enterprise was often discouraged, christian missionaries were the only private agency in the field of education.

Under the above mentioned circumstances a band of patriotic and enterprising young men in Pune launched the New English School on 1st January, 1880. These young men were Chiplunkar, Tilak, Namjoshi, Apte and Agarkar. Opening of the New English School proved a new era in the educational and public life of Maharashtra. Bal Gangadhar Tilak and Gopal Ganesh Agarkar later played a vital role in their chosen fields of Politics and Social Reforms. New English School, Pune was singular in having such eminent personalities as its founders. They looked upon education as the surest way to the regeneration of our mother land. In their view, Education was to be the means of rousing the intellect, the drooping will and the slumbering conscious of their countrymen. They kept before the people a very moderate objective of cheapening and facilitating education by starting schools and colleges. This venture was very bold and ambitious particularly in 1880, though it was considered 'mad', 'hopeless', 'criminal' and 'utopian' by Tilak's contemporaries. The founders were too determined and too full of faith to be depressed by apathy or opposition shown by the contemporaries. Through their writings about education they created among youngsters the ideas of patriotism and national self-respect. Tilak and his colleagues achieved the success to the school project through self-sacrifice. All these men had the idealism and enterprise of the pioneers in them. At the time there was a Govt. School and a few private coaching classes in Pune. While the Govt. school was fully supported by the Govt. financing, the private classes conducted by Mahagaonkar, Bhave and others were purely conducted for financial benefits. New English School was different than these. Chiplunkar, Tilak, Agarkar and Apte were so gifted that in their own way they had other things to do than teaching. New English School was extremely fortunate in having them as founders.

A few things are worth noting here at this stage. May be due to the fact that Tilak, Agarkar and their colleagues were educated in the Deccan College where western education was imported, they never thought of going back to oriental education. They accepted what Macauley and the Wood's Despatch had professed. But the starting of New English School in Pune heralded a new movement in Maharashtra. Tilak's influence over the people was so strong that people opened schools in their towns and named them 'New English School'. People were convinced that Education was a tool towards achieving freedom of the country.

Formation of Deccan Education Society

It was essential for the success of the scheme of popular education sponsored by the founders of the New English School that they should form themselves into a corporate body to ensure continuity of effort in that cause and to win public confidence as to the stability and permanence of institutions they might establish. If the public was to be invited to contribute to funds on a scale adequate to the undertaking, the administration of such funds would have to vest in the hands of the organised body, including men interested in education and possessing influence in the Society. From the very outset the founders regarded themselves not as proprietors but as temporary trustees, who on their own personal responsibility and by their own personal sacrifices, would place the school on a firm footing, and then convert it into a public institution, accepting for themselves the status of its life-long servants. When the opening of a college was in sight the formation of a corporate body became a matter of urgency. The earliest mention of the idea of forming a Society occurred in a report of the Superintendent of the New English School for the year 1883. He mentioned in that report that in order to establish a college and to open schools all over Maharashtra it was desirable to constitute a "Board of Trustees with a Managing Committee attached to it". These words gave some idea of the constitution of the proposed Society. When this preliminary work was over, an application for the Registration of the Society was made on 5th August, and the Society was registered on 13th August, 1885 under Act XXI of 1860 (Societies Registration Act) of the Legislative Council of India. The Memorandum of Association stated the object of the Society to be "to facilitate and cheapen education by starting, affiliating or incorporating at different places as circumstances might permit, schools and colleges under native management, or by any other ways best adopted to the wants of the people". The constitution of the Society as originally framed in 1884 provided for setting up three bodies to carry on the business of the Society : (1) Local Managing Boards, one for each Centre, consisting of Life-Members working at that Centre, and entrusted with the internal management of the Societies Institutions situated therein; (2) The Council of the Society for general supervision and control made up of all Life-Members in active service, and an equal number of representatives of the Patrons and Fellows of the Society; and (3)

Trustees to take charge of the permanent funds and property of the Society. This constitution provided for day-to-day management of the Society's Institutions, and initiative as regards the development and extension of the Society's activities for the collection of funds for the purposes of the Society lay with the Life-Members. The Council on which Fellows and Patrons of the Society i.e. those contributing Rs. 200 or more, and those contributing Rs. 1000 or more respectively to the funds were represented and through which they could exert influence on the management of the Society's affairs, had powers of control rather than on initiation. The Council held the purse strings on behalf of the Society and could use that power to exert its influence. Life-Members individually and collectively supplied the driving force to the activities of the Society. The constitution and the working of the Board was thoroughly democratic. Every Life-Member, senior or junior, stood absolutely on the same footing as regards the right of voting and eligibility to office. On their capacity to visualise educational needs and formulate well- considered plans, as also their readiness to carry out these plans depended the progress and prosperity of Society's institutions. The founders of the New English School, Pune succeeded in setting up an altogether new standard of public duty, and made the name of a Life-Member of the Society synonymous with service, sacrifice and integrity. The non-members on the Council had to give a word of counsel now and again, and blessings with their good wishes to any project the Life-Members had put before them. If we look at the private institutions run in Maharashtra at that time, they lacked corporate organisation and consequent lack of guarantees of permanence. They were at a disadvantage as compared to government and missionary institutions. The constitution evolved by the founders of the New English School and Deccan Education Society overcame this difficulty.

We must look at the Constitution of the D.E. Society very carefully. As Tilak, Agarkar, Gokhale and others were involved in framing it, it served as a model to institutions existing at that time as also to those which were started even at later dates. A major weakness of this Constitution, absence of the Governing Council which had a majority of Non-Life Members was pointed out by the then Government and was ultimately accepted by D.E. Society in 1898. Excepting this modification the Constitution of the D.E. Society as framed by the founders continued to function well for over 100 years.

It may be said that the founders of the New English School were influenced by a two-tier management system that prevailed in England for more than two centuries. They had the House of Lords and House of Commons. The administrators came from the House of Commons while the House of Lords had a control over the working of the Govt. Similarly the Board of Life-Members was similar to House of Commons as all the Heads of Institutions were Life-Members. The Managing Council was similar to House of Lords as they had control over the working of the Board of Life-Members. Later on the concept of General Body was also introduced. The General Body had no powers what-so-ever but could express their opinion on the Balance Sheet and Income and Expenditure Statement of the Society. In addition they had the power to elect non-life-members to the General Body of the Society.

Life-Membership was a new concept introduced in the constitution of the D.E. Society. Life-Membership stood for service, sacrifice and integrity. Eventually Life-Members became centres of power in the Society. Life-Members were selected by Life-Members and they continued to be Life-Members till they retired. They had the initiative in every matter concerned with the Society and its institutions. This concept attracted the attention of all the prominent educational institutions in Pune and eventually the Shikshan Prasarak Mandali, Maharashtra Education Society, Progressive Education Society, Modern Education Society adopted the institution of Life-Members. Rayat Shikshan Sanstha, Satara and Vivekanand Shikshan Sanstha, Kolhapur which have schools and colleges all over Western Maharashtra introduced this system in their constitutions. The system has been adopted by many more Societies all over the country. However, like the degradation of political and social systems in the country, the institution of Life-Members also deteriorated. There evolved groupis and nepotism. Life-Members started taking undue advantages and less work. That led to laziness among them. On the one hand life-members became a matter of envy while on the other hand a matter of ridicule. Concentration of power and initiative among the Life-Members was not liked by many non-life-members. Thinkers like Prof. A.B. Shah and Prof. G.P. Pradhan opposed the system on matters of principle saying that selecting Head-Masters or

Principals only from among the Life-Members was undemocratic and it was perpetuating power in the hands of a chosen few who may not be men of efficiency and character. By 1980 some political parties took interest in the affairs of educational institutions in Pune and Maharashtra and amended constitutions of some educational societies in such a way that the Governing Councils were now prominent in the affairs of Societies though the institution of Life-Members remained alive on paper. No doubt Life-Members are the only link between Schools and Colleges and the Management that conducts these institutions. No initiative is now left with Life-Members. However, it must be admitted that the Institution of Life-Members was a prominent administrative system in educational institutions for over a century.

The Fergusson College

When Lokmanya Tilak passed his LLB examination, he had decided to launch educational activity in Pune. He wanted to start a College but could muster enough friends to start a school only when the school started. Because of their social-political activities both Agarkar and Tilak got popularity among the people, got new acquaintances and got donations from princely states. The atmosphere was ripe to start a College. A band of workers like Tilak, Agarkar, Apte, Gole, Kelkar and Dharap were already available for the school. Student strength also grew. Matriculation results of the School were also good. The Deccan Education Society was formed in 1884 and Life-Members were available to it as devoted workers. The time was ripe to open a college.

Teachers who had joined the New English School were efficient teachers in their own subjects; Tilak taught Mathematics and Sanskrit, Agarkar History and Economics, Chiplunkar English and Sanskrit, Apte English and Gole Physics. They were eligible to teach in Colleges also as per the prevailing rules. This impressed the teachers in Mumbai University who included Prin. Wordsworth, Oxenham, Dr. McKikan and Dr. Bhandarkar, Ranade and Telang. They were in favour of allowing the D.E. Society to open a College in Pune.

Shri Vaman Shivram Apte represented the New English School before the Hunter Commission. He stressed the need of (i) Expanding facilities of Education, (ii) Education to be made cheaper, (iii) Improving quality of education imparted in Govt. Institutions, (iv) Independence to private institutions, (v) Freedom to institutions taking grant-in-aid, (vi) Improving education in Indian Languages, (vii) Developing Indian models of education, (viii) Developing Text-Books in India, (ix) Delegating the management of higher education to Indians. The Commission was quite impressed with this deposition. Tilak and his colleagues thought Education, if controlled and imparted by Indians would produce men of quality who would also improve the social and political life of the country. Ultimately that would lead to freedom of the country. They believed that Education was the only force that could bring about material, moral and religious regeneration of fallen countries and could raise them to the level of most advanced nations by slow and peaceful revolutions.

On 24 October, 1884 a meeting of prominent citizens of Pune was held in which the Deccan Education Society was formed. Shri. Apte suggested that opening of a College could be undertaken only when sufficient donations were received from the people. Money thus collected must be vested in the hands of those who were known to be socially and morally of a high standard. In this meeting Tilak proposed a Committee to be formed for that purpose consisting of Mandlik, Telang, Wordsworth, Waderburn, V. M. Kelkar and others. Dr. Bhandarkar in his resolution praised the work of Tilak and six other colleagues.

In December, 1884 the Syndicate of the Mumbai University recommended to the Senate that the D. E. Society be allowed to start a College in Pune and if the College worked well for a period of three years the University should grant it affiliation.

Fergusson College was opened on 2 January, 1885 in Gadrewada near Holkarwada. The D. E. Society had requested the Govt. to allow it to use Shaniwarwada, but the Govt. declined. For some time it was decided to house the College in Budhwarwada. On that occasion Sir James Fergusson made a speech and praised Tilak and his colleagues for their efforts. However, this function proved to be futile as the foundation stone had to be shifted from Budhwarwada to the present site owned by Shirole. From 1892 the College became full-fledged as it was allowed to conduct final year B.A. class. For some time Govt. was inclined to hand-over the Deccan College to D. E. Society but these negotiations fizzled out.

Opening of the Fergusson College was no doubt a triumph for Tilak and his colleagues. The reputation of the College spread all over the country in later years. Many eminent personalities have recorded their appreciation of the work done by Tilak and others. Lala Lajpat Rai, Shriniwas Shastri and Pandit Madan Mohan Malviya have been some of them.

Tilak's Resignation of Life-Membership of D.E. Society

The Fergusson College was started in 1885. While the School and the College were making rapid progress, the internal differences among life-members began to increase. Life-members on whose hearty team-work depended the continued success and progress of the Society's institutions were divided in two opposite camps around Tilak and Agarkar. The difference that now divided them arose partly from differing views about the management of institutions and irreconcilable outlooks upon the social and political questions of the day, and partly from incompatibility of temperament, together working to produce extreme bitterness of feeling. Tilak resigned his Life-membership in October 1890. It was a fateful decision. He cut himself off from the proud handiwork of his own and his comrades' youthful idealism and set out on the rough sea of public life. It was in the circumstances a wise decision, too, because the gulf between others and himself was too wide. It was no use wasting the energies of all in endless friction and opposition. It was the question of child-marriage that first brought the elements of discord to the surface. Not only on the question of child-marriage and enforced widowhood but on others too relating to social reform. Agarkar was a radical, advocating drastic action on the part of the individuals and the Government to root out the cankerous diseases of Hindu Society. In the view of his colleagues, education and the consciousness of social evils it was bound to produce were the most potent instruments of social reform. They were opposed to State-action to accelerate the pace of social reform too much in advance of public opinion. Tilak's opposition to social reform legislation was particularly outspoken and continuous and this circumstance must have tended to produce estrangement between these two persons. This line of cleavage was intensified by other differences regarding the management of the school and the college. In these matters Apte, and later on, Gokhale were one with Agarkar, while Namjoshi and Dharap sided with Tilak. Whatever the grouping of other individuals, Tilak and Agarkar were always to be found on opposite sides on all important issues, and an impassable barrier of thought and feeling gradually raised itself between them.

As regards pay and earnings to Life-Members, Tilak's contention was that the principle of self-sacrifice demanded that the life-members should content themselves with the pay and family provision secured by the Society, and that extra earning should go to the Society. In case of necessity, gratuities might be given to individual life-members, but no regular outside work ought to be undertaken with a view to supplementing the ordinary salary. It were best to put a stop to outside work altogether, because it created divergent interests and imported inconvenient questions into the working of the Society. If outside work was to be allowed, however, it was necessary to rule that profits thereof shall go to the common fund of the Society. Such a rule would secure that outside work shall be undertaken out of disinterested motives purely as a labour of love. Agarkar's views on these matters stood in sharp contrast to Tilak's. He says, "I seriously differ from him on the question of private work. He suggests that no life-member should be allowed to undertake any extensive private work without the consent of the Board. He thinks that such a restriction is necessary in the interests of the Body. Now I am not quite sure that the interests of the Body would be promoted by such a restriction. In proposing the restriction he is solely influenced by the desire that every life-member should expend the whole of his energy on the work of the institutions and that nothing should distract his mind from it. This is extremely desirable; but the restriction proposed will launch us into almost inseperable difficulties ... Further, the strict rules about pay and gratuities may induce some to secretly set aside this restriction to make up their pressing wants, and some may do it for the sake of helping their friends with interested motives or without them. Thus the Board will soon have to convert itself into a most frightful Court of Inquisition producing disgust about it in the mind of every life-member, and thus this restriction will ultimately defeat its own end .... No Body can imitate the discipline of the order of Jesuits without making important modifications in it. No Jesuit is a married man; no Jesuit has private property, nor is he allowed to make any; the Jesuits have a common mess and they lodge in a common house." Life-members were pretty equally divided on the question at issue. It must be clearly borne in mind that the outside work that Agarkar and those of his thinking had in mind was of the literary, journalistic, political or public character. They were not pleading for liberty to engage without let or hindrance in any sort of money-making activities or business, but only in such categories of activities as are indicated above. Traditions have always been held to preclude life-members from the pursuit of business as ordinarily understood. Even private tuition for gain is considered as tabooed to life-members, and regular paid service is ruled out by the pledge of life-membership itself.

It must be remembered that three of the most conscientious and devoted men in the Society Agarkar, Apte and Gokhale were ranged against Tilak in the fight over principles. It is not to be imagined for a moment that they wanted to dilute the principle of self-sacrifice, or lower the standard of devotion to Society. Their own sacrifice left no room for any such misgiving. The Secretaryship of the Sarvajanik Sabha was an honorary unpaid post, and the only gain that Gokhale could have looked for in accepting it was the opportunity of serving a period of political apprenticeship under the guidance of Ranade. For conscientious and unflagging work in the interest of Society's institutions, a greater figure than Apte could not have been found among life-members. If such men differed from Tilak it must have been from disinterested motives, and for worthy objects. They must have considered the vow of Jesuitical poverty impracticable for married men belonging to Hindu Society, with their undefined family obligations to relatives far and near, and in claiming for life-members the freedom to supplement their salaries by extra earnings they were facing the facts of the situation in a spirit of realism. It would have been intolerable to have to place one's domestic difficulties before others and appeal to them for monetary help. A regular system of gratuities would have been most difficult to work equitably. It would have been a source of personal misunderstandings and heart-burnings. It was best to allow a fixed salary and leave to each life-member the freedom to supplement it if he liked and if he could. The Society's work must always be understood to have the supreme claim on the time and energy of everyone; but after that was satisfied, according to such energy of everyone, according to such a standard as his colleagues might apply, there was wisdom in leaving a life-member free to engage in outside work according to his lights. To cut him off from outside work was not the most effective way of making a life-member devote himself absorbingly to the Society's interests. Devotion to academic and administrative work in connection with the Society must come from the urge of his own heart and conscience, and the compelling force of tradition and example. In opposing Tilak on the ground of principle, therefore, Agarkar and Gokhale were striving for the establishment of what was practicable and attainable. The principles they proposed for the working of the Society have stood the test of time, and that their faith in them was deep and disinterested was proved by the events of 1898. The spirit of self-sacrifice did not dry up after Tilak's leaving the Body; it flowed steady and strong and asserted itself again and again in defence of the cherished principles.

The four events described in this essay have influenced the nature and style of management in educational institutions in this country for over a century and would continue to do so for many more years.

Views of Agarkar about Education

Gopal Ganesh Agarkar was contemporary of Tilak and a great social reformer of the nineteenth century Maharashtra. Well-known educationist born on 14thJuly, 1858 and studied in Pune he advocated firmly women's emancipation through education, widow marriage, ban on child marriage and age old traditions, which are a great hindrance to the progress of society. He was the nearest friend of Tilak in the early student life and college but later, due to difference of opinion he left Tilak and the editorship of Kesari and launched his own weekly 'SUDHARAK'.

We must take into account the social conditions in Maharashtra before Agarkar came on the scene. All traditions, customs, social dictates and transactions had religious sanction. Age-old traditions were powerful. The scriptures were the highest authority. The higher castes who wielded religious power dictated the rules regarding marriage, social behaviour and the caste system. Judicial powers were predominantly in the hands of the higher castes. It is in the light of this background that we must assess the work of Agarkar.

Gopal Ganesh Agarkar had planned his future life during his college days, even earlier, at school, when he developed a strong yearning to see as the society. His uncle, Dattopant Bhagwat, has mentioned in his memories that Agarkar had no desire to take up government employment and had informed his mother likewise. On completing his studies, Agarkar along with his colleagues established an educational society and embarked on his lifelong mission of educating the people.

He was the first editor of the pioneering weekly, 'KESARI'. Lokmanya Tilak, Chiplunkar and other colleagues were other willing helping hands. In fact, they were indispensable partners in the venture.

He was determined to use his newspaper to educate the society but mere determination was not enough. As an editor, he had to be prepared to confront the society boldly. Knowing fully well that his views were not understood or accepted by the traditionalists, he had to repeat himself unequivocally. He had to confront hurt feeling, anger and short - sightedness. Many readers threatened him. He however withstood all these pressures.

Reforms : Social or Political ?

Does social reform take precedence over political? This was the main issue of contention between Tilak and Agarkar. When the controversy was raging, the country was still under British rule. The proponents of political reforms argued that the first priority should be to instigate the people rise against their subjugation against the injustice of foreign rule. Did Agarkar not comprehend this simple logic? Did he deny the need for political reforms? What was his stand in this respect? On this issue, Agarkar opined, " All kinds of reforms are classified as social, political or behavioural, mainly for the sake of organising thoughts. They cannot be ranked as first, second or third. They refer to different activities but total reformation of the human being and this country is what we desire and have said so many times. It seems, however, that this is not acceptable to all. Some feel that political reforms are easier and unlike social reforms they are not controversial. The common belief is that since in our struggle for social reforms we are criticised by the people, leading to unnecessary infighting, then it is better that we pitch our might for social reforms. If we agreed to the above statement and still insisted on popular reforms, then we would be worthy of the blame".

Eradication of Untouchability

Agarkar gave some indigenous examples to support his statement. He said that one must think whether an action was performed for profit or because it was one's duty. Once it was understood that one's duty was paramount, there was no sense debating the relative merits of the political struggle versus the social reforms. For example, adhering to the doctrine of untouchability might be in the interest of a few but one must think whether it is right in the name of equality and social justice. If it is not right, then it is one's social as well as political duty to eradicate it. In his words :

> "Those who feel polluted, when they happen to walk in the shadow of an untouchable, insist that we must be independent of English rule. They argue that though Indians are black and the English are white, there is no difference in the caliber because color does not determine one's capability. Why should there be any difference in one's capability? Why should there be any difference if the touchables and the untouchables are not of different colour nor have different physique? How does colour determine the capability of a person? Who introduced this four-structured 'varna'? Who propagated the myth that Brahmins were born out of the mouth of the mythical person called SAMAJPURUSH and the untouchables out of his feet? This unfair shastra must be done away with, and we must learn to sit close to each other - the untouchables and the Brahmins - in our schools. The idea of profitability is utterly futile; our duty as human beings must be our main consideration. It is up to us to see that the unfair distinction between an untouchable and the Brahmin, a widow and a widower, a man and a woman, is rooted out. Yet the conservatives do not wish to do it; why then should they think of abolishing the difference between the victors and the vanquished? Even if they do, how do they hope to bring it about?"

In reality, Agarkar was proud to be, an Indian. He advocated social reforms out of a genuine yearning for his country's progress, hoping that one day the nation would be on equal terms with the more developed western societies.

Emancipation of Women

Agarkar gave prime importence to strengthening of the institution of family life in his programme for social reforms. Because if such an institution is sick, there can be no concern about the status of women in the family. He stressed the importance of women's education. He believed that a husband and a wife were equally important members of the family. For hundreds of yeas, it had been traditionally accepted that men should earn a livelihood by working, may be away from home, while women should stay at home to look after the young ones and the elders in the family. When the needs of the society were few and the lifestyle simple, both men and women accepted the system. With the passage of time, their obligations as members of the society increased and the means of livelihood became complex. In the process,men began to assume a higher status in the family with the consequent decline in the status of women. Women's independent identity was scorned; the sole purpose in life was to serve the husband, produce children, and not meddle with work outside the home . It came to be accepted that the man should be the head of family, assume leadership in society, exercise control over communal organisations and assume proprietorship of income.

The societies decreed that a woman follows all the rules imposed by the institute of marriage even before she had acquired an understanding of what marriage involved. Nobody even remotely considered it an injustice in marrying a very young girl to a much older man. Since, the scriptures strengthened the belief that anyone who flouted the norms of morality laid down by religion was a sinner and would have to pay for his sins in the next life, it adversely affected a woman's position in the family. It was but natural that a progressive man like Agarkar whose independent thinking focussed on social progress should find the inequality of the family structures highly unjust. He suggested several measures for the emancipation of women. He particularly emphasised on the importance of women's education.

Restriction of Child Marriages by Law

Agarkar, believed that if girls stayed longer with their families and acquired proper education, their mental and intellectual growth could be better. After marriage an educated girl would exercise a better cultural influence on her new home. Child marriages burdened very young girls with family responsibilities, making it difficult for them to cope with married life. Child marriages affected boys as well, rendering them mentally and physically weak.

With genuine fervour Agarkar advocated restrictions on child marriage by suggesting the Bill of Consent as the ultimate solution. The conservatives in society raised a hue and cry against it.

While advocating restrictions on child marriage, Agarkar emphasised the need for widow remarriage. The ban on widow remarriage existed among the higher castes, like Brahmins and especially Marathas. A widow's life in Hindu society was miserable. Agarkar advocated that the society should accept her remarriage, which would give purpose and dignity for her, life. This would also take care of the problem of forced abortions. In this matter too, Agarkar expounded the need for a law as well as social education.

Compulsory Education

Many articles in the 'Sudharak' exemplify Agarkar's concern for education. In fact, Agarkar spent most of his life in teaching and propagating education. On completing his education from the Deccan College, he joined the New English School on a paltry remuneration and started a career in teaching. Thereafter he joined the Fergusson College, first as a professor and then as a principal. Through his journals he educated the masses for fifteen years with great dedication. Fifteen years after Agarkar's death, in 1910, Gopal Krishna Gokhale reasserted Agarkar's view that not only mere literacy but primary education must be made compulsory for every boy and girl. He placed the proposal for compulsory primary education in supreme legal council followed by a Bill of the same nature, the year after. Because of foreign rule in the country at the time, nobody expected an immediate implementation of the Act. After Independence, a provision for compulsory universal primary education was made in the Indian Constitution, in the year of 1950. However, the provision is not yet fully implemented to this day.

Mass Education

Agarkar firmly believed that mass education was necessary to teach people to think and curb the tendency towards crime. In this context, he said : "What better tool can there be other than mass education for protecting people's property and life?" Whipping a person, confining him to stock, securing his hands at the back, imprisoning him in a dark room, hand cutting or making him lift heavy musket balls, hanging or shooting him, are these the proper ways to punish and deter criminals?

According to him, preventive rather than curative measures for checking crime were more important; the practice of inoculation rather than using strong drugs to cure a patient was better. Similarly, compulsory education to make the people aware of their surroundings was essential. Keeping citizens in ignorance and letting them to commit crimes and then punishing them was wrong and deserved condemnation.

Agarkar cited another similie to drive home his point. He said that if the markets were flooded with rotten fruits and vegetables, then there was every chance of the rot spreading elsewhere. Was it not wiser then to prevent the spoilt and rotten fruits and vegetables from entering the market? In a similar manner, it was necessary to keep undesirable tendencies away by nurturing the mind properly through education and inculcation of noble thoughts.

Ignorance : Root of all Suffering

Ignorance was at the root of all kinds of physical ad mental deficiencies. Who suffered the pangs of dependence? Who found it difficult to earn their daily bread and who languished in poverty? Who suffered the consequences of ill-conceived notion? These were some of the questions raised by Agarkar who felt that the root cause of all suffering was ignorance. He said that the solution lay in the hands of the government. Unfortunately there was a large section of the society which warned the government to desist from interfering in social and educational matters. A hundred years after Agarkar, the percentage of literacy in Maharashtra hovered around 40 to 45 percent; if such is the speed of the progress of education then we still need another decade to achieve cent percent literacy. Agarkar's suggestion that the government had to shoulder the responsibility for providing compulsory primary education has a wider perspective as can be seen from his words below:

> "If you want children can learn at home or in school run by local councils or private schools as seen in Germany or in England, as in county council schools or aided schools. But, unless the Government makes education compulsory for every child between the age of six and fourteen, no adult, man or woman would ever be able to read or write his or her, own letter or sign without the help of someone. No matter, who takes the responsibility of primary education, the Government must see to it that the scheme is important".

To appreciate his views in wider perspective, we may note the following passage, "We .have taken up the cause of mass education because we are sure that of all the means possible for any nation's physical, moral and religious reformation in a slow but progressive manner and also for the country to compete with the developed nations, education is a primary tool better than any other cultural implement available to mankind".

Together and Equal Education

One of the major points in Agarkar's reformist program was providing equal education opportunities to all men and women for the progress of society. He said :

> "If men and women are given the same type of education, men may have to stay at home to look after the children, wash clothes, do the cleaning up, cook and grind flour. It can not be helped. God did not intend that women alone should face the drudgery, and child bearing has nothing to do with such tedious chores".

While referring the argument that because women did all the household chores there was neither time nor need for education of women, Agarkar emphasised on two vital points. One was that there was no need to have a hard and fast rule as to who should do what kind of work inside or outside the house. Besides, men should not feel it below their dignity to take up household chores. Though everybody accepted in theory that a man and women were equally responsible for running a household, in practise it was found convenient that a man shouldered the responsibility of working outside and providing the family.

The issue of women's education is perhaps not very pressing today (though it may not be entirely true) but a hundred years ago there was a dire need for sustained effort to prepare the ground for making women's education acceptable to all. Credit for women's education today goes to Agarkar to quite an extent.

Those opposed to women's education spread the misconception that coeducation would lead to staying at house and attending to household chores, besides looking after the children. Agarkar, answered them back squarely.

All Kinds of Education for Men and Women

He felt that both the men and the women should take whatever education they want for whichever examinations they want and for whichever degree they desire and may, whenever they want and lead their lives the way they want. He was certain that this would happen one day. It can be said that Agarkar's aspirations have been fulfilled at least in principle today. Women's education is not restricted to certain areas alone, for, nowadays girls seek admission to courses like medicine, engineering, chartered accountancy, and different branches of science and even aeronautics. However, in rural areas because of poverty, parents are still not keen on girls' education, although there has been a change in thinking over last few years. Agarkar, was thus a true visionary to envisage a hundred years ago the direction women's education would take.

Although education and freedom for women have been largely accepted in Maharashtra for many years now, subjugation of women continues elsewhere. The struggle for women's liberation continues.

National Freedom

On national freedom, Agarkar wrote, "Loss of national freedom is lamentable. It is like losing the vital part of the brain which controls all the senses in the body. If there is no vital spirit in the body, the body is dead. This is equally true of a nation. The conquered nation, howsoever affluent, is like a lifeless sculpture - it commands no respect, its people have no sense of either belonging, or any real pride in it. The house in which you live may have beautifully decorated rooms, but if you have no right to live there, it is not your home. You do not have any sense of belonging there, and then why be proud of the house, which is owned by someone else?"

According to the modern concept any county is not a nation until the people of the country control and restrain the rulers. None before Agarkar had defined freedom to include a democratic set-up by the government. The concept of nationhood including monitoring of the government by the people and thereby the formation of government by the people, was first conceived by Agarkar and that too a hundred years ago. Freedom meant, a government controlled and monitored by the people a concept, which is most acceptable even today. However liberal the administrators from England were, they could not negate the fact of subjugation.

Agarkar believed that the use of indigenous resources alone could not help much in developing industries. He said, "Our economic conditions cannot improve by discarding machines and machine-based industries and rejuvenating our old handicrafts. Progress by having machine run industries is inevitable. To reject machinery because the British have invented it and continue in the old rut is a hindrance to our progress. We must use scientific knowledge for our development. We must make efforts, be industrious, and experiment in cooperation with others to improve our life financially."

Agarkar studied the social character of the society from various angles. Political subjugation, obsolete traditions, lack of resources and general poverty were the contributing factors to the backwardness of a nation. He was convinced that the society needed to cultivate new values. Rationality, individual freedom, social party, enrichment of life and faith in science were the prime values he stressed on. His thinking was based on humanitarian values, belief in equality and faith in science, and not on charity or religious considerations.

Summing Up

Agarkar's educational outlook was different from other social reformers of his time. His view was established on strong belief, on rational thinking, scientific approach, individual freedom and moral values.

He gave priority to education for all without discrimination of male and female. In short, we can give important points of view regarding education.

1. Necessity and urgency of education to society to eradicate ignorance and old traditions.
2. Society must give importance and priority to education of girls to stop their dependence.
3. Compulsory education to all members of the society without discrimination of rich and poor class or caste.
4. No difference of subjects of study for boys and girls.
5. Co-education to boys and girls and equal education and equal opportunity to all.
6. Primary education is government's responsibility.
7. Provision for higher education of Science, Commerce and Technical subjects. He strongly believed that the old building of society is almost collapsed, so why not construct new one on scientific education? Because education is itself a social institution affected by and affecting all other institutions.

8

TILAK : TEACHING AND LANGUAGE

English Verses Vernacular Language

Education cannot be thought of without consideration of the language. The countries in which the language of their people is adopted from elementary to post-graduate levels, it is automatically developed and enriched. But with the British rule a colonial country like India faces a very unfavourable condition. The medium of instruction, administration, public relations, everything becomes problematic. Earlier Sanskrit was the language of the masses. There are many regional languages, but hardly ever the conditions were favourable for their development. They are inevitable in the day to day life but never got a respectful place under the British rule. Learning in one's mother tongue is a natural process but in India the whole system became an un-natural one. The nationalistic education conceived by Chiplunkar and others had the underlying principle of giving the mother tongue, its due place and respect. Obviously Tilak has written at length about this problem in his articles on nationalistic education. At times his comment is very sharp. In a speech in 1908 on Nationalistic education he says,

> "English is a very strange language. One cannot master it fast. It is not easy. Just because it is the language of the rulers, we have to learn it; it is but a burden for us. We stand to lose because the medium of instruction is not Marathi. Why do we need to speak for two hours in English? Is there even one British officer who can speak Marathi? But hundreds of us speak English. We have

> wasted years on learning English. If the knowledge I got was given in Marathi, all that I have learnt for 52 years could have been mastered at 25 or 30. We waste the valuable years in learning English. Educating a nation through a foreign language is subjugating it. Therefore the knowledge must be imparted in the vernacular. This will save students' life."

In another lecture delivered in 1908 on this topic Tilak says, "Now a days education is nothing but the ability to speak and write English. But knowing the language is not gaining knowledge. Nowhere else do we find this compulsion of learning thoroughly a foreign language. Forced to learn through a foreign language, what could be learnt in a period of 7 to 8 years takes 20 to 25 years. We cannot do away with learning English altogether; but we do not have to be proficient in that language because it is the key to knowledge. Under the Muslim rule we had to learn the Persian language, but it was not burdensome."

In 1891, Tilak had written two articles entitled 'English language and vernacular language'. He stressed that the language of the ruling Britishers that is gaining importance in administration and education was once underdeveloped. Learning French was a matter of prestige in England; but only when the Britishers rejected this foreign language and gave importance to their own language and when it was practised in all the walks of life did English become a developed and enriched language. Therefore the native Indians should realise that for their language to prosper, self-respect is what is needed. It is possible to make available the knowledge into the native languages through translations. English has become the language of knowledge only because the knowledge in other European languages was translated into English. Thus realising this secret of its prosperity we too can enrich our own languages. Instead, the educated amongst us are happy to use English and are neglecting their own language. This indifference of the educated is what is hampering the progress of indigenous languages like Marathi. In his speech in 1906 at the Mumbai Marathi Granthasangrahalaya Tilak had raised some points for the development of the Marathi language. He said, "The prosperity of the Marathi community and the growth of the Marathi language are interdependent. Your language will develop only if you yearn sincerely for it. Superficial remedies will be of no use. The undue importance to English is harmful for the growth of

Marathi. In earlier times Sanskrit Pundits too were against Marathi, but the saints contributed to the progress of Marathi language. The pundits opposing Marathi used to converse in Sanskrit. But the educated of today are subjugating themselves to English and feel proud to use it everywhere. Even the talks on their religion are in English. This will definitely not make Marathi prosper, on the contrary, people will start to dislike it. A child reared by the maid does not care about his mother." Similarly the educated who always turn to English have a contempt for Marathi. This attitude must be changed first. It is not enough that Marathi becomes the language of knowledge; it should also be the language of communication. There is a progress on this front.

On various occasions Tilak has talked about many matters like the education policy of the government, the state of the universities, the low level of knowledge imparted to the students, the attitude of the educated and the government towards the vernacular languages etc. to criticize the selfish educated and the government. As the vernacular languages had no place in the university curriculum, they could not prosper and people started neglecting them. It is not enough to include these languages to study certain books written in those languages; at least some subjects must be taught through them. Then alone the vernacular languages will prosper. Only literary books do not bring about the progress of a language. Only when Science, administration, judiciary and markets uphold the use of a language does it progress. English is not rich only with Shakespeare and Milton, but because it embraces all the fields of life, it has gained its popularity. But the universities here do not intend to act for the cause of the indigenous languages. Their education does not encourage research and scholarly pursuits. What all the universities are doing is only to supply obedient servants for the smooth functioning of the administration. The universities today have become labour suppliers. One more reason for the inferior quality of knowledge is the third or fourth rate professors that are sent from Britain. They have limited knowledge and do not like to teach. In these circumstances it is but inevitable that selfish graduates are churned out. As the number of graduates is increasing more than the jobs available, the government has adopted the strategy of making the examination increasingly difficult and reducing the number of universities. Thus Tilak has heavily criticized the education system with appropriate examples and has substantiated his argument. But he has not blamed the government alone; the narrow minded and enslaved educated are equally targeted.

In 1904 Tilak wrote an article titled 'The prosperity of Marathi language'. In the beginning he has exposed the ignorant prejudice of a British officer named Birdwood regarding the Marathi language. This Mr. Birdwood was of the opinion that "Marathi has become impure because of the Marathi newspapers". On the contrary, Marathi has become very forceful thanks to journalists from the days of Balshastri Jambhekar to Gopal Ganesh Agarkar, insisted Tilak. However he expressed his concern over the contraction of the sphere of its expansion in India. He pleads that the Marathi people, inspiring from the Bengali, Hindi and Gujarati communities, should create a central institution for the protection and development of Marathi.

In his article titled 'Series of text books for schools' Tilak has attracted attention on an important issue. Tilak has heavily criticized the fact that these books are being prepared by the MacMillan Company in England instead of the local writers. The real danger as he saw was the inculcation of 'loyalty to the British' instead of national pride. The British have already weakened the peoples of India by taking away their weapons, now they want to see to it that the children become mentally feeble too. Even the private institutions do not protest in this regard because the education department has gained control over them by sanctioning grant-in-aid.

In 1906 Tilak wrote three articles titled 'The growth of Maharashtrian Language'. Few days before writing these articles was established the 'Maharashtra Sahitya Parishad' a central, representative institution. The first article deals with the birth of Marathi Language, the period of 1000-1200 years of its existence, the dangers faced in the form of Muslim regime, the role of devotion - professing saints in adopting Marathi as the language of expression and there-by protecting and perpetuating the language. He expresses his gratitude towards the saints who helped the widespread of Marathi. The second article recognizes the role of Shivaji and the Maratha Kingdom in the rise of prestige of the Marathi Language. He stresses the fact that a language prospers with its rulers. The Maratha Kingdom was instrumental for the spread of Marathi in the North upto Atak and in the south upto

Tanjore. Other regions attached prestige to the ability to understand or speak Marathi only because it was the language of the rulers.

Marathi lost its importance with the British rule. That is the root cause of its decline. Now people do not feel strongly about their religion nor are they anxious to uplift their language. Having accepted the dominance of the English language, the knowledge in Marathi has become restricted. Translating from English will help only upto a certain limit. Only when our writers will start expressing themselves with a zest for their country and language, will the Maharashtrian language grow in quality.

The then Education Ministry had appointed a committee to prepare textbooks in Marathi. This committee had given some suggestions about the graphemics Marathi (i.e. devnagri). Tilak was against the idea of this committee being allowed to interfere in graphemics and wrote an editorial to express his opposition. If the system recognized by the education department is rejected the situation will be chaotic. In fact, it is the task of the grammarians to state their opinions, there should be a good discussion at length and then alone could be decided what to include and what to reject. And people will accept whatever is reasonable.

The main objection Tilak has raised is quite different. That is why title of his article reads 'Murder of our alphabet'. The committee, while preparing the new textbooks, had suggested that initiation to the alphabet should not be done in the traditional order of 'k' 'kh' 'g', 'gh', but 'g' 'm', 'bh', 'n' instead. Tilak is strongly against this suggestion. This will be but showing deep ignorance about a system recognized to be 'scientific' since the last three thousand years. He quotes Prof. McDonel regarding the Sanskrit alphabet (which is also the alphabet of Marathi).

Tilak questions the authority of the committee to suggest changes in alphabets and its order certified to be scientific even by western scholars. He has appealed to the public to send written protests if such erroneous decision is imposed.

(However, it should be noted that Tilak's objections are based on a misunderstanding. The committee had not suggested any changes in the order of the alphabet; it had only suggested that the graphemes with similar strokes be clubbed together while introducing those letters of alphabet. Tilak never mentioned that the order of our alphabet is phonetically very good but not from the graphemics point of view. That is why he has conveniently misrepresented the committee. Perhaps he disapproved of the appointment of such a committee in the first place.)

Orthography of Marathi

In 1904 Tilak had written four editorials on this topic. In those days there was a controversy among researchers. Three pundits called Mr. Sane, Godbole and Hatwalne had written 'Marathi bhashechi lekhan paddhati' to suggest some changes in the prevailing rules. The conformists had highly objected to these reforms. They were even scorned at as three Munis. Tilak kept from using any abusive language but launched a serious discussion about the academic and theoretical aspects of the problem of orthographic reforms of the Marathi language. Mr. Sane was part of the Books Committee formed to suggest such reforms. Objecting to such an intervention of the government was also one of reasons why Tilak wrote four editorials on this subject. According to Tilak more than grammarians, the final decision lies in the hands of people who use the language. Many forms considered incorrect by the grammarians are found to be in use. The Sanskrit lovers want Marathi to follow the Sanskrit ways of expression, some Marathi lovers insist that rules of Marathi should be according to Marathi alone. Some give importance to the pronunciation, some find it fit to consider the etymology and common practice.

Tilak observes that the Marathi diction is not uniform. It varies from place to place. It is not always possible to write according to the pronunciation. English has contradictions and irregularities par excellence in the spoken and written language. Even in Marathi the /a/ sounds in ghara, matha, natha is not alike. The first is what is termed as 'udatt' or well-articulated and the second 'unudatt' or not well-articulated. But there is no specific symbol to distinguish between the two. Paahaa, Raahaa have their forms in practice as pahaa, rahaa, that is the /a/ sounds here is once not-well-articulated and once well-articulated. The concept of long and short sounds also changes from language to language. In short it is easier said than done to write exactly the way you speak. The grammarians are the rulers of the language, but with limited powers. The final powers must be with the people who practice it.

Marathi is not yet a fully developed language but it is growing. It is not perfect like Sanskrit. Therefore some liberty has to be accorded in its orthography. It is not possible to make, once and for all, all the rules governing this language. It will be obstinate to say that no changes in the orthography are required. But it is not for the government to take any steps. Only expert Marathi scholars should do it. For this a representative institution should be founded. The problem of long and short vowels in Marathi is a complex one. Therefore we have to act with conscious discrimination and not stick to any lop-sided view. Same is the case with consonant ending words. The nasalisation symbols when not in practice should be omitted, but removing all the nasal symbols without discrimination will be wrong. If etymologically a nasal symbol is justified, we can keep it, otherwise not Marathi is a growing language and therefore we should bear in mind that all its rules cannot be determined for eternity.

9

Tilak and Origin of National Feeling

National welfare can be achieved only when there is national awareness in the minds of the people filled with national spirit. And national spirit can be achieved only when there is spirit of nationalism. Nationalistic theory of education is one of the important theories of education which provides strong philosophical base for the field of education.

Nationalism

"Nationalism may be defined as a state of mind in which the individual feels that everyone owes his supreme secular loyalty to the nation or state" (Encyclop Britanica, Page No. 851).

Nationalism, precisely defined as above, is a modern concept. Throughout history men have been attached to their native soil together with the traditions of their parents. But before 18 th century nationalism was not a generally recognised sentiment moulding public or private life. Because of its dynamic vitality and its all-pervading character Nationalism is often thought to be very old. But it is the historical fact that American and French Revolutions may be regarded as its powerful manifestations.

Nationalism as translated into world politics implies the identification of the state or nation with the people. The end of the 18th century observed that Nationalisation of Education and public life went hand in hand with the Nationalisation of states and political loyalties. Poets and scholars were the first torch-bearers who began to emphasise Cultural Nationalism.

The Roots of National Feeling

Before the 18th century there had been evidences of National feeling among certain groups at certain periods. These were the periods of stress and conflict. As far as Indian history is concerned we shall find ample situations of National feeling during the continuous historical stream. But the span of the concept of Nation was limited to a particular period and province or state. In western countries development of Nationalism stressed National awareness as well as national individualism. During the 17th and 18th century, western countries had undergone different critical changes in human life- style. The common standards of western civilisation were - the regard for the universally human, the faith in reason as well as in common sense, the survival of christian and stoic traditions. These standards were too strong to allow nationalism to develop fully and to disrupt society. Thus nationalism in its beginning was thought to be compatible with cosmopolitan convictions and with a general love of mankind.

Nationalism in Asia

The concept of Nationalism began to appear on the Asian Screen after World War I. The progress of Nationalism in Asia is reflected in the history of the League of Nations after World War I. Among the league's original members there were only 5 Asian countries China, India, Japan, Thailand and Iran. After World War II India, Pakistan, Ceylon, Burma and Malaya were the Asian countries getting independence from the British Commonwealth. The period between World War I and World War II was a period of ripening of nationalism in Asian countries.

India as a Nation

India or Bharat as a nation is not only a geographical concept or a political ideology but it is supposed to be a collective soul of all Indians. Yogi Arvind has expressed this idea in his words -

It is always observed and examined by the historians that whether India was a nation in ancient or medieval ages is questionable. Inspite of the fact that India was not geographically a nation, there was strong feeling of patriotic nationalism during those days.

This was the national feeling from the mountains of the Himalayas to the waters of Kanyakumari. During British regime this 'national feel' was being challenged and smashed down by the

British rulers because rise of nationalism was totally dangerous for their foreign rule.

Tilak as Earnest Educationist

Tilak and Agarkar were meditating as to how best to devote themselves to the service of this country after their university education. They came to the conclusion that the spread of education of the right stamp among the rising generations was the best method of working for the country's uplift. Their plans of national education were taking tangible shape in their minds. Both of them were highly impressed by 'Nibandhamala' of Vishnushastri Chiplunkar. Tilak was more kindred to Chiplunkar in spirit, particularly in his vivid sense of pride in India's past and in his utter disdain for the theory of considering the British connection as providential.

The new school of thought came to be known as the 'Tilak School' of thought as opposed to Mahadev Govind Ranade's. Members of the Tilak school of thought were the earnest educationists who had strong faith in education as the tool of social change.

Objectives of the D. E. Society

On 1st January 1880 New English School was started by these ardent educationinsts. The institution was then expanded into 'The Deccan Education Society, which conducted several high schools & colleges in future. The principle object of starting this institution was to provide such education for the coming generations as would create in their minds love for their country, respect for their forbears and pride in India's past. Before the New English School opened, there were many educational institutions in Maharashtra and other parts of the country. But these institutions were Anglicised and there were only the job hunters and clerks who were the finished products of these institutions. The objectives of the founders of the Deccan Education Society, together with Lokmanya Tilak, were to produce through this institution patriotic and self respecting persons. They also aimed at cheapening and rationalising education by a legitimate and natural emphasis on mother-tongue as the medium of instruction. 'Tilak School' was the coterie of young patriotic persons who decided to take up the work of spreading education of proper type in India.

New English School : A Dignified Institution

New English school rose high in the estimation of the Government, the general public and it was highly honoured by Maratha Princes. His Highness, Sayajirao Gaikwad, Prince of Kagal state and many others visited and helped the school. Dr. Willian Hunter who was president of the Education Commission recorded his unreserved admiration in the following words :

> "Throughout the whole of India, I have not witnessed a single institution which can be compared with his establishment. This institution can rival and compete with not only the Government high schools in the country but may also favourably compare with the schools of other countries".

Principal Wordsworth says, "This institution is an embodiment of the new spirit that was rising in India. The school would certainly leave its impression on the future events in India. The Times of India admired the efforts of these educationists (20-2-84) saying that these enthusiastic educationists will preach love of the Country to their disciples".

The Object of National Education

According to Tilak, the object of National Education was not to disturb the freedom of personal expression of the students. To create national awareness patriotism, love for country and national unity for getting freedom were the main objects of National education according to Tilak.

Tilak had to introduce the National Education movement because Lord Curzon had obstructed the right of personal expression of the students. This was against the right of freedom.

Tilak as an Indian Jesuit

Tilak's educational thoughts, especially about nationalistic education, evolved out of his own personality as an Indian Jesuit. Jesuit is a devoted missionary who offers his life for his mission. Tilak, in his later life, evolved as a public leader. But earlier he was an educationist. The first chapter of Tilak's public life opened in the field of education which he entered with the zeal of a missionary. We get a glimpse of his unbending spirit, his tenacity of purpose, his indomitable determination, from his work. When he was living at Deccan College he discussed the importance and practicability of establishing private schools on the model of missionary institutions.

There was no difference of opinion as to the necessity of native private enterprise in education. The only point of discussion was how to make this private enterprise successful. Self-sacrifice was the only means for men in existing circumstances that time. How to maintain the quality work was also a point of discussion. After several rounds of discussion the team of these educationists came to the conclusion that " if we applied ourselves to the task with the determination of carrying out our ideas at any sacrifice, it was not an impossibility, though it might be a long time before it could be accomplished".

Tilak was in a position to make up mind for the cause of awakening of our country in respect of getting out of western impact on public life. The best way he thought, was to rouse people to a consciousness of their own way of indigenous life. Tilak was the leader of the team of promoters of the New English School. The sacrifice and selflessness of the promoters bore fruit and it made rapid progress.

Before Tilak entered the field of education, a feeling had been growing that christian missionaries, though seemingly benevolent, had virtually become masters of the education of Poona children. Self-respecting Indians felt the want of a national system of education. The New English School in a way was considered as a counter-blast to the mission-schools. In this way Tilak & his team played the role of Indian Jesuits in the field of education.

Tilak frequently visited different places and went on lecturing over National Education and swadeshi.

Tilak addressed a meeting at Sholapur and told his audience that national education is that type of Education which would make the students conscious of our Nation. He said that English was a difficult language and a student had to waste many years to gain knowledge through English. He also added that the younger generation must obtain knowledge upto the age of 15 years which the old generation could not gain up to 35. He remarked that Government money belonged to the public. He further stated that Government might not like the idea of national education, and it might put an end to it. After his speech he met some rich people and collected funds for the cause of National Education. People responded well and Tilak was successful in his mission.

On March 3 1908, Tilak visited Barsi. There also he appealed to the rich to help the cause of National Education. Addressing a meeting at Barsi Tilak said,

> "To be able to read and write alone was no education. They were simply the means of its attainment. That which gave the knowledge of the experience of their ancestors was called education. We are not given such education as may inspire patriotic sentiments in us. In America the Declaration of Independence is taught in the fifth or the sixth class. In this way they train their children in Politics".

He insisted on religious education and expressed his frank view about English language teaching. According to Tilak there was no reason why the study of English language should be made compulsory.

Tilak wrote several articles about education in Kesari. These articles were the editorials reflecting Tilak's thoughts on education. There are 31 articles on education, of which 3 articles are specifically on National Education. Though Tilak emphasizes National Education in these 3 articles, all other articles also reflect powerfully his ideas about education. He writes about Military education, as well as he writes his views about the medium of Instruction. He had expressed his strong views about the functioning of the universities. He also discussed the philosophical foundations of education, taking into consideration the aims and objectives of education.

Though Tilak promoted Nationalistic Education his outlook was broad and his ideas were comprehensive about Nationalistic Education. Inspite of being a political leader his concept of education was clear, pure and extensive. He advised that an Independent country should always observe educational progress, educational changes and educational developments in neighbouring countries. Selection, omission and moderation in the field of education should be a usual process in an independent country. According to Tilak, Nationalistic Education doesn't mean neglect of others' educational theory. Nationalistic education always respects the educational systems of different countries. But at the same time Tilak expected that an Independent Nation should evolve its own educational system based on the cultural heritage, history and socio-economic conditions of that particular nation.

Nationalism through Nationalistic Education

Tilak expressed his views about nationalistic education with special reference to inculcation of spirit of Nationalism in the minds of the educands. It is the duty of the educators that they must be able to inspire the educands in respect of the feeling of Nationalism. The spirit of Nationalism gives a peculiar perspective to the nation. Nation gets the direction. There remains no ambiguity about the aims and objectives of education if the starting point of discussion would be nationalism. Nationalism encourages community life; it also inculcates feeling amongst the students.

In a way national education movement was the outcome of swadeshi movement. Tilak emphasised national Education as one of the four pillars of the political movement in India. Maharashtra Vidya Prasarak Mandal was established in 1906. The Samarth Vidyalaya was being conducted under its auspices at Kolhapur. Prof. V. C. Vijapurkar was the torch-bearer of this activity. Samarth Vidyalaya was then shifted at Talegaon, near Poona; it was an institution having nationalistic pattern of education. Prof. Vijapukar was a devoted educationist having unmatched vision and perspective about national education. Tilak had taken much interest in the development of this institution. He had a campaign of lecturing for raising the funds for the institution.

The Samarth Vidyalaya at Talegaon was an idealistic educational institution where bookish knowledge had no place. The students used the text-books but they were made conversant with work-experience. Agriculture, tree-plantation, basic industrial training, physical exercises for physical fitness, and different types of work-experience were included in the curriculum of the Samarth Vidyalaya. The finished product of Samarth Vidyalaya was a perfectly developed person having love for his country, devotion of work and community feeling. Paisa-fund glass work of Talegaon was another venture of nationalistic workers. It was expected that the students of the Samarth Vidyalaya at Talegaon could also be given some technical education in the workshop and glass factory.

Tilak Maharashtra Vidyapeeth (Pune) and many other 'Rashtriya Shalas were the extensions of movement of National Education in India. At Yeola, Apte Guruji had established a National School which was an output of the movement.

These schools could not grow more and there was no acceptance of them in future. The reason was mass education. Most of the institutions were dependent on grant in aid given by the Government. National Schools did not take the grants. They had to raise their own funds. They had to find out their own ways for solving their problem. Gradually national education movement had a set back and it remained then as an illustrative pattern only.

Political Education by Lokmanya Tilak

Power is basically neither good nor bad. A democrat needs power and a dictator also needs power. What is important is the use or misuse of power. Because of the blatant misuse of power, the word politics has got a bad odour.

Political Education, therefore, has remained a neglected area in social sciences and not much work has been done not only in India but also abroad.

J. P. Naik, a well-known educationist and founder of the Indian Council of Social Science Research (ICSSR) and many other institutions, has given a serious thought to the concept of political education in the post-independence period. According to him, education means knowledge, skills and attitudes, necessary for the development of an individual and that of society. Political education, therefore, means knowledge about the political system, skills for the maintenance and growth of the political system, and necessary attitudes and values to bring spirit in the political system. The objective of political education can, therefore, be stated as the training of individuals to be intelligent, effective and responsible citizens through imparting of knowledge, building up of skills and cultivation of values.1 All these three elements are significant and have to be developed together, each conditioning the other. Mere knowledge does not serve the objective of political education which requires effective participation based on appropriate skills. Similarly, unreflective or ill informed participation is equally undesirable; and neither knowledge nor participation will lead to the desired social changes unless they are both governed by a proper value system.

Every political system operates in a given society which has its own political culture, distinct from that of other countries. The political system, for its maintenance and growth, requires certain knowledge, skills and values on the part of the people. The process of political education gives knowledge, tries to create skills and inculcate values congenial for the working of the political system. As the society consists of divergent groups, the dissatisfied section in society can be given political education for the overthrow of the political system. If this attempt gets necessary support by the people, there is a change in the government and in the political system.

J.P.Naik has further explained the concept of political education. He explains the kinds of knowledge, skills and values necessary for Political Education.

Knowledge

Political Education needs knowledge of the following.

1. the existing society
2. the new society that the nation desires to create; its value system etc.
3. the existing government of the country
4. the basic problems facing the country in different walks of life

Knowledge of the facts mentioned above changes according to time and place.

Skills

The essence of political education is participation in action. A citizen must be politically not only intelligent, but also politically effective i.e. he must be able to assist the political system to function properly (or oppose if he wants to create a new system) to correct aberrations therein as well as to devise strategies for influencing and achieving change in the desired direction. This will need the following skills -

1. skills of understanding and education of the present political system
2. skills of problem solving
3. skills of working in groups
4. ability to understand conflicts of all kinds and to develop proper relations to them
5. ability to express himself adequately on political matters.

Values

Every social and political system is based upon its own unique frame of values. Some of these are fundamental and absolute.

Political Education under the British Rule

Under the British rule, the policy was to divide the Indian people and rule. They always argued that the Indians did not deserve a self-government. Deliberately created attitude of superiority dominated till 1947. Their objective, therefore, was to educate a class of persons who would act as the interpreters between the rulers and the ruled. The British preached the superiority of England over India in almost every field and inculcated a loyalty to the crown. The nationalist attitudes and values were ruthlessly suppressed treating them as indiscipline and revolt.

Western knowledge through British education, efficient centralised government, increasing means of communication like post, telegram, construction of roads etc. Maintenance of law and order in the subcontinent helped strengthen the belief of Western superiority and hide the real imperial interests of exploitation. The face of modernisation skillfully concealed the ugly face of imperialism. As a result, the illiterates as well as the literates extended legitimacy to the British raj.

Tilak learnt the following things as the components of knowledge needed for Political Education.

Knowledge of the Existing Society

Tilak witnessed that the Indian people were suffering from an inferiority complex and had lost all hope and confidence. The Indian civilization was passing through a period of uncertainty and disintegration. India was ruled by an alien power for over a thousand years. Through this long age of darkness, the Indian civilization lost its dynamic vitality. The impact of the West in the form of British political domination came as the necessary stimulus to its reawakening. This reawakening created moderates who believed in the Divine dispensation of the British raj with which Tilak did not agree. On the contrary he challenged the cultural superiority of the West that lent legitimacy to the imperial rule. According to him a foreign domination brings a sense of inferiority which constitutes a great source of weakness. Tilak's analysis of contemporary situation gave him the clear perception that politics was a game of worldly people and not of Sadhus (Saints).

Perception of a New Society

Tilak wanted freedom as a precondition for the development of society. 'Swaraj is my birth-right and I will have it' was not just a rhetoric for him or just an emotional tool to achieve independence. He claimed that people had a right to claim freedom just by virtue of their becoming a human society and that no further justification was necessary. "We are human beings and as such we have the right to be free".

He looked up on freedom as the Chaitanya of a nation and maintained that it was vital for the very existence of any human society. He observed that "Just as self emancipation - mukti - is the ultimate aim of any individual, freedom is the ultimate aim of any nation. Freedom is a boundan duty, a moral obligation and 'Purusharth' for every individual."

His conception of swarajya cut across the divisions of castes, sex and religion. In his view caste and religion had no place in public life, though in private life he generally - but not always - observed some of the orthodox practices. The overriding consideration for him in deciding his stand on a public issue was the political unity of the Indian people so as to press effectively their claim to Swaraj. Swaraj for him was not a mere replacement of foreign by native rulers. It visualised more than national independence and was defined in terms of the freedom of the individual; national independence was a necessary, but not a sufficient condition for it.

He asserted that Swaraj was a moral necessity and the achievement of Swaraj was the Dharma of all self respecting men and it was Bharatdharma for the Indians. In his opinion politics can not be separated from religion. The reason for political education and political action was not merely the injustice of foreign rule, not merely the arbitrary partitions of Bengal but achievement of Dharma for every individual.

It was with this firm conviction that Tilak and the Nationalists set out to arouse the nation to political action for the creation of its own destiny. He stressed that history and tradition, religion and philosophy, action and unity were all made meaningful in the concept of love of the country.

This was the vision about Indian society by Tilak and his followers.

Tilak's Views on the Existing Government of the Country

Tilak thoroughly understood the phenomenon of British imperialism and the full implications of Imperial relationship. Emphasing the truth that empires are founded necessarily for promotion of national interests of the Imperial powers, Tilak, intelligently brought out the contradiction of interests inherent and inevitable in this very relationship. He explained that foreign domination was bound to lead to a total moral degradation and material deprivation, a total emasculation of the subject people. This results in the loss of very necessary human qualities which make social and individual living meaningful. He therefore, rightly insisted that it would be nothing but a political naivety to hope that imperial rulers, however liberal and progressive otherwise, would ever perform the role expected of an agent of modernization and development. He did not distinguish between the conservatives and the liberals.

He, therefore, once said, "For the last twelve years we have been shouting hoarse, desiring that the government should hear us. But our shouting has no more affected the Government than the sound of a gnat. Our rulers disbelieve our statements or profess to do so."

The crude behaviour of the British at the time of famines (1875-76) and at the time of plague in Pune (1897) hardened his attitudes towards the British bureaucracy. Tilak clearly saw the attitudes of racial inequality on the part of the British bureaucracy. Even though Tilak knew liberal streams like Individualism, Democracy etc. in the British thought and education, he experienced that ultimately the Imperial interests prevail over the liberal thought.

He also took notice of the fact that the British Government did not respond to the honest demands of Indian politicians as they had hoped. Points of reference on which Tilak's assessment of the situation was based could be cited as 1) a feeling of general despondency 2) deteriorating material conditions - increasing poverty 3) dwarfing of the educated, and 4) apathy, hatred and rude behaviour on the part of the British rulers. Tilak felt the need of exploring the myth of 'benevolent imperialism'. Instead of accepting the British contact as Divine Dispensation and putting his faith in the bonafides of these 'generous' imperial rules, Tilak thought it necessary to investigate the true character of the basic relationship between Great Britain and India. This brought him face to face with many a basic political and social issues.

Knowledge about the basic problem of the country facing in different walks of life. The basic problems which Tilak identified were :

1. need of creating a sense of national pride based on the values in Indian history and culture

2. his belief that the British rule was imperial in nature and in no way of Divine Dispensation. He, therefore, was dissatisfied with the moderates' programme of prayers and petition
3. it was the legitimacy given by the Indian people to the British rule, which was an obstacle in the way of Swaraj
4. understanding of the need of bringing the masses in the mainstream of the national struggle
5. belief that violent revolutions were not successful without enough popular support
6. the need of political education to the masses - though poor and ignorant-for their organisation and politicization. They were only to be made aware of their true potential assuring them that their future rested entirely in their own hands.

Once Tilak obtained knowledge about the prevailing socio-economic and political situation, he used different skills on different occasions for the achievement of the goal of mass awakening. He realised that only possession of knowledge is not enough. Active participation of the masses in the political process is equally important for achieving the goal.

Tilak was a fine combination of a philosopher, an activist and a teacher. He was intelligent, fearless and a man of highest integrity. He practised what he preached. Once he understood the basic problems of the country at different levels, he applied his mind and used different techniques for those problems.

He wanted masses to understand the naked interests of the British rule, inadequacy of the methods adopted by the moderates, awaken the people about their servility and chanelize that awareness towards the desired goal of Swaraj. He was intelligent enough to exploit the contradiction in the British administration. He skillfully used liberal principles in the British administration against the ruling imperial attitudes.

In this process he clearly saw the obstacles and chose and used the techniques accordingly.

In this part, an attempt is made to study Tilak's 1) skills of problem solving 2) skills of working in groups 3) his ability to understand conflicts of all kinds and to develop proper relations to them and 4) his ability to express himself adequately on political matters.

Use of Non-violence

Tilak has been accused of believing in violence, yet it was he who first urged non-violent political action. He advocated the need of mobilizing the people because Indians were, then, not in a position to use arms. He was not sure about the success of violent methods without enough public support. He had sympathy towards the militant revolutionaries because of their cause and not methods.

He visualised that there were three enemies in his way of political education of the masses. They were 1)the British bureaucracy 2) the missionaries and 3) the moderates. He posed a formidable challenge before them.

The British bureaucracy was the vehicle of Imperial policy and Tilak used all possible means of creating unrest against it. We will discuss the same in the following pages.

As far as Missionaries are concerned not only that Tilak disliked their role, but even leaders like Vivekanand and Mahatma Gandhi held that they were the deadliest poison and worried as the missionaries became active at the time of famine. As far as the moderates were concerned, Tilak viewed that they were not going to the masses and were helping the British in their policy of divide and rule. Moreover, the roots of the moderates were not in the Indian soil but in the west. He, therefore, ridiculed them and made their mockery.

Ganapati Festival

Tilak was successful in reaching the masses through the employment of national and religious festivals. His purpose in starting the Ganapati festival in the new form was two-fold. He wanted to provide an alternative to the Moharrum of the Muslims. He also wanted Hindus to come together regardless of caste or education on a common platform. He brought Ganapati on the streets and the Ganapati Worship be came the jubilant festival of all the Hindus. Even the Muslims did not perceive it as communal and they too joined the festival.

Shivaji Festival

Tilak saw that the country had sunk low under the British rule and needed spirit for rejuvenation. He, therefore, started a festival to revive the memory and glory of Shivaji, the liberator of Maharashtra and restorer of Swaraj. Emphasising the spirit of Shivaji, Tilak wrote, "It is the spirit which actuated Shivaji in his doing that is held forth as the proper idea to be kept constantly in view of the rising generation." Everybody at that time knew that Shivaji festival was political in nature. Therefore, it was not held as anti-Muslim and some Muslims participated in the festival.

Tilak worked tirelessly to reach the people and to educate them through the festivals. He carried his doctrine throughout the Maharashtra and waged his battle. Theodore Shay beautifully narrates Tilak's skill in utilising these two festivals for national awakening. He says, "Education through religion and history, through the association in the popular mind with gods and heroes, through recreating an appreciation of the heritage of the past as a guide to the future - this was the way he conducted his battle. He soon became the first articulate spokesman for the no-longer-silent, tradition directed masses of India. He became the defender and the awakener of India's philosophy of life". Through this political education he insisted on the willingness on the part of the masses to meet the problems of the day and solve them morally, which was the greatest need of those days.

These festivals gradually became popular even outside Maharashtra and Tilak's leadership crossed the regional boundaries. Because of his achievements through these festivals, the moderates were pushed back to the rear and the youth were attracted towards Tilak because of his mass political rallies with the help of religious festivals.

Kesari and Maharatta

Tilak did not fail to understand the importance of newspapers for political education of the masses. The news papers started by him 'Kesari' (Marathi) and 'Mahratta' (English) became popular. Especially Kesari made history and became popular even among the illiterates in rural areas. N.C.Kelkar wrote, "Through his paper, the Kesari, he exercised an immense influence over the masses and it is this influence that is mainly responsible for the infusion of a new spirit among the people".

Looking at the rude behaviour at the time of famine and atrocities at the time of plague in Pune by the British burequeracy and police, Tilak wrote fearlessly. He condemned the inhuman aspects of the British anti-plague campaign. His speeches and especially writing in 'Kesari' sent him to two years' imprisonment.

However, as N.C.Kelkar rightly points out, "His arrest and prosecution in 1897 was a sensation that nearly pulled the mind of the country by its roots, as political prosecutions were then extremely rare, and Tilak was, in himself, a man big enough to mark an epoch by his personal misfortune." The British miscalculated both, the effect of this imprisonment on Tilak and on public opinion.

Now He Became a National Hero

For two decades Tilak was persecuted by the British Indian Government as they saw in him the real challenge to their empire in India. But this gave him an acknowledgement as a national political leader. "He emerged from prison with the responsibility of leading the nationalist cause to political self-determination (Swatantrya). He was acclaimed the Lokmanya, the honoured and respected of the people". He was acused by the moderates as 'Telya Tambolyanche Pudhari' (leader of the masses - in present terminology, leader of the other Backward classes OBC's. But now it became an honour for him. He was acused by Valentine Chirole as 'Father of Indian unrest' but it became a feather in his cap and brought glory.

'Mahratta' an English news paper did the same job for the English speaking population, even though on a small scale.

He was careful to confine his agitation within legal limits. His arguments were logically appropriate and convincing so that people could clearly understand their interests.

Trisutri (Three Devices)

With a view to have a base among the workers, Tilak attempted to promote the concepts of Swadeshi and Boycoatt. He was somewhat successful in this attempt.

However, the partition of Bengal provided him the right opportunity to bring the British administration to their sense. Basically the three principles of Boycott Swadeshi and National education were intended for effective and practical political action and gradually they became an integral part of Tilak's programme of political education for the masses.

Boycott of the British manufactured goods was started to bring economic pressure on economic business and jeopardize the foundation of the whole British administration. Then, boycott became a political weapon and became popular through out India.

Swadeshi was intended to be the counterpart of boycott. It meant self-help and self-dependence in Indian economy. National education was provided as an alternative to Western education begun by Lord Macaulay. It involved the establishment of schools throughout the country dedicated to give Indians a truly national education.

The objective of this programme was Swaraj. The above mentioned three devices were developed initially as a reaction to the British partitioning of Bengal. But soon it became an all India programme of political education for national awakening and national liberation i.e. Swaraj. Swaraj became the reason and justification for the entire programme and movement. Swadeshi, boycott, national education and swaraj were not to be separated from each other. Swadeshi, Boycott and National education were the integral parts of Swaraj.

Tilak wrote furiously and addressed numerous public meetings to advocate the Trisutri. He realised the target well and carefully thought about the means to be employed to politically educate the Indian people.

In this campaign he invited Muslims to join him. It is interesting that

1. several Muslims participated in Ganpati festival and Shivaji festival
2. Tilak himself participated in Muslim festival 'Moharrum'
3. Mr. Jinnah became an ardent disciple of Tilak and the later insisted that Jinnah should fight his legal battle in 1908 when he was arrested for seditious editorials.

First Mass Leader of India

In this way Tilak became the first mass leader of India. He became popular in all the castes and all the religions, among the educated and uneducated, among the rich as well as the poor.

After the announcement of six-years sentence, immediately there was a great outburst of popular feeling. Riots swept throughout Bombay, and demonstrations were held throughout India. Tilak became a national martyr and a popular hero, even according to the British press in England. Now even the moderates' faith in British justice became shaky.

Hindu-Muslim Unity

Hindu-Muslim unity was always the major component of Tilak's political education. In 1914 the World War I began and Tilak returned from Mandalay after six years of deportation.

Now it appeared that he became a little moderate and advocated Home Rule instead of 'Swaraj'. But he insisted that

Home Rule was the right of the Indians, the 'Dharma' of the Indians. Nobody can separate Home Rule from the people.

After the return of Tilak the years of political inactivities were over. The Home Rule Leagues were more effective in arousing the nation to political activity than the moderate Congress.

For the sake of Hindu-Muslim unity, he brought about the famous Congress-League scheme, (1916) a joint programme of common and co-ordinated effort for the goal of self-rule. For the first time in the struggle for Indian independence the organised Muslim community worked with the Congress; and the Congress, moderates and Nationalists stood again united.

Raised Issue at International Level

The Treaty of Versailles (1919) is welknown for the principle of self- determination to the nation-states. Tilak wanted to represent India at the Versailles Peace Conference in 1919 in France. But the British Government did not allow him to do so. Theodore Shay observes, "Had Tilak been free to attend the Peace Conference and to discuss personally India's case with the American President, Swaraj would have been attained sooner."

His second attempt of internationalising the cause of India's independence was his visit to England to file a civil suit against Chirole. Unfortunately he lost the case, but during his stay there he made a common cause with many, contributed to the fund of the Labour Party and many supporters to India's cause.

When he returned to India, he came as the uncrowned king of the nation to which he had dedicated his life.

Values in Tilak's Political Education

There was always a value base for Tilak's political education. Even though he was a hard realist and pragmatist his objectives and the methods selected by him for the political education had value orientation.

He looked upon political freedom, the objective of his education, as a moral obligation, not merely as a natural right but a moral necessity. The political freedom was a bounden duty and Purushartha for every individual. He believed that Human mind is a combination of 'Divine' and 'Animal'. He, therefore, wanted to educate the 'Animal' and incarnate Divinity in the human beings. In this way his justification for Swaraj was based on values.

He believed in democracy and therefore always advocated the concept of popular sovereignty. Tilak through various methods and techniques taught to the people that the real sovereignty rested with the people and not the king or a coterie of rulers who were holding formal power. Therefore, he justified 'Praja-Droha' (right to revolt) if the government had no moral support of the people. He linked the urge for liberty and democratic rule with increasing political awareness.

His concept of Nationalism was also not romantic or negative in nature. It had secular bearing and welfare of the Humanity was its ultimate goal. He did not favour aggressive nationalism.

Theodore Shay, therefore, says, "His message, his political philosophy, must not only be remembered but clearly understood, in Maharashtra, in India, and also, because it has a world significance in the world else we shall be the poorer for not using the legacy he has left behind". Lokmanya Tilak, originally a devoted teacher had an urge to educate the people. Naturally when he entered the field of journalism as an editor of 'Kesari' in 1887, he continued his mission as a teacher on a more vast and multi-level field of people's education.

The object of this paper is to evaluate his editorials in 'Kesari' from the educational point of view. His editorials covered various subjects and enlightened the people at large.

The titles, the sarcasm, the use of plain and simple language, proper illustrations from day to day life, oratorical style and quotations from Sanskrit verses, etc. are some of the special aspects of his editorials. He could easily awaken the masses through his writing. He is aptly described as the father of Indian unrest on account of these editorials.

Kesari's Oath is the awakening of the people. It makes Tilak write with affection for the people. To awaken them fully he tries to get them used to writing and reading what is logical and rational. The solid basis of Lokmanya's writing is rationality. Lokmanya uses, a number of quotations, shlokas, sayings, similes and illustrations and linguistic devices. In his editorials he has set-up a model of writing that is measured to the point, logical and based on evidence and proof.

Appaji Vishnu Kulkarni was the writer of Lokmanya Tilak. He has written a book called 'The last eight years of Lokmanya'. On page 28 of this book, he says, 'The editor puts before the people his own intentions through his editorial. It is a kind of one sided dialogue with the people. Hence it definitely requires fluency in language and oratory. Tilak used to dictate his editorial orally and spoke so fast when his mind was crowded with thoughts that the writer found it difficult to take it down'.

A Planned Use of Ingenious Titles

With his very titles Lokmanya seems to appeal directly to the readers heart, e.g. 'Is the government on its senses?' (6-7-1897), 'Principal - the guardian of beasts or babies' (with a pun on 'Pal') (9-7-1918), 'It is dawn but where is the sun?' (9-7-1918), 'What about India?' (8-8-1905), 'Tilak is out what next?' (14-11-1916). These titles show how Lokmanya excelled in giving titles that were interrogative and created curiosity. Similarly he would create interest with strange types of titles like 'The udders of a male buffalo' (3-9-1907) 'The Christian emperor became a Brahmin' (6-4-1915) 'It was good he spoke' (19-2-1907). He used various meaningful maxims also for titles like 'Darkness under the lamp' (26-2-1907) 'Mountain out of mole hill' (18/25-12-1894). 'New bit of a stick, new rule (20-4-1904) 'A mouse out of digging a hill' (3-12-1901). Such titles kindle the curiosity of readers and prompt them to read the editorial eagerly. Moreover, they help the reader to remember them for years together.

Frequently at the beginning of the editorial, Lokmanya used a Shloka or a saying which suggests the trend (direction) of his thoughts. A saying or maxim seems to give to the reader at the first glance the essence of his editorial. In an editorial entitled 'The greeting of Sir R.P.Paranjpe' (16-12-1919) Tilak used a Shloka from the 'Geeta' which conveys the main point in it. 'Anger leads to bewilderment, bewilderment to confusion of memory, that to loss of intellect and that leads to death'.

Such a Shloka from the 'Geeta' used at the very beginning suggests the loss of intellect of a scholarly mathematician like Wrangler Paranjpe. In the editorial obituary written after the premature death of Namdar Gokhale (23-2-1915) Tilak's use of the saying 'Burning for a moment is better than to remain smoking for ever' suggests how Namdar Gokhale's death had created a terrible vacuum. Similarly this quotation from the Mahabharat conveys the pathos in Gokhale's death and some idea of his short but bright life. Writing on 18-6-1895 on the very painful death of Agarkar, Lokmanya tries to soften the grief of readers by quoting the universal truth 'salute to Time who's influence makes everything to come to be forgotten'. In the editorial written on 25-8-1903 after the scholar Professor Juisivale passed away Lokmanya said 'speak the truth, follow religion/duty, do not stray away from your studies'.

Use of Quotations in the Middle of the Editorial

It is not only at the beginning or the end of the editorial that shlokas or quotations are used, they are used in the middle too. In the editorial written on 13-7-1887 to convince the reader of the point that rulers should not boast that they alone are all powerful, there is a quotation from the 16th section of the Geeta 'I am God Almighty, I am the possessor, I am perfect, mighty and happy, I am rich nobly born. Who else is there like me?' This quotation describes perfectly the false boastfulness of the rulers. In a similar manner Lokmanya wanted to point out that the Montague reforms would be of no use to us. He pointed this out in an editorial entitled 'The male buffalo's Udders' (3-9-1907) using a quote from Hitopadesh 'What is the use of the cows that can have neither calves nor give milk?' He thus, convinced the readers that the Montague reforms would be as unprofitable as the buffaloes that cannot be milked.

Lokmanya in his editorial uses very appropriate quotations from Raghuvansh, Panchatantra, Hitopadesh, Mahabharat, Uttar Rama Charitra etc.; because he wanted his thoughts to create a solid concrete impression on the readers' minds. The quotations from influential writers like Kalidas, Bhavabhuti, Vyas, Valmiki helped to create the desired effect.

Proper use of Figurative Language

It has been a traditional practice to use similes, metaphors, illustrations for explaining the thoughts suggested in the editorial. Lokmanya uses this practice at appropriate but very few places. He wrote an editorial on 6-10-1900 'Lord Sandhurst's reign in which he made the point that Lord Sandhurst depends solely on those working under him and yet expects good administration. He expresses the point thus "Lord Sandhurst's administration resembles the careless or foolish bullock cart drivers who trust the cart to the bullocks and expect them to drive it well". Tilak in his editorial 'Mr. Bruin's death' (1-8-1905) describes the position of the suspicious British officials after Rand's murder saying, "Government officers were in the habit of mixing with people but now the state of the government is like the eagle living in the nest built over the volcano of suspicion". Lokmanya implies here that the British government is mighty like the eagle. But this mighty government is without any reason responsible for self-destruction and using the metaphor for 'the state of the government to be like the nest on the volcano of suspicion'; Tilak explains the whole context.

Proper Use of Metaphors

Of and on Tilak's editorials use very naturally metaphors too. In his editorial 'Principal or guardian of beasts or babies?' written in connection with Principal Wrangler Paranjpe (13-4-1920) Lokmanya uses a metaphor, 'The huge elephant of public opinion ready for self rule'. Or in an editorial entitled 'Wanted to do one thing but something strange happened' (26-6-1917) he uses simple short metaphors and several metaphorical expressions like 'The Jambalum of freedom does not drop of its own in the mouth' and also long extended metaphors. Tilak wrote an editorial called 'New small wooden stick (i.e. a play thing) - new rule' (20-4-1920) to point out that the rulers being dependent on the officials will not change unless the officials themselves are changed. Lokmanya says, "The bull that has learnt blindfolded to go round the fort of officialdom will never try to break and enlarge the hole in walls of officialdom and rush into the fort. A new untrained bull is necessary for that." An illustration or extended metaphors like this from the daily life in villages would seem attractive to ordinary people.

Lokmanya tries to convince us about his points in connection with Marathi grammar by giving a lovely illustration, 'The method of writing the Marathi language (6-7-1904). He says "It is the grammarian's duty to remove the mess in the language. Just as it is desirable and necessary for women to comb and braid their hair so is it necessary to refine words in a language". But cutting or shaving of hairs is not included in combing of hair. In the same manner grammatical refinement does not include stopping the growth of words or cutting them off. Even in the present time this illustration is applicable. Several such illustrations are often found in Lokmanya's editorials. They enhance the literary quality of the editorials and at the same time make us realise the necessity of convincing people by using simple illustrations.

Many of the illustrations in this context convince us that an editor must make his readers understand his point with illustrations from daily life. At one place, Lokmanya tries to explain in his editorial 'Lord Curzon's rule' (29-8-1905) what Curzon does in reality when it is said that he loves the Indian subjects, that he cares for them. Lokmanya says in this context that Curzon's love and care is like what we do to our cattle at home - we care for our cattle after we stop getting frightened at them as we make them harmless by breaking or moulding their horns. Everybody used to have milk-cows in those days so that both the readers and the government could appreciate the illustration. Lokmanya tries to make this point clearer in his editorial 'Philosopher and Diplomat' (18-9-1906) and says, "Just as it is a sin to kill a swan laying golden eggs and a milk-cow similarly it is an act of terrible lack of wisdom to harass and displease the people in India when the British have in their hands the golden land of India and get unconditionally Rs. forty crore every year. British diplomats are fully aware that Indians have to be given enough food, just as one of the udders has to be left unmilked for the calf. But if they do it, we must always remember, it is not out of generosity but of selfishness. A milk-cow and calf is a very simple illustration from daily life that Lokmanya uses to make people understand his point.

Use of Folk-Stories

Lokmanya clearly states his thoughts in his editorials referring to stories from Hitopadesh, Panchatantra, Aesop's Fables etc. Really speaking this method was established by Vishnushastri Chiplunkar's Nibandhamala (series of essays). Lokmanya refers to Aesop's Fables in an editorial called 'This is what should happen but will you do it?' written on 16-10-1894. He uses it to convince people that a proud man like Lord Harries will never admit that his conduct is unfair. Lokmanya says in this editorial "Since a man has made the painting he has shown a man holding the lion's mane and to make him bend but what the lion says is very correct i.e. if the lion had drawn the same picture the exactly opposite thing would have been seen". Tilak in refuting the progressive party's argument that without social reforms we would not be competent for political reforms uses one fable from Aesop in his editorial entitled 'Ways of social reforms (28-11-1896). He says it is because of the caste-system that we have retained our Indianness and remained alive for thousands of years though not independent. If we lose our Indianness we would lose whatever we have. Moreover this hare does not exist and the other is not obtainable, we would, like the dog in Aesop's Fables going with a piece of bread in his mouth, be deprived even of food. Not that reform is not desired but its ways are different. This example from Aesop's Fable is easy for readers to understand.

Tilak's writing contains a good deal of sarcasm. The Pune Chitpavan Kokanasth Brahmins are rather famous for their sarcastic speech so are Lokmanya's editorials full of sarcasm. Such sarcastic sentences often contain new strange words that achieve the desired effect. Tilak writes very sarcastically about Pandita Ramabai Ranade in an editorial (12-1-1904) called "The learnedness of Panditabai" - the title itself being sarcastic. He says "She who thinks of Panchagavya (a mixture of five things including milk, curds, butter, urine and dung of cow.) as fake considers 'Baptismodaka' to be sacred. Forming a new word 'Baptismodaka' of a mixed type Lokmanya ridicules in this editorial Ramabai Ranade's basic frame of mind. Criticising her, Lokamnya says "She should remove the Hindu blot in the degree of 'pandita' (a scholar) and use the secret degree of "Reveranda". One of the sarcasms is connected with the mixed strange new word Baptismodaka (Baptisma + vadka - Christian (English) and Sanskrit mixed) and the second example of derision is suggesting the feminine 'Reveranda' of Reverend in place of 'Pandita'. In a similar manner writing sarcastically in the editorial, 'the necessity of an Adopted son?' (20-11-1893) Lokmanya says 'In the perfected stage of man it was necessary to have a son for the continuation of his name but obviously it is no longer necessary now. Is Sambhaji the reason why we remember Shivaji? Is the name of Nana Phadanvis found in history because his wife adopted a son after Nana's Death? Excepting name how many adopted sons in the rising revolt were seen to be good oldies? Tilak has tried to explain to his readers how ridiculous is the idea of the adoption of a son for the continuity of the family name.

Along with such examples Tilak has also used a number of sarcastic words. This sarcasm emerges very strongly when Tilak writes about the British officers Lord Curzon and Sandhurst. Many derisive expressions like 'Sandhurst's Chattering', 'Sandhurst's circle', 'Sandhurst's gift' in connection with Sandhurst. Likewise he has ridiculed Lord Curzon 'Lord Curzon's few cool utterances' 'the talkative (chatter box) Viceroy', 'Twelve great deeds of Lord Curzon', 'Lord Curzon's Advice' are some of the strange and derisive expressions used by Tilak to judge and ridicule the administration of the officials like Sandhurst, Curzon, Harries etc. This style does not resemble that of Acharya Atre. It is his own special style which is more like that of Vishnu Shastri Chiplunkar.

Oratorial Style

Lokmanya uses a number of examples to prove that a certain statement or argument is wrong and thus with his oratorial style reverses the whole sentence. e.g. to ridicule the statement that good (domestic/social) state implies good political state, Lokmanya gives remarkable historical examples. In an editorial (2.3.1886) called - " What first ? Political or Social" Lokmanya says "What several people seem to believe viz. that a certain type of domestic (social) state would lead to a certain type of political state is not proved on the basis of history. Shivaji founded the Maratha kingdom (rule). The Peshwas crossed on horse back the Ganges and the Indus and unfurled the saffron flag - Did they manage it on the strength of girls studying in the fourth standard at school? Were Shivaji, Mahadaji Shinde, the elder Bajirao born to girls married at the age of twenty five ? Did the Marathas and the Brahmins live together at that time ? Or was the word 'Sati' (widow burning herself on the dead husband's funeral pile) unknown then ? There is no proof whatsoever to believe that the social state then was specially good."

Lokmanya often writes referring to or addressing somebody. The titles illustrate this but even the content of the editorials suggests it, since he preferred oral dictation to writing the matter himself.

We have considered some examples of Lokmanya's oratorial style in his editorials. The editorials were orginally not written by him but often dictated and the writer would take them down. Hence, those editorials often create the impression of being purposeful, designed writing with an oratorial style. But the editorial seems like a speech too.

Use of Tables

Lokmanya does not write on any topic without himself getting and collecting complete and detailed information about it. Tilak in his early career had a personal experience of the great fuss made over the adoption by Princes of States, by the then Prime Minister Mr. Barve of the state of Kolhapur and it made him very cautious about things. He collected statistics and included it in a table in his editorials. This statistics is like proof proving what is what - (differentiating Jayadrath from the Sun). Hence, readers can think about the whole thing and with the detailed table take a final decision. He puts before the readers the collected statistics in a tabled form instead of making a loose statement like different principal countries spend lavishly on the army so that readers can easily see for themselves the truth of the matter.

The editorial, 'Is there any hope for reduction in expenditure over the army?' written on 15.4.1902 contains in the title itself such a table.

Tilak does not say vaguely that Britain is spending huge amounts of money for its own expansion and thereby robbing us. He uses a table containing all the huge sums so that readers can understand it. Such a table saves superfluous things and pointedly gives information. Such a thing helps readers to form their own judgement.

To make readers understand all this, Lokmanya Tilak converts the original table in Mr. Datta's book from pounds into rupees, uses it to support his argument. Lokmanya seems to think even about very small things like the reader's lack of knowledge about the British currency of pounds, converts into rupees so as to help readers understand the point. This implies and suggests Tilak's view that an editor must care for the smallest welfare of the readers. This brings the readers closer to the editor and helps them to have mutual trust. In this context it is significant that Tilak was a student of mathematics.

No Poetry but an Occasional Artistic Touch

There is no place for poetry in Lokmanya's editorials but the style shows an artistic touch in the occasional use of similes, illustrations etc. It does have a bit of artistic colour. The following example used to suggest how the Montague reforms were deceptive is important in this context. In the editorial with an interrogative and artistic title 'It is dawn but where is the Sun?' written on 9-7-1918 he says, "The Montague political reforms are like the mental state of the people who wait eagerly for the morning and the sun-rise since the morning breeze is blowing, the chirping of birds is heard, "the cock is crowing and then feel sad because there is no sunrise in spite of the morning." That is to say Tilak shows the emptiness of the Montague reforms by asking the discerning question, "Where is the sun when there is the light" of the

Montague reforms and daybreak. He stresses in fact the point of the meaninglessness of the Montague reforms.

There is one more example that can be considered in this context. Lokmanya answered his opponents when they started asking about what had happened to the fund collected for the memorial of Shivaji Maharaj. This answer suggests the types of experiences one comes to have in public life. In an editorial with a compact title 'The festival of Shivaji's death anniversary' written on 9-4-1901 Lokmanya says, "The wind has to clear off the clouds on the Sun", repeatedly and every public topic to a certain extent is similar to this situation. It is the duty of the organizer of a festival to point out the mistakes in the objections made by some dull-witted people.

Lokmanya Tilak wrote an editorial with the title 'A New Small Wooden Stick i.e. a new plaything - new rule' four months before his death. It, too, contains artistic language. He concludes the editorial on an extended metaphor and thus shows a rather different kind of style. He wanted to point out to the people that for all of us yearning for self rule it was not proper to wait longer. In this connection Tilak says in his editorial 'Navi Viti, new rule', "How can he who wants to be a moth remain for a long time in the state of a caterpillar? Hence busy yourselves with being moths by selecting new ways, new people fit for the present- time and be determined to taste the sweet juice of the beautiful garden of self rule. Our only request is that you should not be deceived by the temptation of a caterpillar". Here too by removing some people and selecting new people and new means (not weapons) i.e. material, he suggests people should fulfil their desire. He thus seems to induce people to be men of action.

Not Humour, But Sarcasm

Humour, like poetry, is found as an exception in Lokmanya's editorials. There is plenty of sarcasm, derisiveness, though these two are the basic weapons of his legal argumentation. But the sprinkling of humour is rare. Observing that in place of the Marathi method of writing a new ugly method of writing was being used Lokmanya wrote an editorial called 'The method of writing Marathi language on 12-7-1904 '. In it he says, "The British government may well rule over us but it is not a law that it should rule over the short and long marks in the Marathi language, nor was it the wish of the government when it was suggested that the alphabet

Ga, Ma, Bha, Na should be taught instead of A, aa, i, ii etc." Lokmanya came out with an editorial called 'The murder of our Alphabet' on 4-10-1904. In it he says sarcastically," Children will learn 'Ga' an easy letter with two lines and if after Ga, Na, Bha, Fa, and Pa are taught it would be convenient to introduce 'Dha' to students (Dha - a pun suggesting dullness). The person who has thought of this strange thing must be completely ignorant of the science of language or a grammarian belonging to the Kha-khu category.'(again a pun on Kha-khu which suggest ironic laughter) such are the very few limited but very fitting instances of humour that we find in the editorials. But these few instances easily give us an idea of Tilak's sarcasm and mild sense of humour. The peculiarity of the style is the total absence of vulgar humour.

Euphemism

Sarcasm is often expressed in a euphemistic manner. Euphemism implies expressing bitter feelings in sweet words. Naturally such speech and writing are sarcastic. In an editorial entitled 'Raobahaddur Ranade's rare skill (agility) of argumentation' (7.6.1887) Lokmanya writes sarcastically "Vamanraoji Modak refrained from peace and forgiveness" instead of "Vamanrao Modak was very angry." At times Tilak uses oblique expression. He says in the same editorial "R.B. Ranade ventured once, in consideration of the country, the time and occasion, to break, to stun coolly and patiently the whole group of scholars with his strange 'Gaudbangal' oratory. It was not at all necessary for us to share his hopeless, despairing contentment. But R. B. Ranade's implied and open challenge has awakened Kesari to prove the leader of the progressives individually faulty and to prove that the assurances given by Vamanraoji and Kesari are evidence based. The sarcasm lies in Lokmanya's reference to 'the Gaudbangal' that is strange, tricky oratory and 'despairing' contentment.

Simple Sentence Structure

Lokmanya's sentence structure mainly contains simple sentences. They are n^ver long sentences but they have a force and a special speed. Such sentences therefore, appeal directly to the readers. These sentences have the speed of the bullets fired from a rifle and moving swiftly towards the target. When Tilak takes the aggressive stance of refuting something these sentences acquire a rare speed, a rare force and passion and then seem almost to run fast one after the other. But when on some occasion

Lokmanya speaks sarcastically his sentences like those of Agarkar, become long, long-winded. The words in the sentences become shy and one feels the strong twist in the sentence. In his editorial entitled 'Government and the Barisal affair' written on 5.5.1906 Lokmanya says, "These days some officers are playing mischief in connection with the swadeshi movement in that on the one hand they fault us externally for our following English discipline and English law and internally manage enviously to keep the government from being tainted with blame by punishing in the name of English discipline funning and expelling a boy because he wears swadeshi clothes or requests others to do so and on the other hand they issue tyrannical circulars like the Lion Circular which are useful to those conducting the swadeshi movement in a constitutional and peaceful manner in danger."

The typical Chitpawan Kokanasth Brahmins are inclined to speak sarcastically e.g. if it is said to a Poonaite that it is very hot or that it is raining heavily he is bound to answer, "well, if it is not hot in the hot season will it be in the rainy season ?" The editorials contains many such examples of sarcasm of mild humour.

Selection of Words

Since Lokmanya wrote for both the ordinary and extraordinary people, he was in the habit of using mainly easy and simple language. His written language resembles more spoken language so that he naturally uses all types of words from daily life. He creates a new alternative Marathi word for the English one but does not necessarily use it. He did not hesitate to combine words from different languages and form a compound one. Nor did he feel it strange to use a weighty Sanskrit word in the middle of words from spoken Marathi. Depending on the occasion he prepares even new words and takes special care to make the whole language business easy and simple. Because of all these factors Lokmanya's style is different by nature from that of his contemporaries.

In his editorial (31.10.1893) called 'The table of the Bombay Province Budget' he has put together in one sentence all the names of departments - 'Civil, Excise, Customs, Salt, Stamps, Revenue, small departments, Justice, Marine, Religion, Medicine, Stationery, Pension etc.' He has used the English words - Famine Code, Budget, Native, Royal Commission, Jubilee, University,

Book, Committee Member - as they are. He has not made the language difficult and complicated by using alternative burdensome, heavy words. But Tilak also uses a word like 'live poisonous particles' for the English word 'Virus'. Similarly Tilak uses an expression like Government labour - factories for Universities printing certificates. He frequently uses English words with Marathi case forms. e.g. 'Deligetani', 'Memberakherij' (without) 'actapramane' (like) etc. The Marathi language in his editorials shows at many places a turn for the court-Nara the language and it is of course very natural e.g. 'if a member is dead, these societies (or assemblies) need not be registered like the Company Act', 'waiting for the successor's certificate' etc. Words from the court or law are very frequently found in his writing - words like a rough draft, condition, order/ decree etc.

When Lokmanya uses a Marathi alternative he gives a group of words explaining the word and not one alternative for another. He uses simple words like 'Shahari' or 'City people' for 'urban' and 'villagers' for 'rural', 'Agricultural Relief Act' is translated into a simple act for making farmers debt-free and not 'Krushak Runvimochan Vidhi' - a different sanskritized translation inspite of his being an excellent sanskrit scholar. That was because his stand was that what readers were to be able to understand had to be written in a simple language by the editor. Lokmanya was not one of those who believed that a new language is created in an artificial manner. He believed that language is a physically habituated thing. Here he has also used an experiment in word like 'tongue habituated' Tilak did not insist so much on words but gave thought to readers in his use of words.

We have always thought and still think of Lokmanya Tilak's image as that of a lion, a fearless fighter. This fighter's strategem sometimes contains a small battle at other times a fight with the enemy; some times an aggressive stance and at times defence tactics. But most of the time it is a straight confrontation, a cluster of arrows flying. Every word in Tilak's editorial has the power like a bullet from a rifle to hit the target-the enemy's vital spot. Yet Tilak's weapons of words never strike at what is good in the enemy, not even unconsciously. He fights with somebody on a specific occasion but as soon as the occasion ends, no enmity remains between Tilak and him; his relations with his 'enemy' do not remain spoiled. He does not retain permanent enmity with anybody. Tilak always admits that principles are bigger than a person. This quality of a journalist is very rare.

He, who has this generosity and appreciation of merit, can guide people through the newspaper and inspire them to do the correct thing. Hence it would not be an exaggeration to say that Lokmanya's editorials of 'Kesari' were like the morning hymns moulding the Indian people's minds in those days. All these editorials bring before us forcefully his editorial personality. An editor should consider personal malice, jealousy, one's own dignity or humiliation, different types of pressures, relatives as subordinate and he should give greater importance to principles, fight for principles, the ultimate welfare of the people - this is the important principle of editorial writing that Lokmanya set down.

The self rule that Lokmanya hoped for was democratic. He continuously laid stress on National education, profound patriotism, loyalty to the country so that our democratic system would be sensible. He accepted journalism for the sake of people - oriented politics to educate people, to make them wise and he took on the role of the peoples' teacher. He started a variety of different things. He had creative leadership. He did not merely keep making suggestions like a non-playing captain nor move about like him with folded hands. When occasion demanded he himself got down in the red soil, in the wrestling ground of conflict and fought with the government. He retained the firmness of words not their shallowness. He himself became the example of an ideal editor. He was not a mere talker nor did he ever adopt the stranger's role of telling a few ingenuous things. He repeatedly proved that he was a creative worker and not a mere word-user.

Another important peculiarity of Lokmanya Tilak's editorial personality is that the work he undertook, was voluntarily accepted for educating people. Lokmanya Tilak was an editor fully aware of the power of newspapers. In an editorial entitled 'The more the coal is whitened, the more it remains black' written on 13.3.1917, Lokmanya says, "It is not the duty of newspaper writers to entertain people with coloured vapid stuff printed on glossy paper." He further says," Influential newspapers in independent countries act as peoples' political teachers". He adds in the same editorial "The true use of newspapers is to check the despotic (tyrannous) government rule (political power). Even today, the role attributed by Lokmanya Tilak a hundred years ago to the true journalists and editor's duty has not changed. Hence one feels like calling him 'The father of editorial writing.' This makes it clear how Tilak had a full understanding of his own work.

'Kesari' started on 4.1.1881 but Lokmanya actually became the editor of Kesari on 23.10.1887. Lokmanya had written some 20-21 editorials during these 6-7 years. The editorial on 'Which first? Political or Social' written in 1886 led to a violent intellectual clash between Tilak and Agarkar. Agarkar left Kesari and started his own independent newspaper called "Sudharak" - i.e. 'A reformer'. Even before Tilak came to take the responsibility of Kesari's editorship on his shoulders Tilak had already become free by resigning from the membership of the Deccan Education Society. He had completely freed himself from the school and the college that he had started out of his intense longing for national education. He had left the educational field and on his own had the daring, the guts to enter the more vast/extensive multi-levelled, multi-purpose field of peoples' education that is the field of the newspaper. The national education phase of his life had ended and what he was to face was the huge problem of the whole nation's life. He saw very clearly the realistic and horrible picture, of the state to which the British government rule had reduced India. Hence, he considered Kesari's aim to be 'to describe the state of the nation' and bring about the enlightenment among the people through newspaper as a medium of education.

The State of Our Country

Vishnushastri Chiplunkar, Lokmanya's teacher, has written an independent essay called 'The loss of freedom'. Lokmanya felt intensely the wretched state of the country due to 'loss of freedom' and foreign rule. Vishnushastri wrote a long article or a series of articles in which he made clear all his observations, his views, his hopes and motives, and showed the direction of the future. Lokmanya wrote fearlessly and in detail on the British government rule, its imperial attitude, its tyrannical / oppressive acts and in a way brought out the state of our country. Lokmanya wrote promptly whenever some incident took place, when some occasion demanded, on the British government system, its emperical spirit, British officialdom, British financial and industrial policy, its treatment of agriculture and taxation, its selfish educational attitude etc. This writing is naturally in the form of reaction. But when a scholar, philosopher and foresighted, bold editor like Tilak writes on such topics, his reaction is not merely an emotional expression but it brings to light the truth of principle behind it. In every editorial of Lokmanya, hence, importance is given to rationalism, intellectual strategy, logical argument, base and evidence behind the writing. Lokmanya's Kesari editorials were written in response to incidents or some cause but they are in essence suggestive of principles.

The Father of Indian Unrest

Lokmanya is referred to as 'The Father of Indian unrest.' This unrest was created by him through the Kesari editorials. Ordinary readers do not deliberately read philosophical books but they do read newspapers. They take interest in the daily incidents that take place around them. The reader is awakened when a journalist points out the different meanings of that incident, and clearing off the mystery behind it, suggests the possible consequences of that incident. Gradually his mind and his opinion get formed and he may even be ready to act. This is what unrest means. Lokmanya created against the British government an unrest system and its officialdom through the editorials that he constantly wrote.

A Life-long Peoples' Advocate

Tilak was trained to be a lawyer. In the beginning he became a teacher, then started Kesari and though not practising as a lawyer in the court, he took pleadership of the people through Kesari for all his life. This pleadership, voluntarily accepted, would not earn him money. On the other hand it would throw him in prison. But this lawyer who cared for the values of the basic rights of the people and their welfare, fought fearlessly against the mighty British empire using all his knowledge of law, his sharp rational power, his scholarship. The British government was the accused and the Indian people his clients. Lokmanya Tilak's constant charge against the British Government was oppression of the Indian people, looting them, breaking the promises given to them, denying them freedom, thinking about nothing else but the expansion of their own empire, refusing every opportunity to the natives and doing injustice to them in every way they could. To prove these charges Tilak presented in his editorials all the necessary evidence, statistics and tables. He presents his case firmly giving all the former instances of the particular context. He quotes from the Puranas, history, Vedas, Upanishads, uses maxims and sayings so that his thoughts can reach the people. He marks the weak points and the precise weakness of the enemy-party and attacks them, praises what is proper and good, but slashes and breaks whatever is bad. He knows well the strong points of the accused which he conveys to the readers though it is not necessary for him to give up his own point.

Lawyer Only for the Truth

Tilak is a pleader of the truth and pleads only for the truth. This lawyer had intense faith in justice and hates injustice equally intensely. He spreads what his mind and intellect felt was the truth and paid little heed when his relatives, his friends, people belonging to his own religion and party became his opponents. Hence he had to fight his own people along with the British government.

Tilak was known as Lokmanya. He has great faith in the power of the people. He has dedicated his "Geeta Rahasya" to Lord Krishna - the soul of the people. He believed that people should take the ultimate decision. He thought that the people should solve the debates over grammar or even the alphabet. The term people includes all from oil man, betel-leaf workers to high class persons. The Kesari editorials are meant as much for the government as for all the people. Warning the government through the incidence repeatedly taking place and praying to awaken the people Tilak has carried on his mission. The suggestion made through the shloka at the head of Kesari, viz., 'Indian people are like the lion asleep in a cave in the mountain, if they wake up they can destroy the elephant of British rule', is implied in every editorial. This shloka echoes in almost all the editorials.

An Ideal Educator of People

While studying Lokmanya Tilak's Kesari editorials, one often realises that by starting and establishing a genuine literary form through his newspaper editorials, he has made an invaluable contribution to Marathi literature. He has laid down a model of how to do this type of writing that has the power to inspire. These editorials have done the difficult job of creating an encyclopaedia of the early act of the freedom movement.

Newspaper writing is incidental, generally written in a superficial manner and hence is forgotten. But this writing of Lokmanya has become ever-lasting because of his original thinking, the continuing philosophical base of the writer of Geeta

Rahasya and the constant, unbroken motive of the enlightenment of the nation. Jayantrao Tilak has called these editorials " the power of the penance of a learned ascetic with the purpose of the upliftment of the country" and readers feel it when they study the editorials.

'The Kesari writer Lokmanya Tilak' is really the sum of rich qualities of his editor's unquestioned power, his sharp intellect, brilliance, fearlessness, love of truth, selflessness, severe sense of justice, visionariness, idealistic practicalism and self-sacrificing attitude. G.T. Madkholkar in his book 'My teacher in the field of writing' has said, " Tilak's personality, his leadership and his editorship were inseparable and identical." It is necessary, hence, to bear in mind the peculiarities of his personality and his leadership while considering Tilak's policies or style as an editor. Tilak himself was a superman and so was his Kesari! Hence 'Kesari' could create an untiring, strong desire in Maharashtra to fight for the nation's freedom. Editor Tilak was the literary image of the national leader Tilak. The sight of this image and pondering over it will undoubtedly always be full of inspiration for the newspaper business.

"A newspaper's pen always writing on different topics serves the same purpose as street lamps and a policeman's rounds serve". The light of his editorial thoughts was continuously thrown on the merits as well as faults of the British rule and officials. Lokmanya Tilak has tried to awaken the hidden power of the Indian people and in a way challenged the British rule intoxicated as it was. Lokmanya has proved to be the father of Indian unrest. The shloka by Jaggannath Pandit at the head of Kesari is very important from this point of view. "Of my friend, Lord of the heard of elephants, with eyes blinded by intoxication, do not for a moment stay here in this thick forest land, for, here in the mountain cave sleeps the lion who shakes huge rocks with his terrible claws mistaking them for elephants." This 'Anyokti' (surface meaning applicable to something else) in the shloka of Jaggannath Pandit has taken shape in Lokmanya's editorials.

From the above discussion we can be sure that Lokmanya was real teacher in his own peculiar style. He is therefore known as 'The father of Indian unrest' in its true sense.

10

Tilak : An Indology Researcher

Tilak was also a great scholar and his researches in Indology were widely recognised by his contemporaries in world.

Lokamanya Tilak's main contribution to Indology consists of three principle works viz. (1) The Orion or Researches into the Antiquity of the Vedas, (2) The Arctic Home in the Vedas, and (3) The Gita Rahasya whereas (4) Vedic Chronology and the Vendanga Jyotish contains his research papers on some topics in Indology. Mention should also be made of his editorials on the Mahabharata which-testify to his versatile genius.

The Orion

Tilak had realised that western scholars were not prepared to accept a high antiquity for the Vedic literature- Max Mueller in particular had assigned the Rigveda to about 1200 B.C. He had divided the entire vedic literature into four strata viz. the Chhandas, Mantra, Brahmana and Sutra. These were placed in the chronological order in which the Chhandas were the earliest to be composed and the Sutra literature was the last, and all this was complete before the rise of Buddhism about 400 B.C. Max Mueller allowed some two centuries for each stage, and thus arrived at 1200 B.C. as the date of the Rigveda. The same method was followed by one Dr. Hang who assigned five hundred years for each of the four stages and placed the Rigveda in 2400 B.C. According to him the Vedic literature developed during 2400-2000 B.C. All this dating by Max Mueller and others was done on the basis of literary evidence, particularly the style which, however, could reveal only the relative chronological position and no evidence was adduced in support of a calendrical date. Tilak was justified in arguing that this method was rather vague and uncertain and could at best be cited as supportive evidence. The entire gamut of Vedic literature was thus hanging in a sort of chronological vaccum.

Tilak was deeply interested in Sanskrit literature, particularly Vedic, as also mathematics. It was at this time precisely that Shankar Balakrishna Dikshit published his Bharatiya Jyotish Shastracha Itihas in Marathi (History of Indian Astronomy) which is a shining example of Indian scholarship. It demonstrated to the world how the Indians had made remarkable progress in astronomy in ancient times. When Tilak came across a reference in the Bhagwad-Gita that Krishna was 'the Margasirsa of the months, (Masanam Margasirsoham) it immediately struck him like a flash that astronomy may offer some clue to the dating of the Vedas and he therefore collected the astronomical references occurring in the Vedic literature. To his great surprise he was proved right and he could therefore develop his chronology of the Vedic literature. He had given two lectures on it in Pune in 1891 and later prepared his paper for the 9th Oriental Congress which was to be held in London in 1892, but it became such a longish essay that it was later in 1893 published in the form of a separate monograph and only a short summary was included in the Proceedings of the Congress. All this was done when he was fully involved in all sorts of political and social controversies. The idea first occurred to him in 1890 as he states in the Preface to the 'Orion' and it took four years to complete.

Tilak's theory is based essentially on the astronomical evidence He states, "We find that the Rigveda hymns had already become antiquated and unintelligible in the days of the Taittiriya Samhita and the Brahmanas. The Taittiriya Samhita places the vernal equinox in the Krittikas, and I have shown that we must fix its date at about 2500 B.C. If the hymns of the Rigveda were unintelligible at this time, they must have been sung several centuries before it."

The expression "I am Margasirsa among months" attracted Tilak's attention because he saw in it some clue to the Vedic chronology for the simple reason that the names of months in the Hindu calendar are derived from the names of nakshatras.

Presently our new year starts from Chaitra, but as Whitney has shown, it began in Margasirsa according to the Surya Siddhanta. Sacrifice (yajna) is the base of the Vedic culture, and is closer, related to the Sun. Hence, for the performance of sacrifice a good knowledge of months, seasons and sun's movements was essential. Everyday the Nakshatra close to the sun was noted, and the time it took to come to the same position was counted as one year. The beginning of the year was the commencement of the sacrifice and it (Satra) continued for tile whole year. According to the Vedanga-Jyotisha, new year starts from winter. This is known as the vernal equinox (Uttaryana), which means the sun's movement from the south to the north. It has been observed that the seasons lag behind by one month after every two thousand years, and this change has to be adjusted in the calendar. This can be proved by the statement that "the sun is in the asterism of Krittikas," which occurs in the Taittiriya Samhita.

The equinoxes are the two days of the year when the Sun is directly above the equator. As the earth moves in its orbit around the sun, the position of the sun changes in relation to the equator. The sun appears north of the equator between the March equinox and the September equinox. It Is south of the equator between the September equinox and the next March equinox.

This happened in 2350 B.C. With this as a fixed datum, the various stages of the Vedic literature have been dated by Tilak. According to him, the oldest Vedic calendar, the oldest Vedic hymn, was sacrificial, and therefore the sacrifice of the year commenced with Aditi at the vernal equinox in or near Punarvasu. The tradition about the old beginnings of the year is mentioned in the Taittiriya Samhita, and the same is corroborated by the oldest traditions and records of the Parsis and the Greeks who also belonged to the Aryan race. On the basis of the evidence furnished by astronomical references in the Taittiriya Sanhita Tilak developed his chronology for the Vedic literature as follows.

The Oldest Period

The oldest period in the Aryan civilization which may be called Aditi or the Pre-Orion period which, according to Tilak, can be provided 6000-4000 BC time bracket. He observes that the Parsis and the Greeks who, though belonging to the Aryan race, have not retained the tradition of this period because "they carried with them the calendar which was in force when they left the common home, while the Indian Aryans have preserved all the traditions with a super religious fidelity and scrupulousness."

The Orion Period (4000 - 2500 B.C.)

This period starts from the time when the vernal equinox was in the asterism of Ardra (Orion) and continues upto the time when it receded to the asterism of the Krittikas. This, according to Tilak, was the most important period in the development of the Aryan civilization. It was pre-eminently the period of the hymns which contain a record of the beginning of the year when several legends were conceived. (e.g. the legend of Vrisakapi).

The Krittika Period (2500 - 1400 B.C.)

This period begins when the vernal equinox was in the asterism of the Krittikas and continues upto the period recorded in the Vedanga Jyotish. It was the period of the Taittiriya Samhita and many of the Brahmanas were composed during this period. According to Tilak, "The hymns of the Rigveda had already become unique and unintelligible by this time and the Brahmavadins engaged in speculations about the real meaning of these hymns and legends."

Pre-Buddhist period (1400-500 B.C.)

This was the period when the Sutra literature was composed.

Tilak concludes his theory with the following statement,

"The astronomical method, I admit, is vague in so far as it does not enable us to determine the exact date of all the Vedic hymns or works, but it is certainly superior to linguistic method inasmuch as it supplies us with certain definite, undisputed facts, for instance, the position of the equinoxes, which can safely be made the nuclei of the different periods of antiquity."

He further adds "thus we find that of all the ancient nations the Hindus alone had well nigh accurately determined the rate of the motion of the procession of the equinoxes."

Tilak records his debt to the Late Professor R. G. Bhandarkar, his teacher at Deccan College, Pune, for explaining to him the views of certain German scholars and Khan Bahadur Dr. Dastur Hoshang Jamasp for Parsee traditions.

In the Orion Tilak has given quite a new and convincing interpretation of some eighty verses in the Rigveda besides shedding a welcome light on many more. These verses had baffled the students of Vedic literature for long even from the time of Sayanacharya. His theory of 'cosmic circulation of aerial waters' properly explained the Indra-Vrtra myth.

Tilak's dating of the Vedas to such an early period in the fourth millennium was not acceptable to a majority of western scholars, as for instance, Max Mueller who was not prepared to go beyond the second millennium B.C. although he had at one stage concluded that it is impossible to determine the date of the Vedic literature and that it may be four thousand or five thousand year old. But there were quite a few who agreed with Tilak. Professor Hermann Jacobi had simultaneously, but independently, arrived at the conclusion that the antiquity of the Vedas can go back to 6000 B.C. Dr. Bloomfield, an eminent American scholar, was sceptical at first but, as he read through, he was inclined to agree with Tilak's views. He confessed that he was convinced in all essential points and that the book was unquestionably the literary sensation of the year.

It will be interesting to examine Tilak's theory in the light of recent archaeological research. Hundred years have passed since Tilak expounded his views. In his time the Indus civilization had not been discovered; but now we know it in all its glory. It must be stated that there are quite a few who identify it as the civilization of the Vedic Aryans10 although the general opinion seems to assign it to a post-Harappan date in the later half of the second millennium B.C. It may not be out of place to mention here that the recent archaeological data have not yielded any evidence for the Aryan invasion.11 Moreover, the beginning of the settled life in the Indian subcontinent now goes back to almost ten thousand years as is clear from the excavation at Mehragh which is located at the mouth of the Bolan Pass near Quetta in Pakistan.12 The excavated evidence points to continuous habitation starting from 7500 B.C. and ending around 3000 B.C. which marks the Early Harappan phase out of which evolved the Indus or the Harappan civilization. The only noticeable culture change in all the four and a half millennia of continuous habitation is between 6000 B.C. to 4500 B. C. which indicates the arrival of a new group of people or new cultural influences. These are precisely the dates that Tilak has assigned to his Pre-Orion period. This may be sheer coincidence and it will not be prudent to read too much into it at this stage, but at the same time it cannot be dismissed out of hand.

The Arctic Home

Tilak's other work is 'The Arctic Home' in the Vedas. While writing The Orion, he came across certain statements in the Vedic literature which led him to ponder over the problem of the original habitat of the Aryans.

However, he could not find the leisure required for such a serious study in the political and social conflicts in which he was engaged at that time. But when he was imprisoned for sedition in 1898 he could devote his attention to this problem. It was at this time that Max Mueller, the greatest Vedicist had sent him a copy of the second edition of the Rigveda edited by him. It is interesting to note that Max Mueller had developed great respect for Tilak's scholarship although he did not agree with his theories. Actually the Oxford Professor pleaded for leniency for Tilak when he was imprisoned. He put his signature to a petition which urged consideration in respect of Tilak. He wrote,

> "My interest in Tilak is certainly that of a Sanskrit scholar for though I do not agree with argument put forward in his 'Orion' or 'Researches into the Antiquity of the Vedas' (Bombay 1883), I cannot help feeling sorry that he should lose the benefit of his labours. I sent him the edition of my Rigveda, but I am told that he is not allowed to read even his Bible and Prayer-book in prison."

Tilak conceded that he was released in twelve months because of thc efforts of Max Mueller and others.

Titak was deeply interested in the edition of the Rigveda which he received from Max Mueller. He was highly impressed by the statement 'suryodayat prak bahuni ahani asan' meaning 'many days have passed before the sunrise'. It was this statement that led him to trace the original home of the Aryans in the Arctic region. He wrote this book when he was involved in the Jagannath Maharaj adoption case. In the Orion, he had shown, on astronomical grounds, that the antiquity of the Vedas can be stretched back to 4500 B.C. Tilak says in the Preface to the Arctic Home, that it is a sequel to the Orion in which it was unmistakably pointed out that the vernal equinox was in the constellation of

Mriga or Orion during the period when the Vedic hymns were composed, and that it had receded to the constellation of the Krittikas or the Pleiades (about 2500 B.C.) in the days of the Brahmanas. The next logical step was to trace the original home of the Aryans.

Tilak began to ponder over the problem and was immersed in thinking about references to the sun, day, night, dawn and so on. He was very happy when he found the statement that many days have passed before the sunrise for it implied a very long day and a very long night. This phenomenon occurs only in the Polar region and the logical conclusion therefore was that the original home of the Aryans was in the area of North Pole. Although the climate in that region is extreme cold, a few studies had appeared in the latter half of the last century according to which it was mild in the Inter-glacial period when human habitation there was possible. This was established geologically and several scholars had therefore argued that the original home of the early man must be sought in the arctic region where the plant and animal life also originated. In fact one Dr. Warren of Boston University wrote a book entitled Paradise Found or the Cradle of the Human Race at the North Pole. Tilak very meticulously employed all scientific evidence very judiciously and developed his theory of the Arctic home of the Vedic Aryans, He argued as below.

1. According to the latest geological evidence, which cannot be lightly set aside, the last glacial period must have closed and the Post-Glacial commenced at about 10,000 years ago, or 8000 B.C. at the best, and the freshness of the Siberian fossil deposits favours this view.
2. There were at least two Glacial and one Inter-Glacial period, and the geographical distribution of land and water on the earth during the Inter Glacial period was quite different from what it is at present.
3. There were great vicissitudes of climate in the Pleistocene period, it being cold and inclement during the Glacial, and mild and temperate ill the Inter-Glacial period, even as far as the Polar regions.
4. There is enough evidence to show that the Arctic regions, both in Asia and Europe, were characterised in the Inter-Glacial period by cool summers and warm

> winters - a sort of what Herschel calls, a perpetual spring; and that places like Spitzbergen, where the sun goes below the horizon from November till March, were once the seat of luxuriant vegetation that grows at present, only in the temperate or the tropical climate.

It has been recently suggested that Tilak's view was influenced by the writings of Reuben Burrow who wrote on Hindu myths in 1789. He was of the opinion that the equator lay further to the north and that temperate climate once prevailed in Siberia. Polar regions had six months' light and six months' darkness and the sun shines in the North Pole continuously for six months. Tilak quotes Dr. Warren who in turn quoted Captain Pim,

> "On the 16th March the sun rises, preceded by a long dawn of forty seven days, namely, from the 29th January, when the first glimmer of light appears. On the 25th of September the sun sets, and after a twilight of forty eight days, namely on the 13th November, darkness reigns supreme. so far as the sun is concerned, for seventy six days followed by one long period of light, the sun remaining above the horizon one hundred and ninety four days. The year therefore is thus divided at the Pole as 194 days sun; 76 darkness, 47 days dawn, 48 twilight."

The characteristics of the Polar region which, as listed by Tilak, are as follows.

1. The sun rises in the south.
2. The stars do not rise and set, but revolve, or spin round, in horizontal planes completing one round in 24 hours. The northern celestial hemisphere is alone overhead and visible during the whole year; and the southern or the lower celestial world is always invisible.
3. The year consists of only one long day and one long night of six months each.
4. There is only one morning and one evening, or the sun rises and sets only once a year.

These phenomena are so peculiar to the North Pole that one may expect their traces in the traditions and myths of the people who once lived there. The idea of the day and night of the gods, each being of six months' duration, is reflected in the Puranas as also in astronomical works. Mount Meru is the terrestrial North Pole of our astronomers. The Surya Siddhanta (XII, 67) clearly states, "At Mount Meru gods behold the sun after but a single rising during the half of his revolution beginning with Aries.19" According to Tilak, "The day of the Gods corresponds with the passage of the sun from the vernal to the autumnal equinox, when the sun is visible at the North Pole, or the Meru and the night with the Southern passage of the sun, from the automnal back to the vernal equinox"20. He is therefore justified in observing that "If the ancestors of the Vedic bards ever lived near the North Pole, the cosmical or meteorological conditions of the place could not have failed to influence the mythology of these people; and if our theory is true, a careful examination of Vedic myths ought to disclose facts which cannot be accounted for by any other theory."

In the 19th century much of the evidence in respect of the Aryan problem was of linguistic nature, and it was on the basis of comparative philology that theories about the antiquity of the Vedas and the original homeland of the Aryans were developed. Tilak's researches brought in a whiff of fresh air in this otherwise stale atmosphere for he employed astronomical references in the Vedas for dating them whereas in the Arctic Home, he marshalled evidence not only of comparative philology but also of geology, archaeology, ethnography and so on.

This in a way is a good illustration of multi-disciplinary approach which is very much in vogue at present. There were a few scholars who agreed with Tilak. Amongst these the foremost was one Dr. F. W. Warren, the then President of the University of Boston in USA, who was impressed by the array of evidence marshalled by Tilak and hence his judgement was far more conclusive than any other put forth by any Indo-Aryan scholar.

The Bhagwad-Gita

Tilak is known more for his Gita- Rahasya than his other scholarly works. He was once asked by his father, who was on his deathbed, to read the Gita to him. He was then a young lad of sixteen in 1872, but even at tender age was thinking as to what was really the message of the Gita23. He was pondering over it and was very much interested in writing on it but could not do so because of his multifarious activities - social and political, and had therefore to postpone it every time. Finally, when he was imprisoned in 1908 in Mandalay, he requested the government to permit him to take some books with him. It was granted and he has noted in the Preface to the Gita Rahasya that in the winter of 1910-11, he wrote out the first draft, made improvements as and when possible, but since he had not with him the required reference books, he finally completed the work during his sojourn at Sinhagad near Pune. Even then he felt that it was not as thorough and complete in all respects as he desired. He was dictating it to his assistant, some 10-12 pages a day, and the latter wrote in long hand as it was in Marathi. He wrote it in four months and published it in June 1915.

Among the ancient commentaries on the Gita, only that by Shankaracharya is available, and it is highly likely that there were others also. It is well known that the Prasthana-trayi consisting of the Upanisads the Brahma-Sutras and the Gita-constitutes the foundation of the philosophy of Hinduism. Sankaracharya advocated advaita, and preached that only sanyasa leads to the final salvation (moksa). Tilak, on the other hand argues that the Gita teaches us to do our duty in whatever station of life we are. The message of the Gita is thus Karma-yoga.

On the battle field, at the very commencement of the Mahabharata war, Arjuna was perplexed that the enemy were his own kith and kin, and was in two minds whether he should fight or not. Hence Krishna, who was also his charioteer, had to impress upon him that he should do his duty, that is to fight. What the Lord emphasizes is that one should do his ordained duty and while performing it, one should not expect any fruit. This is the niskam-karma-yoga of the Gita. In the Gita Tilak found that the cult of sacrifice was replaced by that of Bhakti, and that it gave the message of karma-yoga and not that of sanyasa as propounded by Sankaracharya.

The Gita Rahasya received numerous accolades from different quarters but the most telling was the praise showered by Sri Aurobindo who found the work "an original criticism and presentation of ethical monumental work, the first prose writing of the front rank in importance ... and is likely to become a classic."

Tilak wrote the Gita-Rahasya in Marathi, and when his friends asked him why did he not write in English, he replied that it is not a piece of research, but was written for the common man who should imbibe the karma-yoga as interpreted by him. Moreover, he said that the people in the western world are already practicing karma-yoga and that is why they have prospered; hence they need not be taught it. When the book was first published in 1915, the first edition of six thousand copies was sold like hot cakes, and there were queues outside the Kesari office in Gaikwad Wada. Although a vast majority of the people agreed with Tilak's interpretation of the Gita, there were some, particularly in Pune, who criticized it out of sheer jealousy. Some opposed Tilak's views because they were contradictory to those of Shankaracharya. Be that as it may, the book was immensely popular as the printing history shows, and was also translated into English and many Indian languages.

Research Papers

Besides these major research works, Lokmanya Tilak also wrote a few research papers. The most interesting amongst these is 'The Chaldean and Indian Vedas', which was originally a lecture that he delivered at the Cama Oriental Research Institute in Bombay on 6th December 1904, and was later contributed to the R. G. Bhandarkar Commemoration Volume. Interesting archaeological discoveries were being made in West Asia at the beginning of the twentieth century noteworthy among which were the inscribed tablets unearthed in large numbers in Mesopotamia which, on decipherment, were found to record what scholars have aptly refereed to as the Chaldean Veda. Tilak had come across certain nonsanskrit works in course of his study of the Atharva Veda. Since, according to him, the Vedic and the Chaldean civilization were contemporary, there must have been culture contact between them. He showed how the word 'mana' was borrowed by the Vedic. Much more interesting and ingenious, however, is the similarity in Taimata and Urugula of the Av with Tiamat and Urgala of the Accadian legends. Tilak has discussed some other words which throw light on the contacts between India and West Asia in the ancient past.

Yet another paper deals with 'A missing verse in the Sankhya Karikas'. The Sankhya Karika of Ishwarkrishna contained 70 verses, but only 69 are available. Tilak reconstructed the missing verse on the basis of the evidence of the commentary of

Gaudapada27. There are some more papers which have been published in a book entitled Vedic Chronology and Vedanga Jyotish. Tilak wrote a series of eight articles in the Kesari on the Mahabharata, which, though reviewed C. V. Vaidya's monumental work on the epic, are also important for his deep insight into the subject. Vaidya had dated the Mahabharat war to about 300 B.C., but Tilak has very convincingly shown that the event in all probability occurred around 1400 B.C. which date is in agreement with that proposed by a majority of scholars.28 Many of Tilak's editorials display his wide erudition and keen intellect. He wrote on a variety of subjects such as Ramayan, Bababhatta, Vishnu-sahasranama, Agnosticism and so on which bear eloquent testimony to his versatile genius.

All of Tilak's writings are marked by a remarkable clarity of style, forceful language whether English or Marathi and elegant prose. They also display his wide erudition which is at once interesting and instructive and is free from cumbersome jargon. This is obviously due to his being basically a teacher of Sanskrit and Mathematics. He was gifted with an imagination of a very high order and his genius was comprehensive and subtle. The sheer speed with which he wrote is simply amazing. He dictated almost a dozen pages at a stretch and worked for over sixteen hours a day. This could be possible because of his super-abundant energy and robust health which he has acquired during his student days. He was a true practitioner of the Karmayoga which, according to him, was the gospel of the Gita. The great Indian philosopher, S. Radhakrishnan wrote that "his (Tilak's) real genius lay in literacy work." His essay on 'A missing verse in the Sankhya Karika' is regarded by scholars as a notable contribution to the interpretation of the Sankhya Philosophy. His Orion started the western world. Mahatma Gandhi was highly impressed by his encyclopaedic learning which he carried lightly. Had he been able to devote all his energies to study and research, he would have certainly solved many riddles of Hinduism. He was a great Indologist.

Maratha History

The Marathas who had established their direct or indirect control over a major part of this sub-continent in the 18th century, were the last rulers of India from whom the British wrested power, as James Grant Duff, the first comprehensive historian of the Marathas, has frankly admitted in his book published in 1826.

Lokmanya Bal Gangadhar Tilak, the Father of Indian Unrest, belonged to the generation of the 19th century Maharashtra, who had not yet forgotten that they were the rulers of this country in the immediate past. As a patriot of the highest order, he dedicated his entire life for the liberation of India from the clutches of the colonial rule of the British over his motherland. He must have thought of history, as the most suitable and effective method to mobilize public opinion against the tyrannical rule of the British. He thought that the career of Shivaji, who was not yet forgotten by the people, would be the best tool which could be used to attract masses towards the freedom struggle. This led him to indulge in deep research about the Marathas, particularly of Shivaji.

Tilak's Equipment as Historian

Tilak was not a professional historian. He entered into the field of historical research by sheer accident.

The initial success in the research of the antiquity of the Vedas, encouraged him to do further research and as a sequel to his Orion or Researches into the Antiquity of the Vedas, Tilak produced another original research book, 'The Arctic Home' in the Vedas' in 1898, during the period of his eighteen months imprisonment at Yervada in 1897-98. The book was, however, published in 1903, because of his busy schedule after his release from imprisonment. The main theme of his research was - where was the earliest home of the Vedas? With a view to resolve this issue he studied geological researches about the commencement of the post-glacial period, the historic evidence from the Vedic and the allied literature, the characteristics of the polar region, and produced a book entitled 'The Arctic Home in the Vedas' having 13 chapters running into 450 pages. He presented a mass of evidence to prove conclusively that before the commencement of the post-glacial epoch, the North Pole regions were inhabited by the Aryan race, and that those people migrated from this place southwards in Asia and Europe not by any 'irrestible impulse' but by unwelcome changes in the climatic conditions of their original home.

Plunge in Maratha History

However, the peculiar circumstances that were prevailing in the last decades of the 19th century, made him set aside his prime interest in the researches of Ancient India, and plunge into the history of the immediate past of Maharahstra i.e. the Maratha History.

The intellectuals of Maharashtra had started taking interest in their history. Neelakantha Janardhan Kirtane, a junior student of the Deccan College, assailed Grant Duff's History of the Marathas (1826) in his lecture delivered in the Young Men's Association of the College in 1868. He rhetorically pointed out that Grant's History was no more than an account of the military expeditions of the Marathas, rather than the glorious achievements of the Maratha people, of which the people of this region were proud. Rajwade V.K. another historian of the Marathas, after enlisting many deficiencies and mistakes in Grant's History confirmed the assessment of Kirtane and said further that his history was not more than a chronicle. Grant's history was also translated into Marathi by Captain David and Baba Sane and published in 1829-30. Text books on History were prepared on the basis of information contained in these histories which presented a distorted picture of the Maratha Rule with a view to justify their conquest of the country. It was, therefore, necessary to remove the prejudices developed by the non-Marathi speaking people, through reading the historical writings of the British to whom the Marathas were simply plunderers who thrived on looting other Indian powers.

The British rulers, who strove to inculcate the feeling of distrust among the Indians, and prevent the revival of Maratha power, put restrictions on the researches in the Maratha period, which was a hot bed according to them. This restrictive policy of the British denying free access to the archival material preserved in the Government Archives, induced a group of Marathi scholars to launch a popular movement for collecting historical material from the historically old families of the Marathas in the last quarter of the 19th century. Individual historians like Kashinath Narayan Sane (1851-1927) Vasudev Shastri Khare (1858-1924), Vinayak Kashinath Rajwade (1864-1926) and Dattatraya Balwant Parasnis (1870-1926) dug out private archives of Maratha princes, jagirdars, sardars, ministers, and others to counteract the restrictive policy of the colonial rule and present an authentic and real picture of the Maratha power, and remove thereby the misgivings created by the historical writing of the British. Rajwade V.K., for instance founded the Bharat Itihas Samshodhak Mandal at Pune in 1910 on the model of the German historian Leopold Von Ranke (1795-1886), with a view to collect, preserve, and publishing authentic source material and promote scientific research in Indian history. The latter half of the 19th century witnessed a flood of historical writings including various forms of literature like novels, plays, poetry, epics, miscellaneous writings, besides the publication of source material. Thus, the period from Gopal Hari Deshmukh, (Popularly known as Lokhitwadi) (1823-1892) to Lokmanya B.G. Tilak (1856-1920) produced many historical writings, which helped to awaken the interests of masses in their past history.

Immediate Cause

However the immediate cause which aroused much interest in Shivaji among the intellectuals, elites and masses of Maharashtra was the references to the dilapidated condition of Shivaji's tomb at Raigad, made by a British visitor James Douglas in his work entitled 'A book of Bombay', first published in 1883 and reproduced in his bigger book 'Bombay and Western Indian' published from London in 1893. Douglas visited the Raigad fort in 1883 and when he found the cenotaph (Samadhi) of Shivaji in a dilapidated condition, the temple in a wretched plight, and the image therein thrown on the ground, pathetically observed, "Nobody now cares for Shivaji, not one rupee is spent on the annual repairs of the tomb of Shivaji Maharaj who was master of an enormous kingdom."

Douglas further urged the British Government, who had acquired the Kingdom of Shivaji and his successors to look into this matter, in a note in which he said, "The British Government conserves the architectural remains of Tudor and Stuarts. Will not the Bombay Government do as much for the tomb, the temple and the arch of Shivaji? A few crumbs that fall from the archaeological bureau of Western India would suffice to keep in repair memorials of a dashing and most romantic period."

The efforts of James Douglas, however, did not go in vain. In view of these remarks, and the pressure from the public, the British

Government, not only declared it as a Monument of Protection but also made some provision for its repairs and maintenance.

The remarks of James Douglas about the neglect of the forts in general and Raigad in particular also created a stir in Maharashtra and both the press and the intellectuals resented the Government policy strongly. Raigad was made the symbol of patriotism, and people were reminded by the Press, as early as 1885, of their negligence of patriotism. Justice M.G. Ranade, the author of the famous classic 'Rise of the Maratha Power' organised a public meeting at Hirabag in Pune in 1886 to promote interest in the issue of Shivaji Memorial. It was attended by many important people including the Maratha Sardars, Landlords and even the representative of the Kolhapur State.

Lokmanya and the Shivaji Memorial Movement

Lokmanya Tilak being otherwise busy with several other issues including his own research in Vedic literature, perhaps, did not actively participate in the Shivaji Memorial issue. But an article in the Native opinion of V.N. Mandlik (1895) in which the author after personally visiting the Raigad fort concurred with James Douglas's views which were reproduced again in his book Bombay and Western India in 1893 about the deplorable condition of the shrine of Maharaja Shivaji at Raigad. This kindled the imagination of Tilak and in his article in the Kesari of April 23, 1895 he condemned himself and the sardars and jagirdars for letting the samadhi to fall into decay. He wrote sarcastically, but the sardars and the chiefs knew that they are not likely to be benefited by Shivaji as he is dead and gone. This exhortation had its desired effect in attracting people from all strata of society and raising the funds for repairs, maintenance, a chhatri on the tomb, and annual birthday celebration. He made this a issue of national interest and gave to it the shape of a movement which was later on known as the Shivaji Movement which spread in the other parts of the country like Bengal, United Provinces, Assam and some places in the South as a political movement and a part of the India's struggle for freedom.

Tilak organised a public meeting on 30th May 1895 at Hirabag, Pune on the same lines as Justice Ranade had done in 1886. A Smarak Committee of 50 members including Tilak was appointed in this meeting to raise substantial funds for the Shivaji

Memorial to give a fitting reply to the Bombay Government which had sanctioned a ridiculous grant of Rs. five per annum for the repairs and maintenance of the tomb of the Maratha Chhatrapati. This appeal touched the public and donations started pouring into the Memorial Fund from two annas of a student to one thousand of Maharaj Sayajirao Gaikwad of Baroda, and within a period of six months an amount to the tune of Rs. Nine thousand was collected.

In view of this unexpected response from the public it was decided that henceforth the birthday of Shivaji be celebrated on the Raigad fort itself, instead of the earlier practice of organising it at Mahad. The Committee also framed provisional rules to regulate celebrations to be held at Raigad from 1896 on a large scale, and published them in the Kesari (3rd March 1896).

Tilak had also planned to direct the attention of the National leaders and make the birthday celebrations of Shivaji, a national festival. He organised a meeting on 29th December 1895 at the Reay Market (now known as Phule Market) which was addressed by national leaders like Surendra Nath Banerjee, President of the Indian National Congress, and Pandit Madan Mohan Malviya.

Tilak had decided to hold the Birthday celebrations at Raigad with a double purpose, firstly to take the people to the fort and let them see for themselves the dilapidated position of the Shivaji Memorial and make them contribute generously to the Fund; and secondly, to declare that what government could not do, the people of Maharashtra will do i.e. the repairs and maintenance by raising funds.

Several objections were raised by the Government while granting permission to hold the function at Raigad. The proposal was rejected first on the ground that Raigad was a reserved forest area, and secondly by objecting to the Marathi term Yatra used in the letter of the organizers which was translated into English by the Oriental Translator to the Government as Fair, which was considered equivalent in English to Market and as per the provisions of the Markets and Fairs Act of 1862 for want of sufficient notice, the request of the organisers was turned down. The organisers substituted the word 'Yatra' by 'Utsava' and approached the Government again.

Tilak was an elected member of the Legislative Council of the Bombay Government since 1893. He arranged a personal interview with the Governor of Bombay who was holidaying in Mahabaleshwar in April 1896 and obtained the necessary permission from the Governor by promising him that no untoward incidents would take place during the course of the festival. Thus, with the explicit permission of the Government, the celebrations were held on 15th April 1896, as declared, and the National Festival of Shivajayanti was inaugurated with great pomp and splendour. The Kesari of 21st April 1896 reported that over 6000 persons from various places of Maharashtra had gathered on the fort to witness the festival and pay their humble homage to their great national hero. The press in general reported it as 'the most glorious and successful function that was ever held at the Raigad fort.' Probably since the coronation of Shivaji which was held over 250 years ago, there had been no function similar to the one held this year.

The Government, however, was not prepared to express any opinion in favour or otherwise on this movement officially called 'the Shivaji boom'. To Mr. Nugent, a member of the Council of Governor, 'the entire agitation is purely a Brahmin move. The Marathas have held aloof' (25-7-1897).

Direct Contribution to Research

The initial success in celebrating the birthday of Shivaji, involved him in direct research in Maratha history, particularly regarding fixing the correct date and place of Shivaji's birth. As regards, the place of birth of Shivaji, all historians unanimously accepted the fort of Shivaneri as the place where Shivaji was born; but opinion was divided about the year and date of his birth - whether it was Vaishakha of Shaka 1549 (1627 AD) or Falgun of Shaka 1551 (1630 AD).

V. K. Rajwade, the doyen among the Maratha historians, in his introduction to the Marathyanchya Itihasachi Sadhane vol. IV published in 1900 discusses the issue of Shivaji's birthdate and on the basis of a chronological note submitted by one Kashinath Krishna Lele of Dhar (Dewas) in 1801 for publication in Kavyeitihas Samgraha periodical of K.N. Sane. This chronology of Dhar mentions that Shivaji was born on Monday, the Vaishakha

Shudha Panchami of the Prabhav Samvatsar and the nakshatra (constellation) was Rohini. According to the English calender the birthday falls on 10th April 1627. Grant Duff denies it and says that Shivaji was born in the month May of the Year 1627 which is obviously not correct. He examined the bakhars (chronicles) saptaprakarnatmak Charitra of Shivaji by Malhar Ramrao Chitnis and Shivadigvijya (found in Baroda in 1818, written by an unknown author) suggesting Shaka 1549 Vaishakha Shudha Dwitiya, Thursday as the birthday of Shivaji, and rejected it on the ground that the Rohini nakshatra does not occur on Thursday. Rajwade doubts the motives of the chroniclers in advocating Vaishaka Dwitiya (7 April 1627) instead of Panchami. It was believed in those days that the king must be born on an auspicious day, and as Panchami did not fulfil that, they must have rejected it and conveniently fixed the birthdate on Dwitiya.

Tilak who was anxious to determine the exact birth date of Shivaji, was dragged into this birthday controversy by the above mentioned Introduction of Rajwade. He elaborately examined this issue in his article in the Kesari of 24th April 1900. He read Rajwade's 140 pages long introduction, it seems and appreciated his efforts of collecting all available information and examining it scientifically and carefully and arriving at some conclusions after examining the contradictory views of scholars. He also hoped that Rajwade would continue his research and examine the controversial or doubtful issues and enlighten his readers by supplying proper information.

Tilak was amazed to see that there was lack of consistency in the chronicles and historical documents about the birth date of a person who was born some 275 years ago, and that five to six versions about his birth date differing in the shaka (year) or, samvatsar (era) or tithi (date). On the basis of information that was available for him he could only surmise that most of the sources agree only on the month of birth, i.e. vaishakha but not with the date and other details, and therefore, he says, one can arrive at a proper decision only after critically examining all the issues involved in it.

Tilak critically examined nearly fourteen sources of information, contemporary and of little later period produced between 17th and early 19th century. They included poetic works like Shivaraj Bhushan or Shiva-Bhavani of a contemporary Hindi poet Bhushan of the North India, Shivakaya by Purushottam, bakhars like Sabhasadi, Citnisi, Chitragupta, Rairi, Shivadgvijaya, Shivapratap, Marathi Samrajyachi Choti Bakhar, 91 Qalimi bakhar, Panditrao bakhar, Pratinidhi bakhar, a chronological note from Dhar and horoscope published in Kavyeitihas Samgraha a periodical of K.N. Sane, and a chronology of the Chhatrpatis published in the Bharatvarsha periodical of D.B. Parasnis. This long list of sources alone is enough to show the deep interest taken by Tilak to establish a single point, namely the birth date of Shivaji.

He did not find a single correct date in all these sources which would fulfil all the tests of astronomical calculations. Out of the 14 sources, 9 give 11 different dates, and the remaining five are unanimous on one date but it does not pass the test of astronomy. He thus came to the conclusion that there are four major versions found in these sources and one has to decide the exact date of birth only after examining them. These probable four dates are :

1. Shaka 1549, Prabhav, Vaishakah Shudha 2, Saturday (7th April 1627)
2. Shaka 1549, Prabhav, Vaishakha Shudha 5, Tuesday (10th April 1627)
3. Shaka 1548, Kshaya, Samvatsar, Vaishakh 2, Monday (17th April 1626)
4. Shaka 1548, Kshaya, Vaishakha Shudha 5, Thursday (20th April 1626)

In these four versions, the month Vaishakha is common in all, but there is a difference in the tithi or day. As regards the difference in the year, Tilak rejects the year 1548 on the basis of the references to the date of his death which was shaka 1602, Chaitra Shudha 15, Sunday (4th April 1680) as all sources were unanimous on it, and after calculating the span of the career of Shivaji, he fixed the year 1549 as the year of birth.

He finally accepted a date which was nearer to the bakhar than that of Rajwade and it was Shaka 1549, Pravhav Samvatsar, Vaishakha Shudha Pratipada (nor 2nd or 5th Thursday, Ashwinin nakshatra (not Rohini) equivalent to 6th April 1627. However, he confessed that there was good deal of confusion regarding the date of birth of Shivaji, and appealed to the research scholars to express their views on this issue which he would gladly publish in his newspaper. He requested the organizers of the birthday celebrations to be held on Vaishakha Shudha pratipada from 1900 onwards.

The year and month, thus continued to be followed by the people for a fairly long time till new sources came forward. In the subsequent years two major sources namely the Jedhe Shakavali and the Sanskrit epic Shiva Bharat and epic composed by Kavindra Paramanand the poet laureate of Shivaji. However, when Tilak wrote the article in 1900 non of these sources of information were available to him. His search for getting an authentic source continued and he succeeded in laying his hands on the Jedhe Shakavali which he secured from Daji Saheb Jedhe Deshmukh of Kari (Bhor princely state) by 1906-7 but could not find enough time to analyse it and so published it as he found it with a brief note, in the journal of the Bharat Itihas Samshodhak Mandal (BISM) in 1916. The other source i.e. Shivabharat came to light only in 1927, which confirmed the date given in the Jedhe Shakavali. A learned research scholar Dattopant Vinayak Apte of the BISM considered afresh in the light of these two new sources and rejected the findings of both Rajwade and Tilak, and declared Shaka 1551, Shukla Samvatsar, Falgun Vadya Tritiya, Friday, nakshtra, hasta, equivalent to 19th February 1630, as the correct date of Shivaji's birth. For a long time historians like G.S. Sardesai, Jadunath Sarkar and others, however did not accept the date advocated by the BISM, and the celebrations continued to be held at two different dates. After the information of Samyukta Maharashtra, the Government appointed a Committee of historians in 1960 to give a finality to this long pending controversy. But the majority decision of the committee submitted in 1966 was not implemented by the Government till February 2000, and now it is officially declared that Falgun Vadya Tritiya of Shaka 1551 (1630 AD) approved by the majority and advocated by the BISM as the authentic date for the celebration of Shiva Jayanti. Thus after nearly hundred years i.e. since Tilak wrote his article in April 1900, the controversy is now resolved. Tilak must get credit for this.

Tilak wrote a number of articles on Shivaji and other historical matters connected with Maharashtra since 1895 practically till the end of his life in 1920. During his long imprisonment at

Mandalay (1908-1914) it is discovered from his note book, among other things, like history of Hinduism, Indian nationality, Hindu law, Geeta Rahasya, etc. he had even planned to write a biography of Shivaji. He also jotted down the purpose of his Shiva Charitra. According to him, Shivaji did not establish Maratha power for self but for the people of Maharashtra as a whole; his example was emulated by Peshwa Bajirao I, who by elevating Shinde, Holkar, Gaikwad, to the status of Maratha Sardars tried to show that this Maratha nation was for all. The lesson which Shivaji's life teaches, according to Tilak, was that leaders should not exploit caste, emphasis should be on talent and quality irrespective of the individual's social status.

Indirect Contribution to History

Tilak believed that the historical research should be the first duty of any emerging nation. In his article in the Kesari of 9th May 1915, he applauded the selfless efforts of Sane, Khare, Rajwade and Parasnis in promoting historical research in Maharashtra. He appealed to the younger generation that they should emulate the example of these pioneers, who have sown the seeds of historical research in this land. He warned them in these words, "Your ancestry lost the kingdom; if you lose history, your progeny will lose its dharma i.e. duty; Maharashtra will not only be forgotten, but will be destroyed completely; you should try to avoid this calamity."

He gave opportunities to many scholars to publish their researches, or controversial issues, in the Kesari or the Mhratta and thus encouraged public debate. Rajwade, Khare, Parasnis, Bhanu, Paranjape, Jinsiwale and many others responded to this appeal of Lokmanya.

Tilak had to face many objections raised by his enemies against the Shivaji Movement which he had launched on a mass scale since 1895-96. It was considered by some as a movement not for renovation of Shivaji Memorial, but to establish Shivaji as an incarnation of God; an anonymous person called himself as Historicus, in an article in the Times of India 1899 said, "Shivaji's Raj was destroyed by the Brahmins and they are the leaders now to revive his Raj". To Tilak, according to some, Shivaji was not an academic issue but a political one causing Hindu-Muslim riots.

Lokmanya Tilak strongly refuted all these charges levelled against him. To him, Shivaji was not a god, but a superman, appears every now on this earth, as per sermons of Geeta Sambhavami Yuge Yuge, to surmount the difficulties of humanity. Shivaji is remembered for his nation building activities; biographies of great leaders like Shivaji, are the sources of inspiration to the younger generation.

To those who found fault with the brahmin leadership of the movement and doubted that it might be reduced to Ramnavami festival in the long run, Tilak gave fitting reply in his article Shivaji and Brahmin by citing many examples from history, and charged the critics that their main purpose in calling it a brahmin movement was to create a rift between the Brahmins and the non-Brahmans of Maharashtra.

To the charge that the two festivals namely the Ganesh (1893) and Shivaji (1896) caused Hindu-Muslim riots of 1893, 1894, 1896 in Maharashtra, Tilak gave a strong reply in his article in the Mhratta of June 24, 1906. Shivaji he declared, was not an enemy of the Muslims. Had there been a Muslim in his place under those circumstances, he too would have been honoured. Who was he? Where was he born? are minor issues. One who inspires is great. We are not against a festival being started in favour of Akbar or any other Hero from old Indian History....It is a sheer misrepresentation to suppose that the worship of Shivaji includes invocation to fight either with the Mohamedans or with the Government.

In support of the Shivaji festival, Tilak argued that man had become an animal, and Shivaji made him a human being with a desire to be free, and realize that swarajya was his fundamental right. He, therefore, believed that the purpose of Shivaji festival was promotion of patriotism and nationalism among the people of this country.

Once, a young historian, D.V. Apte, to whom a reference has been made earlier, asked Tilak, "My friends say that all research in History is useless and unnecessary; one would hardly get anything out of it, it is a sheer waste of time, and a great headache, so give it up and do something concrete."

Lokmanya replied, "Listen to your friends and do what you want to do with all might and determination. Research cannot be done by all, it is a privilege of the chosen few. It depends on one's liking and aptitude. Research should be done for the sake of research only. One cannot show the tangible results of historical research immediately. But research is such a thing which should not be avoided by one who is interested in it. Every activity should not be motivated by material gain. Man works both for his maintenance as well as for satisfying his urge for pure knowledge. It depends on the nature and character of man, to which he should give priority. One can hardly explain to a common man the ecstasy one gets through research resulting in the advancement of knowledge."

This summarizes Tilak's views on historical research. For want of time Lokmanya Tilak could not pay much attention to historical research but he knew the relevance of history, and how to reconcile historical research for political purposes, as well as for advancement of knowledge, and therefore, his contribution to historical research deserves attention of scholars and political leaders of modern times.

Women's Education

The last year of the 20th century is an appropriate time to look back and take a review of the historical changes that this century has brought. It was a period of transition and so of confrontation on various social issues. Women's education and overall reforms in women's social status was one such hot issue that had caught the attention of all social thinkers in particular and society in general. Especially the last two decades of the 19th century and the first three decades of the 20th century is the period of the tussle between radical social reformists and orthodox Hindu traditionalists over the education of women - whether they should at all be educated and if so what kind of education they be given. Being a hard patriarchal society, no one thought it worth considering what were the views of the women over their own issues. Women played a secondary marginal role in society and that was mostly of a housewife, who was caught in a trap of various age-old customs and traditions. In this context it would be interesting to see what views did a contemporary nationalistic leader, an editor of a newspaper and basically a teacher of a school and even society like Lokmanya Tilak holds about women's education.

The views of a person on any issue cannot be inspected arbitrarily. Especially when one talks of women's education, it is entangled with various issues of the period like child-marriages, dishevelled-widows, widow-remarriages etc. It is along with these issues that we have to study Tilak's views on women's education. It is also important to see a short history of women's education to get the idea of the social ethos on which Tilak put forth his views. Unless we compare Tilak's views with contemporary exponents of women's education like Mahatma Phule, Principal Gopal Ganesh Agarkar, Vitthal Ramji Shinde and Maharshi Annasaheb Karve, we cannot evaluate Tilak's contribution to women's education. It is also important to note that the family in which one grows, the surrounding society that influences the shaping of one's opinions, the education one takes which decides one's preferences, and one's own temperament plays important roles in confirming one's views. Tilak's views should be examined on these grounds. Tilak was not a staunch radical reformist like Agarkar and the principal aim of his life was independence of India. His opinion that social reforms would take place gradually along with political reforms would have also played a definite role in deciding his views on women's issues. We will have to see his objectives and the way he proposed to achieve them in the light of this bigger aim. Whether what he foresaw turned out to be true would also be an interesting point to observe. It is through these various angles that this paper tries to bring forth an overall picture of Tilak's views on women's education.

Tilak's Views on Women's Educations

It is with reference to this social ethos that the thoughts of Tilak on women's education are to be read. They are mostly expressed in the four editorials he wrote between September to October 1887 about a particular female high school. There is one more special editorial 'Stree Shikshanachi Disha' [The Direction Of Women's Education] written on March 16, 1888. There was a lot of discussion going on in the newspapers about a female high school established in 1884. Tilak thought that the founders of this school were neglecting the criticism against them, thinking that those who write against women's education were uncultured, uneducated and obstinate people. If the curriculum of this school had been made public before the school began, Tilak thought there would not have been misunderstandings about the school. The attempt to educate women would be successful according to him if the consent of the people is honoured. He, like other so many people of his time, did not deny the necessity of education for women, but differed with the contents and the way it was given. He thought that the exponents of education should first think of the contemporary society and opinions of the masses before allowing their imagination a free play. Again and again Tilak emphasised not to neglect the psyche of the society and that the preferences should be made accordingly. Nothing could be achieved by neglecting the society. The second point he mentioned is that if half of the humanity is uneducated our goal will never be achieved, but that does not mean that the kind of education being given to man is appropriate for woman too. Their duties in this world are different, and so should be their education. Time and situation also demand this difference. The curriculum in the female high school is akin to that of boys' school. If women are forced to take this kind of education, society would never be benefited.

In the second article, he accepts that traditionalists agree with reformists that educated women would do their duties more efficiently; but disagrees about the duties of women in society. Education to woman is not a new concept in our society. There are examples of scholarly women in our Puranas. But, sending women to schools to receive formal education like boys is a new concept borrowed from the English, and as in the case of other concepts borrowed from them, here too we are in the wrong. If English rule and education would continue for more than a hundred years, our families would imitate their lifestyle. He accepts that society is not stable, it should change according to time, situation and ruler but is of the opinion that attempts to bring reforms would never be successful if social conditions are not taken into consideration. Our families are different from English families and so should be our education. Their girls do not marry at an early age, they stay with their parents till they reach the prime of their youth. They do not depend on their parents economically if they are educated and, and they get sufficient time to educate themselves as they marry late. They, like boys, help their families by earning money. Women can complete education in such social situations. What is the use of education in our society? Our girls have to marry before puberty, they have to live with in-laws after marriage. So, they do not require education for earning money. At the most, they have to be taught how to be good housewives, and the school which does not teach that, is useless and would never prosper. He does not like the criticism of some people when they say that educated women would wear boot and stockings like English madams and roam in Bund Garden with their Sahibs. His basic argument is, when the education given to boys is not wholly beneficial the consequences would be doubly harmful, if the same is given to girls. We imitate the English, but English women themselves are getting education only for the last twenty years or so, then why should we hurry to give it to our women? He thinks that the time is not ripe for women's education, and very sarcastically he adds, when marriages would take place at a later stage, when there would not be joint families, when restrictions of religion and morality would be loose, when middle class people would have enough to spare, when the English educated women, singing on piano, dancing a kindergarten dance, telling stories of Grace darling and Elizabeth, instead of Seeta or Ahilya, then only English educated women would be honoured in society. We require women who care for our religion and household work, who know some reading and writing. The schools which will not produce such women are not required. Educate women for two or three hours in the interval, after they finish their daily chores. This education should be according to the laws of the Hindu religion and feminine duties. Such schools, where women of all religions come together and are taught by the English madams may suit the rich or the destitute, or to those women who have to earn their livelihood. This school will be a nuisance to middle class people. If reforms are brought about suddenly, they break the society and female schools are stepping on the same lines. Reforms are to be carried out very gradually, caring for the psyche of the society. Otherwise, reforms will never take root, and you will be cut off from the society.

In the third editorial (published on Oct. 11, 1887) Tilak warns the founders of female education to re-examine their objectives and to make appropriate changes in their curriculum. He also raises the question as to why people and government should spend money on such schools which are of doubtful use. Like boys' schools, girls' schools are already well settled. There is a scope for reform in these schools, but that does not mean there is a need to open new schools. We already have a female training college, with the thought that these women would teach in girls' schools. This high school does not have either young girls or training teachers. According to our religious traditions, girls marry before attaining puberty, and after marriage, they have to do household chores in their husbands' homes. That is why there are no married women in schools. After marriage, they even forget the alphabets which they once knew. This means that society does not get the benefit of educated women through girls' high school. If the female high school has the objective of doing away with this lacuna, we will have to see how many married Hindu women are there in this school. The total number of married women is twenty. If women of other religions are excluded, one can see how few Hindu women are benefited by this school. He then goes on to accuse the management of the female high school that they have been carried away by imaginary reforms and have neglected completely the contemporary social situation. He is of the opinion that even if high school education is the extension of primary education, it is not useful in general, for our women. It may be useful in England, where women can be clerks, lawyers, doctors or editors. He does not think that women should remain slaves in the hands of men, but he thinks that at least five hundred or even a thousand years should pass before the situation is changed. He underlines that marriage is a social contract in Western countries. Women marry at a later stage, and there too only a few years have passed when they have started taking professional training. Do we want our women to be clerks or writers? Those who are proud of the woman community would never like to think of our women as clerks being kicked by English Sahibs. In summary, the education in female high school is useless except for a very few rich women, who, if they choose, can be writers. Our women should be given education to improve the household work. They should improve themselves by reading scriptures. As for the artists, their profession is the main thing and education subsidiary, so for the women, household work is the main thing and education is secondary. They are not supposed to neglect the work and run to school from 11 to 5 taking the guidance of Christian teachers for Western education. No one would be ready to spend the first fifteen or sixteen years of their life for such education. The house of in-laws is a workshop. The practical education that she will get here, no school can ever give. We are in need of that education which will not bring her out from this workshop, but which will teach her something suitable from our religion. In addition to this, if some people want western education they can avail of it.

The fourth editorial [Oct.25,1887] sarcastically addresses the reformists of women's education and elaborately puts forth his ideas. He says that he drastically differs from them about the duty of a person towards society. The reformists claim that a "man and a woman are both like a wheel of a cart called family. If one lags behind, the cart will fall into a ditch. A woman is a fellow-friend of a man. A man could never go forth keeping her behind. Education would not do harm to women as it has not done to men. " Tilak belittles the reformists saying that they live in dazed condition of mind and are blind to the actualities of our society. It is important to think of how life of human beings would be after one thousand years but that does not mean to start the reforms immediately accordingly. As they say women would be free like men to choose their profession, there would not be slavery in marriage and the nation would prosper because both educated men and women would be working together. This may happen but after 5 to 10 hundred years. The problem with which we are concerned is what kind of education should be given to our women to bring some change in their position. We are in search of such an institute that will give them more than primary education but will not hinder their womanly duties. Those who say that I am against women's education are perverse and prejudiced. It will take time to change the tradition of marriage before puberty. There can be a woman like Dr. Anandibai Joshi who will be educated and would do a profession like a man with the permission of her husband, but it will be an exception. We accept that if there are women like her we should help them go forth, but that will not achieve anything in general what we can achieve by a number of cultured women. They should be educated without disturbing their marriage life. Women's education in the real sense of the term will not begin till a number of married women are being educated. Reformists of women's education should never forget this. Formal education in high school is for boys, not for girls. They require different type of education that would help them to be good housewives. He thinks that the founders of female education know this, but turn a deaf ear to this reality. Sarcastically he remarks that he should admire them for their strategy in opening a boarding school in Pune for women. The question is would the quality women take admission in it? Would they declare how many girls above the age of 14 to 15 are there? He is sure that people will never send their married daughters in such boarding schools. At the most there would be some poor destitute women who want to become teachers. How is the internal management of the boarding school is not yet known. Those who have thought of such a boarding school must have been blind by the ideas of reforms. It may turn into a widow-house like the one Pandita Ramabai is going to open.

As religious reforms require mingling with masses, so does women's education. The women's community will not improve, if one or two women become M.D. or M.A. So thousands of rupees that are being spent on female high school are only for the benefit of five to ten women. We do not envy them, but the Govt. should first see the welfare of the common masses and then of the rich. If they do not have that much funds, preferences should be given to reform the majority of people. It is surprising that at the end of this article he says that his thoughts may be incorrect but instead of pointing at his lacuna if someone obstinately and arrogantly calls him hypocrite, he will never tolerate it and will expose him before the society.

Two months after the publication of these articles Tilak thought that he should make his views more clear. He decided to write one more article [March 6, 1888] because his opponents vehemently criticized him for his conservative attitudes. He begins the article saying that he is much more an exponent of women's education than anyone else of his time. By nature his tendency is for women's education, but he thinks that as men and women have different roles to play in life, their education should also be different. Career women would always be minority so the founders of women's education should not think only of their needs. Housework and married life are the principle duties of a woman, she should be taught to read and write, but to make her study after the age of 16 is against her femininity and so is harmful. His main point was this, but according to him no body could point out any mistake in his thinking. Some objected that he is short- sighted and his thoughts do not go with his English education. These objections he thinks do not point any flaw in his thinking process and so he need not answer them, but as the lion does not hide in fear of an elephant, so does not he. He defends himself for the satisfaction of his opponents. He then quotes an article in a book published in the month of February of the same year called 'Nineteenth Century.' The article is by one Miss Sivley and is about the curriculum in female high schools in England. She says, "that the duties of men and women differ and so should the courses. English schools do not keep this in mind and teach the same curriculum to boys and girls up to the age of 18. This happens because some scholars do not think there is difference between men and women. It is alright when they are small, but when they start growing the difference is visible. Boys are strong, stout and boisterous. They love outdoor activities, where girls are by nature simple. They love indoor games. This difference develops with the age and is completely opposite at the end. A grown up person goes out of the house in search of a job, whereas a woman though married or unmarried looks after her house. As it is a duty of a man to earn money it is the duty of a woman to do the household work and to look after her children. This does not mean that men should dominate over women, but one should not interfere in other's field.Each one should take care how he or she excels in his or her duty. The curriculum in schools should be such that would teach them the excellence in their respective fields". At the end of his editorial Tilak notes that it is his modest request to reformists of women's education to think of these points seriously and bring the appropriate changes in practice.

To sum up, Tilak is of the opinion that there should be separate education for women that would make them better mothers, and better housewives. There is a lurking fear behind this position that the life-style of society would change by English education and by the imitation of western culture. He therefore rejects the concept of serving women and firmly believes that education plays a secondary role in women's life.

There are two types of reformists, those who want to impose reforms in spite of resistance and the others, who think social reforms will follow gradually with the changing time and political reforms. Tilak is the second kind of leader who did not want to disturb the contemporary social set up. The careful reading of his articles shows that he is not against women's education, but that he is afraid the haste of the reformists would disturb the public opinion against it. Tilak knows very well the psyche of our traditional Hindu society, and would oppose any decision taken hastily without probing the pros and cons. He is of the opinion that reforms are to be introduced according to the time, situation and the opinion of the masses. If the masses are behind time, try to change their opinion, but never neglect them or never try to bring reforms without their acceptance. He insisted on the same view in the case of other social problems of the time. He strongly opposed any interference of government in the Hindu laws and traditions. Not only that he did not want law to be imposed against the shaving of widows, but that he did not even want our people to bring pressures on bringing an end of this custom. Deenbandhu the news paper of Satyashodhak Samaj invoked the barbers to refuse to shave women. Agarkar also called the Brahmin society to take the warning seriously. Tilak on the other hand expressed his dislike for such invocations. He expressed his views that pressures should not be imposed on women, leave the question to them, and allow them to take their own decision. If one is ready to shave her head let her do so, At the same time he brought the stark reality on the social front that prohibiting this custom will not improve the condition of widows. Unshaven widows will suffer more. As they cannot remarry we should think positively about finding the means of their livelihood. If forced not to shave, they will prefer to die like Sati. These views show that Tilak knew the cruelty, wickedness, undue passion and selfishness of our men folk in depth. Even if he sounds orthodox traditionalist, he is more balanced and thoughtful on same occasions.

In cases of widow remarriages Tilak holds the same view of not stirring the feelings of society. When Agarkar congratulated Shri R. B. Joshi for remarrying his sister against the wishes of his parents, Tilak sympathizes with the parents and says that sons have no right to make their parents unhappy in an old age by going against their wishes. Indirectly it shows that he was against widow marriages. In 1893,when Dhondo Keshav Karve remarried a widow called Godubai Joshi, Tilak has written: "One has no right to pinch the society. In this we differ from the reformists. Parents are to be respected even if they are foolish. In the same way convictions of the traditional society also have to be respected. Society claims honour because it is always big in number." The last sentence clearly indicates why Tilak is called 'Telya Tambolyanche Pudhari'. He has contacts even with the lowest strata of the social setup and knew very well that one can never lead unless one gets their backing. In a way sometimes he seems to cater to their tastes even against his will, but it's a part of his political strategy and he faithfully sticks to it, accepting compromises.

It may be noted however that in his own personal life he carried out the reforms he advocated. He educated his daughters in the same female school which he criticized. He did not stick to Deopuja, Sandhya and other such everyday rituals. He attended widow remarriage parties, he freely interlined with men of any creed, community and religion. Tilak was not at all a champion of orthodoxy. He stood for hastening slowly in bringing about social and religious reforms, and was against any sudden violent break with the past. He was a good progressive conservative Hindu, his beliefs were firm and this policy secured for him the support of the general masses.

Tilak was uncompromisingly against the attempts of Mr. Byramji Malbari to bring reforms through legislation. Ranade, Bhandarkar and Agarkar held that if the reforms initiated by the Government were calculated to serve the best interests of the people, they should not be opposed simply because the foreign Govt. sponsored them. Tilak was the only public man of his day to be wholly against the bill of the Age of the Consent. Here too, the way in which he spoke and wrote would show that he was quite reasonable and earnest about the cause of social reforms. He did not want to rush his people and get headlong into it. In this case of the Age of Consent, he suggested that the attainment of puberty should be made the legal age for consummation of marriage. As a spokesman of the common people, he wanted the Govt. to bend down to the will of the people. In the 'Kesari' and the 'Maharatta' he carried on an incessant campaign against Mr. Malabari, the social reformers and the Govt. Although the campaign failed and the Govt. carried through the legislation in spite of his opposition, he moved a resolution in the Bombay Provincial Social Reform Conference condemning the Govt. for not respecting legitimately and widely expressed public opinion.

He was beyond doubt in favour of social reforms but all that he wanted was that the initiative in that respect should be taken by educated Indians and they should primarily be achieved by educating the public. He inveighed against legislation to force the pace of reform among the ignorant masses because he believed that the method would not work and all such legislation would remain a dead letter. In the public meeting in Tulshibag under the presidentship of Rao Bahadur Nulkar, he put the proposal of social reforms, like girls should not be married before the age of 14,and boys before the age of 20. A man marrying again should marry a widow but no one should marry after the age of 40. Dowry should be abolished and widows should not be disfigured. Respecting masses does not mean accepting even the evil customs. In many of his articles he has censured the aged people who generally married girls under the age of 14,with a sharp edge of his pen and has tried to emphasize the status of wife in one's life. A woman, he says, is not a machine of producing children, nor a maid servant to devote her whole life in household work. How could a man be so empty headed like cattle to marry immediately after the death of his wife, whom he has accepted with the pledge Y } M, AW} M, H$m { M, who shared his life through thick and thin, who took half of the responsibility of his family on her shoulders and with whom he had sexual intercourse for so many years? He occasionally admires the reformists that their objective to bring equality between men and women is praiseworthy, but instead of encouraging widow remarriages he suggests that they should bring a change in the tendency of men to marry even at the later stage of their life. Both men and women should be aware of the glorious life of Sanyasashram, which our religion insists after a certain age. To lessen the undue excessive importance of marriage is the true path towards reforms and is in defence of Hindu religion. His merciless logic and proficiency in Sanskrit lore adds such grace to the scholarly advocacy of his views, that even if one does not agree with his views, one becomes powerless in expressing one's disagreement. But Tilak's efforts were futile because he found out that no one wanted to suffer and make sacrifices for his convictions and it dawned upon him that most of those who called themselves social reformers were not serious about practice and indulged merely in precept. In yet another episode of Pandita Ramabai, Tilak did not like her activities of opening a residential school, but Agarkar, Ranade and Bhandarkar were very enthusiastic about it. In the beginning, Tilak enrolled his name among the sympathisers of the school after satisfying himself that the Indian girls were not compelled to attend Christian prayers, and the education was only secular. He soon discovered that the condition was not being observed and the institution was functioning as a proselytizing body. He protested against it. The Sudharak wrote tauntingly about Tilak, questioning his motives and calling him an opponent of women's education. Ultimately, Agarkar was convinced of Ramabai's double dealings, and quietly removed his niece from the school. Tilak's triumph was indisputably established in this controversy. It was his intelligence, insight and thorough understanding of the motives of the people that lead him to see through some contemporary cases.

Tilak was born and brought up in a traditional Brahmin family of Gangadhar Shastri, well known for piety and learning. In general his views about women were never liberal. He agreed with what Manu said "Z ór ñdmV§Í` hoV". He naturally symbolizes the deep-rooted patriarchal culture of Hindu society where women have a secondary and marginalized position. It is not surprising therefore, that Tilak adhered to the side of Dadoji against Rakhamabai. In an article on March 19. 1887, in Kesari, Tilak criticizes Rakhamabai very harshly as a foolish hater of our customs and traditions. He calls her act as a licence for extra-marital relationship, and holds her responsible for sowing the seed of dissatisfaction in hundreds of otherwise happy families. In comparison he has showered his praise on Anandibai Joshi for devoting her whole life for the cause of betterment of Hindu women and foresees that she will remain immortal in the hearts of Hindu men and women.

Tilak's views on women's education, if compared with his contemporary reformists, can be evaluated in the light of history of women's education. Mahatma Jyotiba Phule, though preceded Tilak, had opened a school for girls in 1848 in Pune. He was strongly opposed by society and even by his own parents. He taught his wife Savitribai, who afterwards became a teacher in this school. Both of them continued their work of women's education up to the lower levels of society. The then education officer Cady gave financial assistance to this school in 1852.

Agarkar, a radical reformist in Maharashtra was an exponent of women's education, who held such strong progressive views which were not easily acceptable to the contemporary society. He was an individualist and firmly believed in the equality of sexes. He was of the opinion that women's education should be made compulsory by law. If a woman has to take care of her child, it is a crime to keep her illiterate. He laughs at Tilak's statement that we had a tradition of women's education. There is no proof that women were given formal education, nor were they taught to read and write at home. In all developing countries, women are getting education, while we have kept them locked in our houses. We should encourage them to come into the light, choose a profession they like, secure higher degree, and marry when they like. He was very sure that these reforms would take place very soon and the credit to foresee this correctly should be given to him as the present position of women shows, whereas Tilak thought it will take at least five to ten centuries to bring about the educational reforms in women. Agarkar was against child marriage and asked the society how could a woman continue her education if she is married at an early age, if she delivered a number of children and was expected to look after them. Either they should not marry till they complete higher education or the in-laws must give them liberty like unmarried women to continue their studies. He says that our society suffers and does not prosper because half of its number has been prevented from making use of its intelligence. Boys and girls should be given co-education so that there would be a healthy competition among them and each one will get a position according to his intelligence.

Agarkar's thoughts were poles apart from those of Tilak's. Both of them harshly criticized each other over their views. Agarkar had the courage and daring to say whatever he felt right despite the opposition of the masses whereas Tilak always found the golden mean, made compromises and stuck to the orthodox Hindu tradition. Another of his contemporaries Maharshi Annasaheb Karve was an activist in the real sense of the term.

He married a widow, opened a primary and high school for adult women, a boarding school for destitutes and widows. The culmination of his work is seen in the establishment of a unique university only for women. He introduced subjects like Home-science, child-development in the curriculum of the degree examination. In his memoirs, he mentions that he met Tilak and told him about this university but Tilak refused to give him anything in writing in recommendation of this university. He said education has made men sceptic, he did not want women to be come so. In actual fact, Tilak's ideas about women's education were being brought into reality by Karve, but there was a basic difference in the view of these two thinkers. Karve believed that in terms of intellectual qualities, there is no difference between man and woman. They are equal yet their fields differ so should their curriculum. Another thing was that he wanted women to do jobs and become economically independent, the idea Tilak would never tolerate.

Tilak was of the view that he too was a reformist but his ways are different than the radical reformist like Agarkar. Tilak's speculations about women's education failed. In spite of his opposition, the female high school prospered and there were more such schools where women started taking English education. It means that the society did not wish to keep its women in their traditional status. Whereas Agarkar thinks of women in general, Tilak's views are confined only to middle class brahmin women. He opposed compulsory primary education for girls. But a big procession of women under the leadership of Vitthal Ramji Shinde followed by thousands of untouchable women and Ramabai Ranade followed by thousands of higher class women proved that general masses were for compulsory primary education for women. A meeting was called in Kirloskar Theatre under the presidentship of Chief Officer Shankarrao Bhagwat when Tilak was a special invitee to convince people of not making primary education compulsory for women. Vitthal Ramji Shinde opposed Tilak and suggested him not to deliver a lecture. Tilak neglected him and started to talk, when people threw eggs on him. He was saved by Vitthal Ramji and his son. The meeting was adjourned. The next meeting of this type in Gayakwadvada also ended in commotion. The two incidents show that time was changing and Tilak could not estimate it.

One thing has to be noted in justification of Tilak that Tilak's views about women's education came as a reaction to the extreme views of the reformists. It was in defence of the Hindu traditional cult that he had to take this position as a representative of its past glory. There is no separate theoretical presentation on this issue. So his views are limited and confined only to the occasional incidents. Tilak afterwards concentrated his energies more in politics and less in social reforms. He felt it more prudent to attack the foreign rule and concentrate upon capturing political power and use it as a means of bringing about social reforms. He became a national leader and tried to revive nationalistic spirit among people. If Tilak had joined hands with reformists about women's education, his public image would have helped the spread of women's education earlier. But then Tilak as a political leader would not have emerged as strongly as he did.

11

TILAK AS CONGRESS PRESIDENT

The Nationalists decided to put forward Tilak, the Lokmanya, the greatest leader of the people, as their candidate for president of the forthcoming session. The Moderates had only one possible candidate who they hoped would be able to prevent Tilak's presiding at the Calcutta session. That man was Dadabhai Naoroji, one of the founders of the Congress, and widely accepted as the Grand Old Man of India. The Nationalists could not openly oppose the candidacy of such a venerable leader. The Moderates were successful; Tilak declined to stand for office and Naoroji was selected president of the session. But regardless of who occupied the presidential chair, the Nationalists were resolved to bring about a revolution in the Congress, Writings in the Kesari on the eve of the session, Tilak set forth the Nationalist programme : 'If the Moderates think that we are easily disappointed and lack grim determination they are entirely mistaken. We have lost faith, not in the ultimate result, but in the dilatory activities of the Congress.... Not that we have no faith in constitutional agitation. We do not want to overthrow the British Government. But political rights will have to be fought for." The Nationalist spirit pervaded the atmosphere of the whole Calcutta session, and the popular strength of the Nationalists was overwhelming. The leaders had decided that this was the time at which to put forward their entire programme and, if it were accepted, to place the Congress in the leadership of the independence movement.

The Nationalists first presented resolutions on Swadeshi and national education. Both resolutions were passed. Tilak added to the swadeshi resolution the phrase that swadeshi would be followed 'even at a sacrifice.' Then Pal rose to the platform to second the resolution on boycott. This time the Nationalists would not accept a restricted interpretation of boycott as a purely economic device, or a limited acceptance of boycott for use only in Bengal. Pal lucidly explained the Nationalist position when he announced to the assembled delegates. 'You will have observed the word "boycott" is attached to the word "movement". The word "boycott" is left severely alone, and the only qualification which the authors of this Resolution have attached to the word "boycott" is that it shall move from point to point, move from city to city, move from division to division, move, I hope, you will allow me to add, from Province to Province.... You will see that the omission of British goods in relation to boycott was intentional. As a statement of fact it was necessary, because in Bengal we have not only tried to boycott British goods, but also, so far as it may be a convenient phrase, all honorary association with the Government also. That is the meaning of boycott which will move from point to point until God knows where. I originally opposed the introduction of the term "boycott" in ,our politics and political life, but in the course of a few days we found that, whatever objections might be taken to the word, the thing was exceedingly useful not only economically but politically as well.... I ask you in the name of God, in the name of your nation, in the name of the future emancipation and realization of the highest destinies of your people, to lend your support to this movement now, and when you go back to your Province, there, so that, as I have said, this thing may proceed from point to point, from city to city, until the whole of India is ablaze, not with the fire that ruins and kills, but with the fire that brings plenty, patriotism and progress'. This was boycott in its fullest meaning, and it is obviously the precursor to the non-cooperation movement.

The moderates could not bring themselves to accept all of Pal's implications., They struggled with all their parliamentary powers to modify the boycott resolution, and at last a compromise was effect to the extent that the Congress would approve of boycott as a political weapon throughout India, but not quite to the extreme degree Pal had advocated. In effect, the Congress want on record that 'the boycott movement was and is legitimate'. Again the Nationalists were victorious in fighting for the nation's political rights. There was to be a resolution on Swaraj. The Moderates had manoeuvred Dadabhai Naoroji into the presidential chair to contain the Nationalists on this, their most revolutionary proposal. Naoroji had been a constant advocate of the Moderate programme of prayers and petitions to the Government. He had worked for years in London on behalf of the Congress. He had a record of loyalty to the British spirit and of twenty-one years of service to the Moderate cause. If any man in India could stop Tilak in his drive for Swaraj, the Moderates believed it was Dadabhai Naoroji. Before the Nationalists could present their resolutions, including the revolutionary one on Swaraj.

Naoroji delivered his presidential address. He told the assembled delegates of his twenty-one years of work on behalf of the Moderate programme, and then he said he was disillusioned. He was disillusioned with both the Moderate programme and the British spirit in which he had always believed. He went further and proceeded to denounce the British Indian Government 'as a barbarous despotism unworthy of British instincts, principles, and civilization? Then with an explosive force hard to imagine today, Naoroji announced to the session, to India and the world that he supported Swaraj as the goal of the Congress. This was the greatest possible victory for Tilak and the Nationalists. 'Tilak's phrase had been adopted, and "self-government" was now put forward as a right'. In effect, the Congress at Calcutta accepted Swaraj (though not defined as absolute self-rule) as the ultimate goal of the national movement.

The Congress did not disallow a continuation of the Moderate programme of prayer and Petition for the redress of grievances, but the Congress give leadership to the nation for the Nationalist programme to fulfil the Nationalist goal of Swaraj. After the Calcutta session, Tilak said, 'Swadeshi, Boycott, and National Education are the three most potent weapons given into our hands by the National Congress, and with these we must establish Swaraj.' The 1906 session adjourned with the Nationalists victorious. The Moderates were convinced that at the next session of the Congress the Nationalists would endeavour to define more broadly swadeshi as a further Indianization of all things, and boycott as an expanded dissociation with all things British, and Swaraj as self-rule, within or without the framework of the British Empire. The Nationalists became apprehensive that the Moderates would endeavour to retrench, to qualify and modify further the resolutions taken at Calcutta, and to recapture the Congress for the old Moderate programme. From the beginning of 1907 until the Congress session in December, both parties were manoeuvreing for positions of strength.

Surat Split

Originally, the Congress session of 1907 was to have been held at an appropriate city in the Punjab. Judging from the strength and popular support of the Nationalists in 1906, the Moderate leaders were afraid that the extended Nationalist programme would be passed if the Congress to be held in Lala Lajpat Rai's province. Rai had aroused tremendous popular support for the Nationalists in the Punjab. Sir Pherozeshah Mehta controlled the Congress committee in charge of planning the 1907 session, and being an astute politician, he was able to persuade the committee to move the session from the Punjab to their relatively quiet, central Indian city of Nagpur. Nagpur was one of the few cities in which the Nationalists had not begun to develop wide popular support, and the Moderates felt that there they would have a ,chance perhaps to modify the stand taken in 1906, without incurring popular displeasure during the session. As soon as this shift was planned, the Nationalists, who hoped to elect Tilak as president of the session, began to develop their strength in the Nagpur area. By November, they had so successful that the 'political backwater' of Nagpur was transformed into a Nationalist stronghold.

The Moderate controlled Reception Committee was greatly alarmed and, casting about for some means to thwart the Nationalists, again changed the location of the session. This change took place in mid-November, only about a month before the session was to convene. The session was moved to Surat in peaceful Gujarat, for Surat was considered an 'entirely safe' Moderate stronghold, one that had the added advantage of being far removed from turbulent Bengal. In the summer of 1907, the British had arrested Aurobindo Ghose on a charge of sedition. The indictment failed due to the refusal of Bipin Chandra Pal to testify against his colleague. But while Aurobindo was freed for lack of evidence, Pal was imprisoned on a charge of contempt of court; and his strong voice was lost to the Nationalist cause for the 1907 session. Rai was sentenced to transportation in the spring of 1907 for his Nationalist activities, and it appeared for a time that a policy of governmental repression would seriously undermine the

Nationalist cause. The other leaders did not sit back quietly during all of the Moderate parliamentary manoeuvres to change the locale of the session. The Moderate plan became more and more clear. To the Nationalists everything indicated that they were about to capture the Congress and retreat from the firm stand taken at Calcutta. As Aurobindo Ghose's paper warned. '... the Bombay Moderates... want to wipe away the colour given to the Congress during the last two years and go, back to the old and effete programme of prayer and petition. They want to crush the spirit of Nationalism and the desire on the part of Indians to stand independent of foreign help and go back to servility. They want to disregard all sense of self-respect and lick the dust of the foot that kicks. This is what Sir Pherozeshah and his satellites now that they have shifted the scene of the Congress to a sleepy hollow, want to do.' But the Moderates were not only concerned with holding the session in a safe place, they were firmly resolved to elect a Moderate to the presidency of the session. Pherozeshah Mehta and the Reception Committee selected Babu Daswehari Ghose.

Lala Lajpat Rai had recently returned from exile, and Tilak withdrew as the Nationalist candidate for president in deference to-Rai who was the great national hero after his release. The Reception Committee would not agree to accept Rai. The Punjab leader hated discussion and finally felt called upon to ask not to be nominated. Because of all these manipulations, considerable bitterness was being engendered between the two groups. Until the middle of December, the Nationalists were not resolved even to attend the Surat session since they could argue with considerable evidence that it was being rigged against them. But it was finally decided that they must not cause a rupture in the Congress and that they must attend Surat in an effort to hold the line against reaction. As the Bande Mataram reported. 'When Mr. Tilak and Lala Lajpat Rai, fresh from exile, were in favour of attending the Surat session, there could be no further question of course. It has been decided, then, to attend the Surat Congress in what force we can muster at this short notice and do our best to hold the ground we have gained.' The atmosphere at Surat at the convening of the Congress was tense.

The first issue after the Chairman of the Reception Committee had welcomed the 1600 delegates was the nomination and election of the president of the session. According to the Moderate plan, Dr. Rashbehari Ghose was to be installed as president. While the Nationalists did not object to Dr. Ghose on personal grounds, they objected to the principle of undemocratic selection and to what they believed was an obvious sign of the Moderate manoeuvres to undermine the Calcutta resolutions. Lokmanya Tilak, as the leader of the Nationalists, requested permission to speak before Ghose was installed. He sent a note to the chairman and followed it with a reminder that it was his right to address the delegates before the voting. The chairman refused to recognize Tilak's rights by ignoring his requests to speak. When this became apparent, Tilak began to make his way to the platform. Certain Gujarati Moderate volunteers endeavoured to block his way. He gained the platform and endeavoured to speak, but the Moderates would not permit him to. A newspaper account in the Calcutta Statesman then said that while Tilak with arms folded wanted to speak, 'a Gujarati rushed to attack Mr. Tilak on the platform." Aurobindo Ghose, in charge of the Nationalist delegates, saw that Tilak would not be allowed to speak and that he might be done bodily harm, and so he gave the signal to the Nationalist delegates to storm the platform and rescue their leader. Immediately the session exploded into pandemonium. Moderate volunteers fought with Nationalist delegates from Bengal, Maharashtra, and the Punjab. The great tent in which the session was held became a confusing background. The meeting was suspended. Immediately the two factions caucused. The Nationalists met 600 strong under the chairmanship of Aurobindo Ghose, while the Moderates gathered to hold a closed conference. Tilak spoke to the nationalists saying that 'a speedy reunion would be possible,' while in the Moderate meeting, Surendranath Banerjee declared 'the Congress was dead'.

The Nationalist meeting unreservedly accepted the principles established at the Calcutta session and reaffirmed their belief in swaraj, swadeshi, boycott and national education. The further nominated a committee headed by Tilak to bring about a reconciliation with the Moderates. In their closed session, the Moderates set about to rewrite the Constitution of the Congress. They included a Creed of the Congress as the Constitution's first article. The Creed stated: 'The objects of the Indian National Congress are the attainment by the people of India a system of government similar to that enjoyed by the self-governing members of the British Empire and a participation by them in the rights and responsibilities of the Empire on equal terms with those members. These objects are to be achieved by constitutional means by bringing about a steady reform of the existing system of administration and by promoting national unity fostering public spirit and developing and organizing the intellectual, moral, economic and industrial resources of the country'. Acceptance of this Creed became mandatory for Congress membership. It represented a complete retreat from the stand taken a year earlier. No longer was Swaraj the goal but rather a system of government similar to that enjoyed by the self-governing members of the British Empire... by bringing about a steady reform of the existing system of administration. The Nationalists were shocked. It appeared to them that the entire unfortunate split at Surat had become a premeditated provocation. The Bande Mataram commented: 'This last move of the Moderates has completely floored us. Inexplicable are the ways of these Moderates ... the country knows what importance should be attached to the resolutions passed at such a Conference. But the move has done one good it has made the Loyalists show their hand, and we know now that boycott, swaraj and national education had no place in the Congress they hoped to hold.' The Nationalist attempts to bring about a reconciliation were completely thwarted. The Moderates appeared to have achieved their goal in ridding the Congress of the Nationalists and in retreating to their old policy of prayer and petition to the bureaucracy. The split of Surat created two parties or two organizations in the Indian political scene. The Moderates by their parliamentary manoeuvres had retained control over the Congress.

The Nationalists kept the support of the people, and since they alone offered a dynamic programme of political action, the Moderates had won a hollow victory. Plans were laid in the early part of 1908 for a great new Nationalist party under Tilak's leadership which would be used to organize and lead the people in their struggle for Swaraj. Tilak was still interested in bringing about a reconciliation and a reunification of the Congress, but if this were not possible, the Nationalists were prepared to continue their struggle through a new organization stronger and more dynamic than the Moderate-dominated Congress had ever been.'

Congress Session at Surat

At the end of 1907 the leading agitators of the Bombay Presidency, with a considerable following from other parts of India, made an attempt to force the Indian National Congress to accept their views. It is unnecessary to give here any general account of the Congress, as the proceedings are regularly published in the press and in the annual reports issued by the Congress itself. The twenty-third meeting of the Congress, which opened at Surat on 26th December 1907, was however of special importance, for it was at this meeting that a definite and public cleavage took place between the Moderates and the Extremists, or Nationalists as they preferred to call themselves, and it was the fact that the latter were unable to control the policy of the Congress that was put forward by many of them as a justification of their resort to, violence. After the proceedings were over the Moderates issued a press communique on December 27th, and the Extremists on December 31st; they are of course on many points contradictory, but where they are agree the common version may be accepted. The split took place ostensibly over the election of the President, but really, as will appear later, over the general policy of the Congress. When the Congress met on December 26th, the Moderates say "over sixteen hundred delegates were present," while the Extremists state that "there were about thirteen hundred and odd delegates at this time in the pandal, of whom over 600 were Nationalists, and the Moderates' majority was thus a bare majority."

After the split took place only some 300 delegates attended the Extremist meeting, so it would appear that this estimate of their following in the Congress was exaggerated. Dr. Rash Behari Ghose having been proposed as President, the Chairman called upon Babu. Surendranath Banerjee to second the motion, but he was not allowed by the Extremists even to start his speech and the uproar was so great that the sitting was suspended for the day. The leader of the Extremists was B.G. Tilak of Poona; and their object was to propose as President Lala Lajpat Rai, who had been recently released from deportation. When the Congress met next day Tilak sent the following note to the Chairman by the hand of a "volunteer" :

Sir,

I wish to address the delegates on the proposal of the election of the President after it is seconded. I wish to move an adjournment with a constructive proposal. Please announce me.

Yours Sincerely,
B.G. Tilak
Deccan Delegate (Poona)

The Chairman received the note, and what followed is thus described in the Moderate communique : "The Chairman considered a notice of adjournment at that stage to be irregular and out of order. The proceedings were then resumed at the point at which they had been interrupted yesterday, and Mr. Surendranath Banerjee was called upon to conclude his speech. Mr. Banerjee having done this, the Chairman called upon Pandit Motilal Nehru of Allahabad to support the motion. The Pandit supported it in a brief speech and the Chairman put the motion to the vote. An overwhelming majority of the delegates signified their assent by crying "all, all" and a small minority shouted "no, no." The Chairman thereupon declared the motion carried, and the Honourable Dr. Ghose was installed in the Presidential chair amidst loud and prolonged applause. While the applause was going on, and as Dr. Ghose rose to begin his address, Mr. Tilak came upon the platform, and stood in front of the President. He urged that as he had given notice of an "amendment to the Presidential election," be should be permitted to move his amendment. Thereupon it was pointed out to him by Mr. Malvi, the Chairman of the Reception Committee, that his notice was not for "an amendment to the Presidential election", but it was for "an adjournment of the Congress", which notice he had considered to be irregular and out of order at that stage; and that the President having been duly installed in the chair no amendment about his election could be then moved. Mr. Tilak then turned to the President, and began arguing with him. Dr. Ghose, in his turn, stated how matters stood, and ruled that his request to move an amendment about the election could not be entertained. Mr. Tilak thereupon said, "I will not submit to this. I will now appeal from the President to the delegates." In the meantime an uproar had already been commenced by some of his followers, and the President who tried to read his address could not be heard even by those who were seated next to him. Mr. Tilak, with his back to the President, kept shouting that he insisted on moving his President, and he would not allow the proceedings to go on. The President repeatedly appealed to him to be satisfied with his protest and to resume his seat. Mr. Tilak kept on shouting frantically, exclaiming that he would not go back to his seat unless he was "bodily removed." This persistent defiance of the authority of the chair provoked a hostile demonstration against Mr. Tilak himself, and for some time nothing but loud cries of "Shame, Shame" could be heard in the Pandal]. It had been noticed that, when Mr. Tilak was making his way to the platform, some of his followers were also trying to force themselves through the volunteers to the platform with sticks in their hands. All attempts on the President's part either to proceeding with the reading of his address or to persuade Mr. Tilak to resume his seat having failed, and a general movement among Mr. Tilak's followers to rush the platform with sticks in their hands being noticed, the President, for the last time, called upon Mr. Tilak to withdraw, and formally announced to the assembly that he had ruled and he still ruled Mr. Tilak out of order and he called upon him to resume his seat. Mr. Tilak refused to obey, and at this time a shoe hurled from the body of the Hall struck both Sir Pherozeshah Mehta and Mr. Surendranath Banerjee, who were sitting side by side. Chairs were hurled towards the platform, and it was seen that Mr. Tilak's followers who were brandishing their sticks wildly were trying to rush the platform which other delegates were endeavouring to prevent. It should be stated here that some of the delegates were so exasperated by Mr. Tilak's conduct that they repeatedly asked for permission was to eject him bodily from the Hall; but this permission was steadily refused.

The President, finding that the disorder went on growing and that he had no other course open to him, declared the session of the 23rd Indian National Congress suspended sine die. After the lady-delegates present on the platform had been escorted to the tents outside the other delegates began with difficulty to disperse, but, the disorder having grown wilder, the Police eventually came in and ordered the Hall to be cleared." The Extremist maintain that Tilak got up to make his amendment immediately after Surendranath Banerjee had finished speaking, and deny that Dr. Ghose was duly elected amidst loud and prolonged applause. "All this", they say, "if it did take place, as alleged, could only have been done in a deliberately hurried manner with a set purpose to trick Mr. Tilak out of his right to address the Delegates and move an amendment as previously notified." They also state regarding the attitude of Tilak's followers, "Chairs were now seen being lifted to be thrown at Mr. Tilak by persons on and below the platform, and some of the Nationalists, therefore, rushed on to the platform to his rescue." Although Dr. Ghose's speech was never delivered it was published in the Calcutta press, and telegrams received on the evening of December 27th by the Extremists in Surat showed, according to them, "that he had made an offensive attack on the Nationalist party therein." This diminished any chance of a compromise, but next morning Tilak gave a delegation of the Moderates the following assurance in writing, which states very succinctly the points of difference between the parties.

Surat, 28th December, 1907

Dear Sir,

With reference to our conversation, and principally in the best interests of the Congress, I and my party are prepared to waive our opposition to the election of Dr. Rash Behari Ghose as President of the 23rd Indian National Congress, and are prepared to act in the spirit of forget and forgive provided, firstly, the last year resolutions on Swaraj; Swadeshi, Boycott and National Education are adhered to and each expressly reaffirmed, and secondly, such passages, if in Dr. Ghose's speech as may be offensive to the Nationalist Party are omitted."

Yours, and c.,
B.G. TILAK

Proposals of Self-government or Swaraj

The most important difference related to the drafting of the Swaraj or Self-Government resolution, and to show what it amounted to the proposal passed the previous year in Calcutta, and the draft resolution at Surat, are printed side by side :

Calcutta Resolution, 1906

That this Congress is of opinion that the system of Government obtaining in the Self-Governing British Colonies should be extended to India, and that, as steps leading to it, it urges that the following reforms should be immediately carried out, (Here followed certain administrative reforms such as simultaneous examinations in England and India, and the reform of Executive and Legislative Councils, and of Local and Municipal Boards.)

Surat's Draft Resolution, 1907

"The Indian National Congress has for its ultimate goal the attainment by India of Self-Government similar to that enjoyed by other members of the British Empire, and a participation by her in the privileges and responsibilities of the Empire on equal terms with the other members; and it seeks to advance towards this goal by strictly constitutional means, by bringing about a steady reform of the existing system of administration, and by, promoting national unity, fostering public spirit and improving the condition of the mass of the people."

"Those who accept the foregoing creed of the Congress shall be members of the Provincial Committee."

"All who accept the foregoing creed of the Congress... shall be entitled to become members of a District Congress Committee."

"From the year 1908, delegates to the Congress shall be elected by Provincial and District Congress Committee only."

After the adjournment of the Congress the parties held separate meetings. The most important leaders on the Moderate side were Dr. Rash Behari Ghose, the late Sir Pherozeshah Mehta, Surendranath Banerjee, and the late Mr. G.K. Gokhale; curiously enough Lala Lajpat Rai, whose proposed election as President was the nominal source of all the trouble, joined the Moderate camp. On the other side Aurobindo Ghose presided at the meeting of the Extremists held on December 28th, and the most prominent persons these were B.G. Tilak and G.S. Khaparde; it is significant that at this meeting, in the absence of Lala Lajpat Rai, special honour was paid to the other Punjab deportee, Ajit Singh, who was publicly presented by Tilak with an embroidered cap.'

It is clear from the Swaraj resolutions quoted above that the question which really divided the Congress was whether the agitation for Self-government was to proceed on constitutional lines or not; but the importance of this incident at Surat from the point of view of revolution and sedition is that it was taken by the revolutionary leaders as the signal to begin the campaign of violence. If the "sweets" letter sent by Barin Ghose to his brother Aurobindo on December 27th, 1907, be accepted as genuine this point needs no further elaboration; Aurobindo Ghose's own words in the leading article "New Conditions", published on the day of the first revolutionary assassination, leaves the matter in little doubt, and is itself a confirmation of the genuineness of the letter. The argument of the Bengal revolutionaries that the policy of the bomb was adopted because their attempt to control the Congress at Surat was a failure is, however, demonstrably false; it is completely refuted by the single fact that they sent Hem Chandra Das to Paris to learn how to make bombs over a year before this eventful meeting of the Congress took place.

Leading Agitators

If a list of the leading agitators of the West of India were made out it would be found that the great majority were Brahmins belonging to Poona and the neighbourhood; of these there are two main classes, the Konkanasth or Chitpavan Brahmins, who trace their origin from the Konkan, the strip of low country between the Western Ghats and the sea, and the Deshasth Brahmins, who belong to the plateau of the Deccan which slopes Eastward from the Ghats. B.G. Tilak and most of the prominent followers belong to the former caste, which consequently has a bad reputation for loyalty, but, as in many similar cases, it would be a mistake to brand as disaffected a whole community to which some of the most able and loyal servants of Government belong.

The Poona Brahmins are at least the equals of any other Indian community in education and intelligence ; it is therefore not surprising to find that they are very advanced in their political views. Though many of them clearly expressed themselves in favour of turning out the British Government, the real leaders do not seem to have approved of the immediate resort to violence; even Tilak, who apologised for the revolutionaries of Bengal, is believed to have considered their proceedings premature, and, in short, although many of them are in favour of a revolution, they, as practical men, refuse their support to methods which do not appear to promise success. This perhaps partly explains why, while the Poona Brahmins may be fairly regarded as the brain centre of the revolutionary movement, the number of revolutionary outrages in the Presidency has been comparatively small; at the same time the firmness with which both the Government and the High Court of Bombay dealt with revolutionary agitation and violence, for instance in the Nasik Conspiracy case, and in the conviction and removal from the scene for six years of Tilak himself, doubtless had its effect in moulding the opinions of the older men and restraining the impetuosity of youth.' The year 1916 was the most eventful in Tilak's career. The session of the Indian National Congress was held at Lucknow during this year. Tilak's role in this session is indeed unique. Since the days of the Surat split he Congress had been controlled by a prominent section of the Moderates who simply met at an important town, passed the resolutions and dispersed.

The main resolutions were in connection with the improvements in the councils, the creation of executive councils in the Punjab and the United Provinces; the prevention of the extension of communal representation to local bodies; the abolition of the system of indentured labour and the removal of intolerable restrictions and humiliating conditions under which thousands of emigrant Indians had to live and earn their livelihood. "In one word, the Congress resolutions had proved utterly ineffectual ... Such was the depressing balance sheet of Congress achievements up till 1916, when once again it met at Lucknow under the presidency of the Moderate leader A.C. Mazumdar. Tilak travelled to Lucknow with more than three hundred delegates in a special train known as the 'Home Rule Special'. When it reached Lucknow.

Tilak was received by thousands of his admirers. They virtually besieged his car, showering roses on him, garlanded him throughout the long route upto the Congress pandal. So far so, the people drew the carriage themselves, shouting his slogan, 'Swaraj is my birthright and I shall have it'. When Tilak took his seat on the dais, he received a very warm ovation. Indeed he was deeply overwhelmed by the warmth of the reception. He put forward a resolution on selfgovernment. He explained, 'It may not be Swaraj in the widest sense of the word, but it is far better than Swadeshi and boycott ... All that is included in this one resolution on selfgovernment, and I would ask every one of you to carry-out this resolution with all your effort, might and enthusiasm'. Regarding Muslim representation in the central and provincial councils, he showed much generosity. He declared emphatically. 'It has been said by some that we Hindus have yielded too much to our Mohammedan brothers. I am sure I express the feeling's of the Hindu Community all over India when I say that we could not have yielded too much. I would not care when I say that we could not have yielded too much, I would not care if the rights of self-government are granted to the Mohammedan community only ... I would not care if ,those rights are granted to any section of the Indian community. The fight then will be between them and the other sections of the community and not, as at present, a triangular fight. When we have to fight against a third party, it is a very important thing that we stand on this platform united; united in race, united in religion, united as regards all different shades of political creed. That is the most important event of the day.' To give separate representation to the Muslims posed a ,problem. The United Provinces opposed it, but after a heated debate, it was accepted. But many leaders opposed the idea of half of the total representation. Tilak prevailed upon M.A. Jinnah and Madan Mohan Malaviya and his appeal for a via-media was accepted. He thus achieved Hindu-Muslim unity :and Tilak's generous gesture of granting a liberal representation to the Muslim was, greatly applauded.

The Lucknow Pact, Tilak opined, was for a united India marching forward to attain its freedom. Indeed his vision was not of Hindu domination in any sense. 'The Lucknow Congress finally buried the hatchet between Hindus and Muslims and between Moderates and the Nationalists and, above all, gave birth to a demand for Swaraj, Home Rule, on a truly national scale ... Tilak himself regarded the Congress achievements at Lucknow as something in the nature of a miracle'. This ceaseless round of activities kept Tilak busy from morning till midnight on 27th 28th and 29th December. The part Tilak played as a peacemaker evoked appreciation from all sides. Shri C.S. Ranga Iyer has graphically described Tilak in the Subjects Committee meeting thus : "In the Subject Committee. Lokmanya Tilak in the Subjects Committee of the Congress was an interesting suy. When the angry speakers were foaming on all sides, he was calm as a rock ... I remember the remarkable composure of Tilak in the Lucknow Congress when the Moderates and the Extremists, the Hindus and the Muslims were unusually agitated the Moderates over the forward step that the advanced politicians were taking, the Hindus and Muslims over the communal representation and the Pact. Pandit Madan Mohan Malaviya was very much upset. He would not reconcile himself to the Pact, and the Hindu enthusiasts, who invaded his spare hours, were assured by him that, if there was a need and if it was proper, he would hold a huge demonstration against the Congress, if it surrendered to the Muslims. The leader of Maharashtra . . would not listen to any argument against the pact. Not that he was enamoured of it himself, but, if it would satisfy he Muslims, if it could bring them to the Congress, if it could replace their extra-territorial patriotism by many Nationalism, the agreement was worth reaching. Loka-Indian Tilak's attitude was the deciding factor in the Hindu-Muslim settlement, the last word on the subject so far as the Hindus were concerned. Pandit Malaviyaji's contemplated demonstration against the Congress did not come off and. Panditji himself wisely lowered the flag and bent before the gale."

Outside the Subjects and the Open Session, Tilak's influence was accepted as the cementing factor by all. Shri Kamini Kumar Chanda who, according to his reminiscences of Tilak, stayed almost in the midst of the camp of the great Muslim leaders has testified to the confidence of the Muslim leaders in Tilak. He has recorded how an emissary was once sent to Tilak at night and an urgent meeting with him was arranged by Jinnah and Mason Imam. Even after all these negotiations, the resolution on Self-Government had a stormy passage in the Subjects Committee, Jinnah had moved an amendment requiring the deletion of a sub-clause in that resolution. Mrs. Bement wanted to stand by the original draft.

The Jinnah-Besant tussle grew in bitterness and Jinnah threatened to move his amendment in the Open Session. If it was defeated in the Subjects Committee. At this stage, Tilak, Mazhar-ul-Haq and some other leaders persuaded Jinnah to accompany them to a place outside the meeting. Pandit Malaviya appealed to the Subjects Committee to compose differences at the Subjects Committee stage. Jinnah returned to the Subjects Committee ready for an adjustment. The Self-government resolution was finalised on 28th December and the next day that resolution loomed large as the major item in the Open Session of the Congress. Besides Surendranath Banerjee, who got the unique honour of moving the resolution, there were sixteen speakers who either seconded or supported it. Bipin Chandra Pal, Mrs. Bement, P.M. Petit, Baptista-these and the other, speakers allowed the audience to enjoy what was veritably a sumptuous feast of first-rate eloquence.

When Tilak appeared on the platform, there was such a warm and enthusiastic reception that he had to stand still for a few-minutes before quiet was restored and he could address the audience. Using the 'enthusiastic reception accorded to him as the starting point of his memorable speech, Tilak said : "I thank you sincerely for the reception that you have given me on this platform; but, let me tell you I am not foolish enough to think that this reception is given to me personally. It is given, if I rightly understand, for those principles for which I have been fighting. The resolution which I wish to support embodies those principles. It is the resolution of Self Government. It is that for which the Congress has been fighting for the last thirty years.

The first note of it was heard ten years ago on the banks of the Hugh and it was sounded by the Grand Old Man of India, that Parse patriot of Bombay, Dadabhai Naoroji. Since the note was sounded, differences of opinion arose. Some said that the note ought to be carried on and ought to be followed by a detailed scheme at once, that it should be taken up and made to resound all over India as soon as possible. There was another party amongst us that said that it could not be done so soon, and the tune of that note required to be a little lowered. That was the cause of the dissensions ten years ago, and I am glad to say that I have lived these ten years to see that we are going to put our voices and shoulders together to push on this scheme of Self-Government. Not only have we lived to see these differences closed, but to see the differences of Hindus and Mohammedans closed as well. So we are united, in every way, in the United Provinces and we have found luck in Lucknow." Replying to the charge that the Congress had yielded too much to the Mohammedans, Tilak continued :

"I am sure I represent the sense of the Hindu Community all over India when I say that we could not have yielded too much. I would not care if the rights of Self-Government are granted to the Mohammedan Community only. I would not care if they are granted to Rajputs. I would not care if they are granted to the lowest classes of the Hindu population, provided the British Government considers them more fit than the educated classes of India for exercising those rights. I would not care if those rights are granted to any section of the Indian Community. Then the fight will be between them and another section of the community, and not, as at present, a triangular fight." Explaining the potentialities of the scheme which there solution embodied, Tilak declared : "It may not be complete Home Rule but it is more than a beginning of it. It may not be complete Self-Government but it is far better than Local Self-Government. It may not be Swaraj in the wider sense of the word, but it is far better than Swadeshi and boycott. It is in fact a synthesis of all the Congress resolutions passed during the last thirty years, a synthesis that will help us all to proceed to work in a definite and responsible manner." Warning the delegates that the acceptance of the resolution ought to make them earnest, Tilak remarked :

> "Nothing can be gained by passing resolutions on this platform, by the simple union of races and parties. The union is intended to create a certain power and energy among us, and unless that power and energy are exercised, you cannot hope to succeed. Great are the

obstacles in your way. You must now prepare to fight on behalf of the scheme."

Finding that the Self-Government or Home resolutions had been unanimously and enthusiastically accepted by the Congress, Tilak submitted to the Subjects Committee a resolution that the Congress should carry on Home Rule propaganda both in England and India, that it should raise funds for that purpose and that it should appoint small committees in various parts of the country for propaganda work and for the collection of funds. This resolution was ruled out on the ground that the constitution of the Congress did not allow such a resolution to be discussed. Tilak, however, persuaded the AICC to appoint, from among its own members, a special committee to devise means for carrying on continuous, educative propaganda.

Differences and Commonness between Tilak and Gandhi

The great durable principles that provided the common foundation to the lives and work of these two great leaders are far more important than the tactical differences or differences of attitude that might have existed. The first such principle was love of country. Tilak had always been a nationalist first. To him India was the Mother, the past, the present and the promise of the future, the image for which he demanded the nation's sacrifice and for which he sacrificed himself.

Humanitarian principles often motivated Gandhiji's actions, but he recognized that what he did for humanity was of value to the extent that he acted for India, for India was the 'action-environment' in which the universality of his faith and his principles could be demonstrated and proved. Because of this he, too, became a great and devoted son of the Mother. It has been said that Tilak was a national leader and that Gandhi was an international leader; and though each man had a world message, it was for India and for the people of India that both men lived and worked and died, it was to a universal and eternal philosophy of life that each dedicated himself. It has been urged by some that the greatest difference between Tilak and Gandhiji lay in their personalities. In effect, this thesis proposes that Tilak was, after all, a Brahmin politician and Gandhiji was a casteless saint. But the difference is far more apparent than real. Each man, because of his love and understanding of India, performed a role in the independence movement that was valid in terms of the roles of leaders in India's history. Tilak was a Brahmin, but this did not make him a slave to Orthodox rigidity; rather he fought against atrophied orthodoxy and the divisiveness of caste-ism; he was a scholar devoted to learning, to teaching and to guiding the people, to awakening the spirit of India, to sacrificing himself in the performance of his duties to the highest purpose of life. He lived humbly, he dedicated himself to the cause in which he believed.

Gandhiji's role was that of the saintly seeker after Truth, the humble, dedicated man of the people who identified himself with the lowliest, and who sought in the remotest villages of India that Truth which India has always known. Action for a high purpose, self-sacrifice and dedication, the classical precepts of the noble life, were the guiding principles of each man. Tilak was scholar, teacher and awakener; Gandhiji was seeker, man of the people, inspirer. Tilak was the Lokmanya; Gandhi was the Mahatma. Each fulfilled the obligations of his Swadharma. The lives of each were understandable to the people of India, each communicated directly with the people, because each lived a life related to the classical values and seeking the Purpose of life which the people understood. The Moderates were never able to communicate their vision of India's role in the world precisely because their vision was not based on the value system of the people. The vision of Tilak and Gandhi was communicated because it was based on India's own vision. Tilak and Gandhiji taught the classical message of perfect yourself, dedicate yourself to the highest aspirations of man, live in Truth, live in your True Nature, strive for the fufilment of the Purpose of life.

Their political philosophy was founded on this philosophy of life. Self-reliance 'courage and willingness to sacrifice motivated each man and was a part of their message to all men. The willingness to act, to meet the challenges of the world and to make of the world a better place in which to live guided each man and was a part of the message of each. They each relied upon the people, their wisdom and their willingness to act, to bring about their common goal. They each sought to unify the people by stressing the common bonds that united rather than the forms, customs, conventions and institutions which separated. And by united popular action based en courage born of self-reliance and dedicated to the common goal, each man taught that Swaraj could be achieved. These were the elements of the common foundation that united Tilak and Gandhi and the nation. Gandhi gave vent to his feeling about Tilak in his speeches and writings. He showed much respect for him and recognised his services for the country. In fact Tilak's involvement in the national cause was at a time when Gandhi had been busy in South Africa before the first global war. Gandhi praised Tilak's efforts for the foundation of the Home Rule League and its functioning in a major portion of the subcontinent. The following texts would show Gandhi's deep regard for Tilak's, patriotic enthusiasm and fervour.

National Union Meeting Speech at Bombay

January, 13, 1915

At a meeting convened by the Bombay National Union at Hirabag (Bombay) on the 13th instant to welcome Mr. and Mrs. Gandhi, Mr. Tilak was present, though no formal invitation was sent to him. The meeting was attended by about 250 persons. Mr. Tilak addressing the gathering said that they were only doing their duty in honouring Mr. and Mrs. Gandhi, as they had fought for the honour of India in a distant land. He said that India ought to produce more men and women of the self-sacrificing spirit of the honoured guests, and impressed upon the audience that this was the lesson they had to learn from the career of Mr. Gandhi.

Mr. Gandhi's speech was colourless and formal; he expressed the gratefulness of the Indians in South Africa to the mother country which contributed lavishly to the fund for their relief during the late struggle. He said it was a pleasure to meet Mr. Tilak in Bombay as he fully intended to pay his respects to him when he visited Poona.

Mr. Baptista said that it did not matter whom Mr. Gandhi selected as his guru (this refers to a remark made by Mr. Gandhi that Mr. Gokhale was his guru), so long as he always held before him the ideals of honour and self-respect as he had done throughout his life. Both he and Mr. Ali Muhammad Bhimji referred to the gallant conduct of the Indian troops in support of the cause of right in the present war.

April 30, 1916

Belgaum Speech

A large gathering of people (about 1,000) assembled in Khotibis Wada in Raviwar Peth, Belgaum, on the night of the 30th of April, to hear Mr. M.K. Gandhi speak on the subject of

"The Depressed Classes". The audience was mainly composed of Lingayats and "Untouchables". R.S. Shivmurti Swami Kanabargi presided.

Mr. Gandhi then rose and said that as was ill, he-would, only speak to them for a minute. He deprecated their opposition to the holding of the Provincial Conference in Belgaum. The principal object for the holding of the Conference was to effect a reconciliation between the two political parties. Home Rule must be granted to India and all classes should present a united front in demanding it. If Home Rule should be granted, no particular class would dominate, otherwise it would not be Home Rule. He for one would oppose any party or class that wanted to set itself above the others. He made no distinction between the higher and the lower classes and did not look with disdain upon a man simply because he was a sweeper or a barber, nor did he look up to anyone merely because he was a Brahmin. His religion taught him to consider all men alike, without distinction of class or creed. Home Rule would not be granted so long as there were differences between them. He promised to do all in his power to remove their disabilities.

Bombay Provincial Conference Speech at Belgaum

May 1, 1916

Mr. Gandhi spoke as follows in Hindustani... He was an outsider in the sense that he was not a member of the nationalist party or for that matter of any party. He had no mental desire for listening to the speeches or to his own voice but he had felt it his duty as an aspirant for national service to study all the institutions he could and hence it was that he found himself at the Belgaum Conference. He was desirous of being present there as he was anxious to see the inauguration of an era of peace between the two great parties which, he was assured would take place at Belgaum. It was a matter to him, therefore, of great pleasure that the foundation for unity was being laid at the Conference. He heartily supported the resolution moved by Mr. Tilak. He was sure he was not expected to endorse every word of the resolution on the report that was adopted. It should be enough that he found himself in agreement with the main draft of the resolution. Had the wording of the resolution been in his own hand, he would probably have omitted some expressions. Mr. Tilak's speech left nothing to be desired and he if worked as he was sure he would, and the nationalist party as a whole also worked truly in the spirit of the resolution and Mr. Tilak's remarks, he was sure that the coming union would be a great blessing to the motherland. It was for that reason that he found himself in disagreement with Mr. Baptisa, who seemed to be so much in tune with the pleaders. If they approached the question in the pleaders' spirit they would be constantly picking holes. What was needed was to approach the national question as common men. They would then overlook the faults and defects in their erstwhile opponents but would ever seek points of agreement and contact. Indeed if the party returned to the Congress fold with an absolutely honest and selfless spirit, ever thinking of the country and its cause and never thinking of party or personal gain, God would be with them and with God with them the nation could then (go) forward in the face of the world's opposition.

Gandhi wrote to Tilak

Ahmedabad
July 27, 1915

Dear Mr. Tilak,

I have your note. I have not given anyone any authority to use my name in connection with the interviews I had with you. I have not even read the things you are referring to. The conversations between us were private and must remain so. The draft sent by you hardly does justice to the interview. I never said that I spoke for the Congress party or with its authority. I simply came as a friend and admirer and for friends. I did not know what view the Congress party would take. I simply put a tentative proposal before you.

I hope you will respect my wish not to be drawn in a newspaper controversy and that you will in no case publish the interview.

I am,
Yours sincerely,
M.K. Gandhi

At Ashram

March 17, 1918

The step I have just now taken is a very grave one, but at the back of it there stands a great idea. It is grave because, on hearing of this all those who know me in India will be very much pained, be almost in an agony of grief. But, at the same time, I have here an opportunity to convey to them a beautiful idea, and

I should not miss it. This is the motive behind my action. I have been getting quite impatient for the last two days to explain it to you but I could not get enough quiet time for that. It would make me very unhappy to miss the morning and evening prayers in the Ashmore. And, besides, yesterday the music maestro dropped in and so I just would not forgo the pleasure of hearing his strains. I have swum past many a lure but many hungers still persist in me. At present I get here all that I long for by way of music and, therefore, although it was Anasuyabehn's express wish yesterday that I should stay on there, I insisted on coming over to the Ashram. At a time like this, the music here has a very soothing effect on me. This is in deed the best occasion for me to unburden my soul to you. At other hours, you are likely to be busy with your work and to make you leave that and assemble here-that won't be proper either. From the ancient culture of India, I have gleaned a truth which, even if it is mastered by the few persons here at the moment, would give these few a mastery over the world. Before telling you of it, however, I should like to say another thing. At present, there is only one person in India over whom millions are crazy, for whom millions of our countrymen would lay down their lives. That person is Tilak Maharaj. I often feel that this is a great asset of his, his great treasure. He has written on the inner meaning of the Gita. But I have always felt that he has not understood the age-old spirit of India, has not understood her soul and that is the reason why the nation has come to this pass. Deep down in his heart, he would like us all to be what the Europeans are.

As Europe stands on top at present, as it seems, that is, to those whose minds are steeped in European notions-he wants India to be in the same position. He under went six years' internment but only to display a courage of the European variety, with the idea that these people who are tyranizing over us now may learn how, if it came to that, we too could stand such long terms of internment, be it five years or twenty-five. In the prison of Siberia, many great men of Russia are wasting their whole lives, but these men did not go to prison in obedience to any spiritual promptings. To be thus prodigal of one's life is to expend our highest treasure to no purpose. If Tilakji had undergone the sufferings of internment with a spiritual motive, things would not have been as they are and the results of his internment would have been far different. This is what I should like to explain to him. I have often, with great respect, spoken about this to him, as much as I could, though I have not put the thing in so many words orally or in writing. I might have, in what I wrote, watered down my meaning, but Tilak Maharaj has so penetrating an intellect that he would understand. This is, however, no matter to be explained orally or in writing. To give him first-hand experience of it, I must furnish a living example. Indirectly, I have spoken to him often enough but, should I get an opportunity of providing a direct demonstration, I should not miss it, and here is one. Another such person is Madan Mohan Malaviya. Amongst the present leaders of India, he is a man of the holiest character-that is, amongst political personages and amongst those whom we know. Unknown to us, there may be many such indeed. But although he is so holy in his life and so well informed on points of dharma, he has not, it seems to me, properly understood the soul of India in all its grandeur.

I am afraid I have said too much. If he were to hear this, Malaviyaji might get angry with me, even think of me as a swollen-headed man and take a dislike to me. But I feel no hesitation in saying what I do because it is quite true. I have spoken to him many times. I am bound to him by ties of affection and hence I have even indulged in frequent wranglings with him. At the end of all my arguments, however, he would merely say that all I had said might be true but that he was not convinced of it. I have this opportunity to provide him, too, with a direct demonstration. I owe it to both to show now what India's soul is. For the last twenty days, I have been mixing with ten thousand millhands. In my presence, they took a pledge in the name of God. At the time, they did so with great enthusiasm. Whatever type of people they are, they all believe at any rate that God exists. They thought that, when they had observed the pledge for twenty days, God was bound to come to their help.

When that did not happen and God prolonged the test, their faith faltered. They felt that, led by this one man, they had suffered all these days but gained nothing whatever, that if they had not allowed themselves to be prevailed upon by him but had turned militant, they would have had their 35 per cent, or even more, in a much shorter time. This is my analysis of how their minds work. I can never bear to be in such a situation. That a pledge once taken, at my instance, should be so lightly broken and that faith in God should decline means certain annihilation of dharma. I simply cannot live to be a witness to this in any activity to which I am a party. I must impress upon the minds of the mill-hands what it is to take a pledge. I must show to them what I can do for a pledge; if I did not, I would be a coward. For a man who brags of clearing seven feet, not to clear even one is impotence. Well, then, to keep those ten thousand men from failing, I took this step. This was why I took the vow and its impact was electrifying. I had never expected this. The thousands of men present there shed tears from their eyes. They awoke to the reality of their soul, a new consciousness stirred in them and they got strength to stand by their pledge. I was instantly persuaded that dharma had not vanished from India, that people do respond to an appeal to their soul. If Tilak Maharaj and Malaviyaji would but see this, great things could be done in India. I am at present overflowing with joy. When, on a former occasion, I took such a vow, my mind did not enjoy the peace it does today. I also felt at that time the pull of the body. This time I experience nothing of the kind. My mind is filled with profound peace. I feel like pouring forth my soul to you all but I am beside myself with joy. My pledge is directed to making the mill-hands honour theirs and teaching them what value to attach to a pledge. For people in our country to take pledges whenever they fancy and break them at any moment betrays their degraded state. And for ten thousand mill-hands to break faith with themselves would spell ruin for the nation.

It would never again be possible to raise the workers' issues. At every turn they would quote this as an example and say that ten thousand mill-hands endured suffering for twenty days with a man like Gandhi to lead them and still they did not win. I was thus forced to consider by what means the mill-hands could be made to remain firm. How could I do this without suffering myself ? I saw that it was necessary to show them by example how, for the sake of one's pledge, one had to undergo suffering. So it was that I took this pledge. I am aware that it carries a taint. It is likely that, because of my vow, the mill-owners may be moved by consideration for me and come to grant the workers' (demand for) thirty-five per cent increase. My desire is that they should grant the demand only if they see its justice and not out of charity. But the natural result would be that they would do so out of charity and to that extent this pledge is one which cannot but fill me with shame. I weighed the two things, however, against each other : my sense of shame and the millhands' pledge.

The balance tilted in favour of the latter and I resolved, for the sake of the mill-hands, to take no thought of my shame. In doing public work, a man must be prepared to put up even with such loss of face. Thus, my pledge is not at all by way of a threat to the mill-owners; on the contrary, I wish they clearly understand this and grant the 35 per cent to the mill-hands only if they think it just to do so. To the mill hands, too, I would say that they should go to the owners and tell them as much.

Gandhi wrote to Viceroy

Delhi,
April 29, 1918

Sir,

As you are aware, after careful consideration, I felt constrained to convey to Your Excellency that I could not attend the Conference for reasons stated in my letter of the 26th instant. But after the interview you were good enough to grant me, I persuaded myself to join it—if for no other cause, then certainly out of my great regard for yourself. One of my reasons for abstention—and perhaps the strongest—was that Mr. Tilak, Mr. Besant, and the brothers Ali, whom I regard as among the most powerful leaders of public opinion, were not invited to the Conference. I still feel that it was a grave blunder not to have asked them, and I respectfully suggest that the blunder might be partially repaired if these leaders were invited to assist the Government by giving it the benefit of their advice at the Provincial Conferences which, I understand, are to follow. I venture to submit that no Government can afford to disregard leaders who represent large masses of the people, as these do, even though they may held views fundamentally different. At the same time, it gives me pleasure to be able to say that the views of all parties were permitted to be freely expressed at the Committees of the Conference, For my own part, I purposely refrained from stating my views, either at the Committee-on which I had the honour of serving-or at the Conference itself. I felt that I could best serve the objects of the Conference by simply tendering my support to the resolutions submitted to it—and this I have done without any reservation. I hope to translate the spoken word into action as early as the Government can see its way to accept my offer, which I am submitting simultaneously herewith in a separate letter. I recognize that, in the hour of its danger, we must give—as we have decided to give-ungrudging and unequivocal support to the Empire, of which we aspire, in the near future, to be partners in the same sense as the Dominions overseas. But it is the simple truth that our response is due to the expectation that our goal will be reached all the more speedily on that account-even as the performance of a duty automatically confers a corresponding right.

The people are entitled to believe that the imminent reforms alluded to in your speech will embody the main general principles of the Congress League Scheme, and I am sure that it is this faith which has enabled many members of the Conference to tender to the Government their whole-hearted cooperation. If I could make my countrymen retrace their steps, I would make them withdraw all the Congress resolutions, and not whisper "Home Rule" or "Responsible Government" during the pendency of the war. I would make India offer all her able-bodied sons as a sacrifice to the Empire at its critical moment; and I known that India by this very act would become the most favoured partner in the Empire and racial distinctions would become a thing of the past. But practically the whole of educated India has decided to take a less effective course, and it is no longer possible to say that educated India does not exercise any influence on the masses. I have been coming into most intimate touch with the ryots ever since my return from South Africa to India, and I wish to assure you that the desire for Home Rule has widely penetrated them.

I was present at the sessions of the last Congress, and I was party to the resolution that full Responsible Government should be granted to British India within a period to be fixed definitely by a Parliamentary Statute. I admit that it is a bold step to take, but I feel sure that nothing less than a definite vision of Home Rule-to be realized in the shortest possible time will satisfy the Indian people. I know that there are many in India who consider no sacrifice too great in order to achieve the end; and they are wakeful enough to realize that they must be equally prepared to sacrifice themselves for the Empire in which they hope and desire to reach their final status. It follows, then, that we can but accelerate our journey towards the goal by silently and simply devoting ourselves, heart and soul, to the work of delivering the Empire from the threatening danger It will be national suicide not to recognize this elementary truth. We must perceive that, if we serve to save the Empire, we have in that very act secured Home Rule. Whilst, therefore, it is clear to me that we should give to the Empire every available man for its defence, I fear that I cannot say the same thing about financial assistance. My intimate intercourse with the ryots convinces me that India has already donated to the Imperial Exchequer beyond her capacity. I know that, in making this statement, I am voicing the opinion of the vast majority of my countrymen. The Conference means for me, and I believe for many of us, a definite step in the consecration of our lives to the common cause. But ours is a peculiar position. We are today outside the partnership. Ours is a consecration based on the hope of a better future. I should be untrue to you and to my country if I did not clearly and unequivocally tell you what that hope is. I do not bargain for its fulfilment. But you should know it. Disappointment of the hope means disillusion. There is one thing I may not omit. You have appealed to us to sink domestic differences. If the appeal involves the toleration of tyranny and wrongdoing on the part of officials, I am powerless to respond. I shall resist organized tyranny to the uttermost. The appeal must be to the officials that they do not ill-treat a single soul, and that they consult and respect popular opinion as never before. In Champaran, by resisting an age-long tyranny, I have shown the ultimate sovereignty of British justice. In Kaira, a population, that was cursing the Government now feels that it, and not the Government, is the power when it is prepared to suffer for the truth it represents. It is, therefore, losing its bitterness and is saying to itself that the Government must be a Government for the people, for it tolerates orderly and respectful disobedience where injustice is felt.

Thus, Champaran and Kaira affairs are my direct, definite, and special contribution to the war. Ask me to suspend my activities in that direction, and you ask me to suspend my life. If I could popularize the use of soul-force, which is but another name for love-force, in the place of brute force, I know that I could present you with an India that could defy the whole world to do its worst, In season and out of season, therefore, I shall discipline myself to express in my life this eternal law of suffering and present it for acceptance to those who care. And if I take part in any other activity, the motive is to show the matchless superiority of that law. Lastly, I would like you to ask His Majesty's Ministers to give definite assurances about Mohammedan States. I am sure You know that every Mohammedan is deeply interested in them.

As a Hindu, cannot be indifferent to their cause. Their sorrows must be our sorrows. In the most scrupulous regard for the right of these States, and for the Muslim sentiment as to places of worship, and in your just and timely treatment of the Indian claim to Home Rule, lies the safety of the Empire.

I write this, because I love the English Nation, and I wish to evoke in every Indian the loyalty of the Englishman.

I remain,
Your Excellency's faithful servant,,
M.K. Gandhi

Gandhi wrote to Lord Willingdon

Bombay,
June 11, 1918

Dear Lord Willingdon,

I trust you will not misunderstand this note.

I venture to think that your stopping of Messrs. Tilak and Kelkar yesterday was a serious blunder. They had been informed on your behalf that they could offer criticism but they could not move an amendment. Your having stopped them will be resented as an insult to a great and growing party in the country. Your action has made the position of workers delicate and difficult and if Mr. Tilak is an enemy of the Government or of the Empire you have undoubtedly strengthened his hands in the pursuit of his course. But if you had allowed him and Mr. Kelkar to have their say, they would have gone away satisfied and it could have been said that you had given fair play to all. Will you not publicly express your regret for the blunder or send for both of them, expressing your regret to them, and invite their cooperation and discuss their viewpoint ? You will lose nothing and you will gain greatly in the estimation of the people, enhance your prestige, increase your capacity for securing help from the people and possibly win over the Home Rule party, and also nip in the bud an agitation that is bound to spring up in the country.

I repeat my request that you will not misunderstand this note, which is prompted by nothing but goodwill.

I remain,
Your faithful friend
M.K. Gandhi

Ahmedabad Speech

June 24, 1918

You all know the purpose of this meeting. You also know that Bombay has protest against the insulting behaviour of His Excellency the Governor towards members of the Home Rule League at the War Conference. At the Bombay meeting, too, I was in the chair and, having expressed my views there, I shall not take much of your time. This meeting is for, two things : one, to support the action of Bombay and, two, to explain the position to those who do not read newspapers and, since even newspaper reports are often fragmentary and incorrect, to place the facts before newspaper readers as well. This is what today's meeting is for. His Excellency the Governor was faced with the question whether or not to invite Mr. Tilak and other swarajists to the War Conference. Since Mr. Tilak and Mrs. Besant had not been invited to the Delhi Conference, the question was an unusual one for Lord Willingdon and he gave it careful consideration. In the end, he invited them and Mr. Tilak accepted the invitation. The latter enquired whether he would be free to address the Conference and whether any amendments would be in order. He was told in reply that no amendments to the resolutions could be moved but that, after selected speakers had addressed the Conference on the resolutions, he would be free to speak and comment on their views. His Excellency sincerely meant what he said and there was no ambiguity in his words. And so Mr. Tilak and others went to the Conference. But what was their experience there ? Before Mr. Tilak had completed his second sentence, His Excellency the Governor interrupted him-stopped him from making any criticism. He did not know what Mr. Tilak wished to say. He knew nothing, of course, about what the speech would be like. And yet, believing that the sentence which Mr. Tilak had commenced with a 'but' would be objectionable, the Governor did not allow him to complete it and stopped him from proceeding further. Not that His Excellency would not have been within his rights in doing so, on some other occasion. It was, however, improper of him to have thus stopped a guest whom he had invited to his place to address a meeting and, in doing so, he has offered a gross insult to Mr. Tilak and the other distinguished guests, in fact to all the people of India. Mr. Tilak is no ordinary man. He is adored by the whole of India. It is really intolerable that he should have been ordered in this manner to resume his seat. We have assembled here today to demonstrate that the people of Ahmedabad too cannot tolerate this and to support Bombay's action. In this we are but doing our duty and showing ourselves to be true swarajists. It must be one of the implications of swaraj that any insult to India should be treated as an insult to Indian independence. We have come together today to call the Governor to account for having insulted Indian independence. We should tell him that he has offered us a serious insult and that he should apologize for that. With few exceptions, there is no newspaper in India which has approved of the Governor's action. They have all condemned it. Even The Pioneer has done so and said that when the need of the hour is to enlist the cooperation of the people such an incident should not have taken place. It has gone further and advised the Governor to swallow the bitter drought and get on with the work. The object of this meeting in Ahmedabad and the resolutions it is to pass are quite in order. One of the resolutions calls upon the Governor to apologize and says that, should he fail to do so, His Excellency the Viceroy should intervene and express his disapproval of the Governor's action, and further that, unless this is done, Home Rulers will not attend any meeting presided over by Lord Willingdon. We do not wish to extend our displeasure with him to the Empire nor to run away from our present duties. In the second resolution, we point out the difficulties we encounter in helping the Government. Our intention in it is to assert that we wish to help it, but cannot do so fully because there are certain things which need to be done, and which only the Government can do, before we can help. In saying that it cannot afford to ignore the educated classes and that the Indian soldier will not rest satisfied with rights inferior to those enjoyed by the British soldier, we also point to our difficulties and argue that, if we have not been able to help, the reason lies with the Government itself. Let this cause be removed and we shall then withdraw our charge against it. This is not enough, however.

There are certain things we must ourselves do. If we do not, we shall fail in our duty as swarajists. We pray to God to grant us swaraj this very day. But God tells us that we shall get it when we deserve it. If He were to give us all that we pray for, there would be complete chaos in the world. We have to prove our fitness for swaraj. We have ample material with which to 'silence our enemies, but it is our duty to see our defects as they are. If, being angry with the Government for these defects, we keep thinking of its shortcomings and sit back with folded hands, we shall never come to enjoy swaraj. Travelling all over India, I have gathered that her people want to live, as those of Canada and Australia do, as citizens having equal rights with the Government. We want it to obtain our consent for carrying on the war and only then ask us to contribute men and money. If our intention is not to leave the Empire, it is to our advantage to Work with the British as partners. Our first and last duty is to join the Empire in making sacrifices and to make them courageously. It is only thus we shall succeed in getting swaraj early. Our duty is two-fold : to resist injustice and take the necessary steps to end it and, at the same time, to stand by the Government in its hour of difficulty. If we mind these two duties, we shall have proved our bonafides. If we want to disprove the charge against us, we should give it no reason to doubt our loyalty-this is the only real way to punish it. There is another aspect to this resolution, which, too, you should consider. I have had a letter from Mr. Tilak in which he says that, if the Government of India would place the Indian soldier on the same footing as the British soldier, he would be prepared to give 5,000 men in six months and, should he fail, to pay a penalty of Rs. 100/ - for every man (short of that figure). For this purpose, he has also sent me a cheque for Rs. 50,000, 1 have had talks with Mr. Jinnah and Mrs. Besant, too, on this subject. They have admitted that we should supply the required number of men to the Empire. Mr. Tilak believes that, if we make definite conditions with the Government for helping it, no room would be left for any misunderstanding afterwards and that, therefore, that is the course we should adopt. I hold, on the contrary, that we lose nothing by trusting, and so I have no hesitation in advising people to join up. We shall, by doing so, get what we have been demanding. I believe in trusting people and my advice, therefore, is that we should proceed on the basis of trust. I have attended this meeting to tell you that, if your chanting of the swaraj mantra is to be efficacious, you should do your duty. To wipe out the blot on the face of Gujarat, people should take to careers in the army. This is the best way of learning to defend Ahmedabad, should it ever be raided. We do not propose to turn this into a recruitment meeting but, when such a meeting is called, you should not fail in your duty.

Gandhi wrote to Maganlal Gandhi

Bombay,
Ashadh Sud 6 (July 14, 1918)

Chi. Maganlal,

I could not return (to the Ashram) after seeing Mr. Pratt, for I heard that Jagjivandas had been taken ill and I had to go to Nadiad. At Pratt's, a number of Englishmen surrounded me and started talking very pleasantly. They expressed a desire to go and see the Ashram. I invited them to come over on Saturday. Most probably, I shall be there. If I can start in time, I may arrive by the afternoon train on that day. Even if I don't, you should expect them. They may be there any time in the evening after five. I have told them that they would see things better if they could stay till prayer time. See that the boys, or the leading ones among them, are taught the English hymns. Sing Lead Kindly Light. If they come at five, show them the kitchen, etc., and the food.

I write this letter from Bombay. I came here directly from Karamsad. Tilak Maharaj is here. As it has been suggested to me that I should give out my views on the Reform Scheme only after seeing Tilak Maharaj in Bombay, I am busy seeing people. I shall be back in Nadiad on Wednesday evening. I shall leave here on Tuesday evening but shall be going to Godhra on my way. From there, I shall go to Nadiad the same day.

Blessing from
Bapu

(Ps.)

You must be putting the accounts in order. Get someone to help you in this, if necessary, and do so.

Karamsad Speech

July 14, 1918

(Gandhiji) said at the outset that he was there to give them an unpalatable dose and he hoped that they would not turn away from it all at once, bearing in mind that one of the principal characteristics of a self-governing and liberty-loving people was to give ear to all counsel and to choose one that appealed to them most. What, he asked them, was the meaning of swarajya ? Our villages are no better than dung-hills; we cannot defend ourselves and our families against robbers or wild beasts; nukhis and rawanias coerce and oppress us as they will; we have no arms and we do not know the use of arms. Is this swarajya ? And yet, this is the natural order throughout India.

Imagine the tidiness and the atmosphere of quiet and healthy independence of an English village and think how miserably an Indian village compares with it. It is because every Englishman can stand on his legs and can defend his home and his village against any invader that the English village appears so incomparably superior to ours.

The first essential of swarajya is, thus, the power of self-protection. I am fit for swarajya only when I am able to defend myself and to shed my blood for my country, and India could be said to be living only if five lakhs of men lay down their lives for her. A seed must lose itself in earth in order that numerous seeds may spring up from it. Even so, from the ashes of the thousands dying for India, will spring up a living India. We Indians visit temples every morning and evening and pay our obeisance to gods-gods who, we say, descend on earth to protect the weak and succour the oppressed, when virtue subsides and vice prevails. It then ill becomes us to go to these temples. If we have not the spirit and the capacity of self-defence in us. And what verily did our Ramachandra and Krishna do ? They modelled heroes out of common clay and equipped them for self-defence. The golden opportunity for acquiring the power of self-defence has come to us and it behooves us to seize it and profit by it. An Empire that has been defending India and of which India aspires to be the equal partner is in great peril and it ill befits India to stand aloof at this juncture.

Madras Speech on Non-Cooperation

August 12, 1920

Mr. Chairman and Friends,

Like last year, I have to ask your forgiveness that I should have to speak being seated. Whilst my voice has become stronger than it was last year, my body is still weak; and if I were to attempt to speak to you standing, I could not hold on for very many minutes before the whole frame would shake. I hope, therefore, that you will grant me permission to speak seated. I have sat here to address you on a most important question, probably a question whose importance we have not measured up to now. But before I approach that question on this dear old beach of Madras, you will expect me-you will want me to offer my tribute to the great departed, Lokmanya Tilak Maharaj. (Loud and prolonged cheers.) I would ask this great assembly to listen to me in silence. I have come to make an appeal to your heart and to your reason and I could not do so unless you were prepared to listen to whatever I have to say in absolute silence. I wish to offer my tribute to the departed patriot and I think that I cannot do better than say that his death, as his life, has poured new vigour into the country. If you were present as I was present at that great funeral procession, you would realize with me the meaning of my words. Mr. Tilak lived for his country.

The inspiration of his life was freedom for his country which he called swaraj; the inspiration of his deathbed was also freedom for his country. And it was that which gave him such marvellous , hold upon his countrymen; it was that which commanded the adoration not of a few chosen Indians belonging to the upper strata of society but of millions of his countrymen. His life was one long sustained piece of self-sacrifice. He began that life of discipline and self-sacrifice in 1879 and he continued that life up to the end of his day, and that was the secret of his hold upon his country. He not only knew what he wanted for his country but also how to live for his country and how to die for his country. I hope then that whatever I say this evening to this vast mass of people, will bear fruit in that same sacrifice for which the life of Lokmanya Tilak Maharaj stands. His life, if it teaches us anything whatsoever, teaches one supreme lesson; that if we want to do anything whatsoever for our country, we can do so not by speeches, however grand, eloquent and convincing they may be, but only by sacrifice at the back of every word and at the back of every act of our life. I have come to ask everyone of you whether you are ready and willing to give sufficiently for your country's sake, for your country's honour and for religion. I have boundless faith in you, the citizens of Madras, and the people of this great presidency, a faith which I began to cultivate in the year 1893 when I first made acquaintance with the Tamil labourers in South Africa; and I hope that, in these hours of our trial, this province will not be second to any other in India, and that it will lead in this spirit of self-sacrifice and will translate every word into action.

Why Non-cooperation?

What is this non-cooperation about which you have heard much, and why do we want to offer this non-cooperation? I wish to go for the time being into the why. There are two things before this country. The first and the foremost is the khilafat question. On this the heart of the Musalmans of India has become lacerated. British pledges, given after the greatest deliberation by the: Prime

Minister of England in the name of the English nation, have been dragged into the mire. The promises given to Muslim India, on the strength of which the consideration that was accepted by the British nation was exacted, have been broken and the great religion of Islam has been placed in danger. The Musalmans hold and I venture to think they rightly hold-that so long as British promises remain unfulfilled so long is it impossible for them to tender whole-hearted fealty and loyalty to the British connection; and if it is to be a choice for a devout Musalman between loyalty to the British connection and loyalty to his Code and Prophet, he will not require a second to make his choice and he has declared his choice.

The Musalmans say frankly; openly and honourably to the whole world that if the British ministers and the British nation do not fulfil the pledges given to them and do not wish to regard with respect the sentiments of 70 millions of the inhabitants of India who profess the faith of Islam, it will be impossible for them to retain Islamic Loyalty. It is a question, then, for the rest of the Indian population to consider whether they want to perform a neighbourly duty by their Musalman countrymen and if they do, they have an opportunity of a lifetime which will not occur for another hundred years, to show their goodwill, fellowship and friendship and to prove what they have been saying for all these long years that the Musalman is the brother of the Hindu. If the Hindu regards that before the connection with the British nation comes his natural connection with his Muslim brother, then I say to you that if you find that the Muslim claim is just, that-it is based upon real sentiment, and that at its background is this great religious feeling, you cannot do otherwise than help the Musalmans through and through so long as their cause remains just and the means for attaining the end remains equally just, honourable and free from harm to India. These are the plain conditions which the Indian Musalmans have accepted and it was when they saw that they could accept the preferred aid of the Hindus, that they could always justify the cause and the means before the whole world, that they decided to accept the preferred hand of fellowship. It is then for Hindus and Musalmans to offer a united front to the whole of the Christian powers of Europe and tell them that weak as India is, India has still got the capacity of preserving her self-respect, she still knows how to die for her religion and for her self-respect. That is the khilafat in a nutshell; but you have also got the Punjab. The Punjab has wounded the heart of

India as no other question has for the past century. I do not exclude from my calculation the Mutiny of 1857. Whatever hardships India had to suffer during the Mutiny, the insult that was attempted to be offered to her during the passage of the Rowlatt legislation, and that which was offered after its passage, were unparalleled in Indian history. It is because you want justice from the British nation in connection with the Punjab atrocities; you have to devise ways and means as to how you can get this justice. The House of Commons, the Lords, Mr. Montague, the Viceroy of India, everyone of them knows what the feeling of India is on this khilafat question and on that of the Punjab; the debates in both the Houses of Parliament, the action of Mr. Montague and that of the Viceroy have demonstrated to you completely that they are not willing to give the justice which is India's due and which she demands. I suggest that our leaders have got to find a way out of this great difficulty and unless we have made ourselves even with the British rulers in India, and unless we have gained a measure of self-respect at the hands of the British rulers in India, no connection and no friendly intercourse is possible between them and ourselves. 1, therefore, venture to suggest this beautiful unanswerable method of non-cooperation.

12

TILAK : AN OVERVIEW

The Personality and Life-Philosophy of Lokmanya Tilak

The personality and life-philosophy of Lokmanya Bal Gangadhar Tilak had a profound effect on his society.He had contributed to almost all important fields like politics, social reforms, philosophy and education. The objectives of education were not very clear to many people. For Tilak, learning was not just acquisition of knowledge useful in preparing for native clerical jobs. The creation of educated men through the learning process was certainly beneficial to the alien rulers for running their administrative machinery. People so turned out, welcomed the golden fetters, by entering in to Government jobs. To break through this British black magic was the first and foremost need of the hour. The venerable Vishnushastri Chiplunkar was one such social leader, who had crushed these fetters of Governmental service, and, started the monthly publication of his 'Nibandhamala' ('Series of Essays') through which he used to impart real instruction to the people on their 'Mother Land, Language and Religion'. Through his writings he used to expound forcefully the significance of the loss of 'freedom' and of Self-Government.

All this happened when the British rule was, of half a century old. People, as well as, their leaders had come to look upon the British rule as a Divine Gift and British as their respected preceptors and such ideas had become firmly rooted in their thinking. They had got excited and captivated by the wholesome results of the British Rule. Slowly however, the wicked intentions of the rulers were getting clear, and with it, dawned the realisation, that loss of freedom stood for, not mere loss of political power, but for total destruction of the indigenous culture, religion and language. The enlightenment of the true difference between slavery and independence, and consequential awareness of the responsibility to awaken the masses to this reality, were at work in the founding of an independent school by leaders like Chiplunkar, Tilak and others.

Tilak and other leaders established the New English School (1880), The Fergusson College (1884) and The Deccan Education Society (1885). The curriculum, the teaching methods and the examination system, were the same old ones, but with the difference of having the Management, the teachers, the atmosphere, all being Indian. Tilak was one of the founder members of this Institution and was also on its teaching faculty. But in the course of time he came to realise that he could not be totally at one with its policies and practices; and, when his differences mounted high, he dissociated himself from the D.E. Society. Lying open before him then was a vast field of social service at school, college or university levels and at the levels beyond, all totally untitled and demanding the services of an efficient ploughman. What was being carried earlier through 'Nibandhamala' by Vishushastri Chiplunkar, was undertaken by Tilak with great vigour and tenacity and on a comprehensive scale. Of these duties he was quite clear and cognizant in mind, right from the moment of his founding the school. Almost simultaneously and within one year after the establishment of the school, that is in 1881, the weeklies Kesari (in Marathi) and Mahratta (in English) were started. In 1889 Tilak devoted himself wholly to the responsibilities of the Kesari, and thus commenced his life of rigour as a Nation-educator. Tilak became a national-teacher.

What is the content of National Education? During the days of bondage, the first and foremost aim of education, is to arouse among the masses an urge for freedom and to prepare them for a fight for freedom; to arouse the complacent masses with an awareness of their dormant potential and to employ that in the fight for freedom. This was the objective that motivated Tilak and in what was reflected allegorically in the motto chosen by Tilak for the Kesari. The verse runs thus :

What is it that constitutes National education? It covers everything that records the country's glorious past in the fields of religion, culture and literature, also an examination of its present-day-ills, and, above all, an anxious thought to the ways and means of fighting of their root-cause viz. the foreign rule- the syllabi of national education comprise thoughts to the indigenous, the foreigners, the Nation, the independence, means of winning independence, as to who can be the rightful claimants of self-rule, the nation's strength, and spots of strength and weakness of the foreign-rule. The study material thus includes all the above, plus the up-to-date information on the ever-moving current of affairs in various fields. National education involves correct decisions amidst ever-fluctuating situations and exact guidance to people of different dispositions, rising united with a lion's strength. What Tilak did was the awakening of such a lion of the populace who was burning with the fire of Inward-Strength. His roaring proclamation as - "Self-Rule is my birth- right and I shall not fail to achieve it" - started reverberating through the caves and dens of the minds of the Indian people. Never must have, allegorical verse-lines been put to such effective use among the masses.

Successing this mission demanded a varied combination of tremendous intelligence, unswerving faith, utter fearlessness, steady mind, selflessness, firmness, high courage and readiness to go behind the bars. And all this in turn demanded a firm philosophical foundation and practical awareness. It also needs the skill and resourcefulness in a judicious use of strength and tact while leading the masses in fighting with the foreign rulers. For, politics is not a unisided affair, but one which touches and enters all compartments of life, of the society, and, is double-faced through its spontaneous and circumstantial rules. This requires strategy in both speech and writing, facing challenges of all nature and unfailing shooting of the target much like Rama's arrows from the ever full-quivers.

Earlier newspapers and periodicals in Maharashtra had carried the movement of spread of education. Knowledge brings about new awakening and new sharpness, but not necessarily a will to act. This latter part requires a countrywide philosophy and application of intellect. What Lokmanya Tilak did, was putting an end to mere propagation of knowledge and starting an era of actual activity. He transformed the newspapers into viewspapers and verily into missiles. This needs a basis of a different kind of intelligence and mental power from the one, in the field of mere academic education.

Three media of mass-education were current in Tilak's times; educational institutions, religious platforms and news-papers or public lectures. If he wished Tilak could have been quite successful in the first two; he could have been a teacher of high order with his intellectual and scholarly capacities; he could also have been a good teacher imparting religious discourses in the cause of the nation, knowing fully well its effectiveness and power (as he once remarked about his preferences in life). He does not exclude using the temple-institutions in the service of the Nation, and gave a wide social base to the institution on religious discourses. Festivals likeand represent only new, extended, religious and national forms of the same. These festivals contributed largely in creating Tilak's image as a National Teacher. A new concept viz. that of 'National-Devotee'() arose and the old one of a 'Religious-Devotee'()received social and national dimensions. We thus realise how Tilak's concept of education was extensive enough ranging over the whole of country and combining tradition with modernity. He was ever inventing new and newer media to be put to service in his mission.

This mission of national education and social organisation which he carried with unflinching faith and spiritual strength was the outcome of the life-foundations he secured from the 'Bhagwadgita'. One can know the personality and life-philosophy of Tilak best through his marvelous book 'Gita-Rahasya'(). This was not written just with the help of ancient commentaries, which no doubt he had well gone-through, but in addition, he had studied the Upanishads, the theistic as well as atheistic systems of Indian philosophy, the Great Epicsp Ramayan and Mahabharat and the Puranic literature. Further, through comparative study of the Eastern and Western doctrines, rose his deep conviction that the yoga propounded in the Gita was the 'Yoga of self-less Action' (). The sub-title he gave to his book was 'The Hindu Philosophy of Life, Ethics and Religion', requesting the readers to refer to his book for answers to questions on correct duty () or its reverse (.)

He has dedicated his work not to any dear one, a preceptor or a deity, but to the 'Mankind Deified' 'To the Divine Lord united with the Populace' that makes clear how he treated the Society as Divine Manifestation, and how his writing of this book stood for his life-philosophy.

That the life-breath of the Gita was 'Desireless Action' was Tilak's firm faith and the key-teaching of the Gita is condensed, according to him, in the stanza-

"Your authority extends only as far as doing the duty it is not within your perview to think of fruit thereof; hence, never pin your eyes upon the results of your action; neither insist on not doing the action".

This stanza through its four quarters, which are beautifully complementary to each other, makes a wonderful Quadruplet for the philosophy of 'life of Desireless Action'. Tilak's commentary on this stanza is worth constant contemplation. Says he, that after stating that one must stop at doing duty, there is a natural expectancy of one's rightfully enjoying its fruit also. So the next line was needed to the fruit, and also the third line asking not be motivated by the fruit while doing the duty. The last line emphasises one's not abandoning action and asks never to entertain such a thought, for one must do the assigned duty, at all cost. 'Duty one must never run away from, neither perform it with attachment,' is thus the gist of the Quadruplet.

This 'Desireless Duty' that is taught here is an introduction to the 'Soul Steady-in-Reason' referred to in the following stanza -

'When one casts away all the longings of the mind,' and gets contented with one's own state, then one is called as 'One of Steadied Intellect'.

Three qualities are essentially needed to attain this state of mind :

(1) Discriminative faculty,

(2) Benigness towards all creatures,

(3) Unification and welfare of society,

The first one is apparent in the judgement of desirable and undesirable nature of actions. For it is a thought upon the pros and cons or the propriety and impropriety of an act that gives rise to the will to act. Those whose discerning faculty is not steady, go on continually receiving waves of new and newer ideas and thus can not gain concentration on anything. Their thinking is called 'arresting thinking' which, to be transformed into discerning thinking, needs a clear knowledge of what is meritorious or otherwise, moral or immoral, selfish or selfless. This requires having eyes ever fixed on universal good and on how to attain it. A person with such an attitude alone can show discrimination in right and wrong actions. The outburst "I am immersed in concerns about the universe coming from Samartha Ramdas can be said to be representing this very mental make-up. In truth, those are sages of high spiritual attainment, who are ever engrossed in the furtherance of welfare of all creatures; but those who translate this spiritual practice in to the life of worldly activities must be looked up on as persons of a superior order. They are actively working for the uplift of the entire society.

The significance of social unification and welfare has been explained at length and with a number of illustrations by Tilak. (Geeta Rahasya - pp-326-334) It does not mean merely assembling people, but linking them with similar ideals and aspirations and with the bonds of affection. This task involves constant thought on and working for their mental nourishment, their physical wellbeing, and ways and means of assuring these. Also it stands for leading to virtuous paths as for averting from going astray - "were I to abandon action, there will be world-wide catastrophe".

So says Lord Krishna, for, the common man imitates the actions of distinguished leaders. So it is the bounden duty of the wise, to set example in conduct to the society. Says Tilak in the same vein; "learned people are the very eyes of the society, and so their shirking from duty will lead to social destruction through mental blindness and imbalance" . Further; "the wise constitute the eyes of the society even its preceptors, mending the society when and where needed, so as to suit the changing times and region."

Tilak was engrossed in fixing the nature of his undertaking in arousing the strength of the masses and in reflecting on putting to effective urges suited to local conditions. Through his pen, he acted as a powerful watch-dog to every act on the part of the rulers. He analysed very meticulously and explained the results thereof to the society as well as to the Government. As a teacher performing this mission to the common man and to the intelligentsia, he was truly a National Teacher.

It was not that Tilak disapproved that the Gita brought about a reconciliation of 'Knowledge, Action and Devotion' . What was however important, was to which one of the three, he attached primacy. Concisely, he views the Gita as a religious text expounding 'life of action with Basis in Knowledge and Stress on Devotion . Here, the substantive 'Life of Action' he qualifies with the word Desireless' or 'detached'. Hence his most condensed description of the final teaching of the Gita is - 'Desireless Life of Action', which is also the fine thread running vibrantly through his entire life-activity. In its application this principle takes different shapes suiting different regional and temporal contexts, as has been explained at length by Tilak. His editorials deserve to be studied from this angle, highlighting a firm philosophical foundation, perfect awareness of practical situations, width of vision, exact analysis, vision of the consequences, impartiality in treatment and love for righteousness. . These qualities of his editorials, answering mainly the contemporary situation, raised them to all-time-relevance and permanent value. Thus Tilak did not give birth to a news-paper named 'Kesari', but to a 'Missile' in the form of editorials, which was put to effective use, also by those who came after him in the field.

Through these editorials Tilak imparted an education on 'what constitutes a nation?', 'Duty to Nation', and 'How to perform it.' His Gita-Rahasya is not a work expounding sectarian doctrines nor a commentary in the fashion of ancient commentators. Tilak is an expositor of the Gita, expounding deep 'Humanitarian Religion', especially enlightening on its practical aspect, beside its familiar spiritual one.

Before Tilak were the above solemn lines 'that is Duty which brings about material prosperity as well as spiritual good.' The Gita has praised King Janak as an ideal illustration of this.

"The word 'Dharma' is derived from the function of sustaining. Society is sustained through . So that in true Duty, which performs the function of sustaining (the society)." This was Tilak's view of Duty. In his reflections on Duty, we get beautifully combined the remarks from the Gita and from (in theof the).

From Tilak's discussion it is clearly felt that, if the Gita be called the 'Text of Spiritualism', the 's words sound its vivid Applications and that both the works proclaim identical principles.

Similarly, "The crux of duty is concealed in a cave. (Hence) the path followed by distinguished persons is (to be accepted as) Duty". This is the final advice, which stands for discrimination, exact analysis and guidance, as Tilak did after a close study and life-long experience. The range of Tilak's thinking was comprehensive and multifarious. He wanted to turn the train of the entire nation on to proper rails and also to speed it on.

Tilak's views on life and duty rested on the Eternal Law and theistic faith. While propagating, in practical life, the 'Desireless Life of Action' he believed in 'Final Emancipation' as the ultimate aim of man's action.

Agarkar, on the contrary, was a rationalist out and out, and was not ready to accept anything that went beyond reasoning. He threw asunder the credibility in word . A thorough secularist, he took God as an invention and as an aberration of mind. He was at the same time for liberty of thought. The first and the last tenet of humanitarianism, according to him, was "those who are dedicated to universal religion, the furtherance of welfare of mankind must fearlessly communicate to others, whatever they felt as correct, commendable and salubrious, and practice it as far as possible." He opted for the scientific mode of comparing and classifying observed situations and for ascertaining the rules working behind them, rather than entering into a metaphysical reasoning about them. What inspired the frame of his mind was the line of thinking of Comte, Mill and Spencer. viz to restrict thinking strictly within the bounds of proven facts, from direct perception and drawing inferences based on these alone.

Agarkar was a thinker of self luminous intellect. He firmly believed in intellect being the only reliable means to determine what is proper or improper, good or bad, and in the verdict it gave. To him all argumentation drawing authenticity from the Veda or Vedic tradition was futile and frivolous. Fanciful beliefs and practices rooted in the society were fought by him, tooth and nail, and so to castism and women's enslavement.

Tilak too, did not side with fantastic religious ideas and practices, and in principle, did not oppose Agargar on castism or on womens' plight. He however did not find reason to treat the crucial Hindu texts and doctrines as lacking in authority. On the contrary, he strongly believed these fundamentals as securing human-welfare, in this life and in life after death. Hence, he did not feel it necessary to flout the testimony of Veda and could not be blind to the fact that pure rationalism does not help realise the Ultimate Truth, and that pure intellect can not reach this height. He was a staunch upholder of Reason-based, Devotion-propelled Life of Action. Thus while not opposing the reforms in Hindu religion, he would not brook disowning the fundamental principals of Hindu Faith- He has elaborated his stand and ideas on the theory and practical conduct of Hinduism in an extensive article on the 'Character of Hindu Religion' and condensed that in the following three verses—

"Faith in the testimony of Veda, multiplicity of the Paths, (to reach the goal), freedom of Objects of Worship- this summarises the nature of Religion. Adhering to this religion and consecrated by the prescriptions of Law, as adumbrated in the Vedic and its ancillary traditional texts; or as befitting the course of time, ever engaged in practising the assigned duty, in full faith and out of full respect to the traditional texts - such alone could be called a 'True Hindu'".

Mahatma Gandhi has treated Gita as a text book on the 'Life of Detachment', . Lokmanya Tilak on title-page of his Gita-Rahasya quotes the Gita verses -

("Hence tirelessly perform (your) assigned duties in a detached mind; for so doing the duties, man attains the highest reward.") 'Desireless Life of Action' (of Lokmanya Tilak) is the same as the 'Life of Detachment' (of Gandhiji), though with a subtle distinction between the two. Gandhiji's theorisation, which is based on Truth and Non-violence demands utmost purity of conduct, as both untruth and violence are motivated by some kind of attachment of objects, or rewards in mind, and hence purity of means becomes necessary. It is different with the Desireless Life of Action (of Tilak) : Truth or Untruth and Violence or non-violence are to be contextually decided and adopted accordingly; even falsehood and injuriousness become lawful and righteous if circumstances demand those. The very genesis of the Gita is for the purpose of a correct (theoretical and practical) understanding of the lawfulness or otherwise in inflicting injury to beings. Bheeshma's Verdict on man's duty given at the end of the 'Mahabharat-War', clearly explains the distinction between the theory and practice of Duty, and the Mahabharat-stories also often bring about the meritorious nature of Violence in peculiar situations in life. Armed revolt thus becomes an act of duty under some circumstances. In the life of a nation, Krishna, the teacher of Yoga, as well as Arjun, the valiant warrior, both have honoured places, complementary to each-other and as exemplifying an integrated picture of 'Virtuous Life' . Religion if practised, protects the life of man, this is the axiom at the base of righteous life.

"For protecting the righteous and for annihilating the vicious, I take birth in each and every age". This promise from the Lord clearly makes room for violence where needed. These very words form (for Lokmanya Tilak), the base of the 'Life of Action' in his struggle for freedom. Rooted in truthfulness, but taking different forms, in different conditions, it is not degeneracy in values, or dishonesty or cruelty or cowardice that is preached by him; but the inward conviction of the strength and freedom of spirit and nourishment it bestows upon the nation at large. His Pran-mantra "Self rule is my birth-right and I shall seize it." was far more powerful than an incantation of Vedic sages. Casting off inertia and awakened to his potential strength, what wonders a Lion can do, was impressed by Lokmanya Tilak, in the minds of his country-men, throughout his life.

Though a pious-religious person, he never opted for adopting modes of religious worships in any of his activities. He principally believed in discriminatory thinking and elastic application of the laws of conduct While he ever strived for universal good and translated philosophy in to action, he was a social reformer at the same time. He always proclaimed in clear terms : "Staunchy respecting the great traditions, and with no harm to them, reforms must be carried out as suited to the times."

The allegation made upon him that, he compromised upon his principles in order to woo the masses is far from truth. He was the man who could swallow whatever fell to his lot, with spirit undaunted.

The nation respected him as the "Father of National Unrest" and spontaneously honoured him with the title 'LOKAMANYA' - (World-Acclaimed). He utilised the national unrest thus aroused as a necessary step in the ensuing fight for independence. He threw open all the gates all the highways and byways, and all directions amidst this all-sides training to countrymen. He thus prepared a base-land for further work by those, who succeeded him in the undertaking. What nationalistic education can be and what a national teacher should be is, for the first time in history, exemplified in the form of Lokamanya Bal Gangadhar Tilak.

Bibliography

Annie, Besant, *India Bound or Free? A World Problem*. London, 1926.

Aurobindo, Ghose, *On National Problems: The Views of Sri Aurobindo, Ghose*. Calcutta, 1950.

———, *The Foundations of Indian Culture*. New York, 1952.

B.C., Pal, *Nationality and Empire: A Running Study of Some Current Indian Problems*. Calcutta, 1916.

Bal Gangadhar, Tilak, *His Writings and Speeches*. Madras, 1922.

———, *The Arctic Home of the Vedas*. Poona, 1925.

Bepin Chandra, Pal, *His Life and Utterances*. Madras.

Chitta Ranjan, Das, *India for Indians*. Madras, 1921.

D.V., Tahmankar, *Lokamanya Tilak*, London, 1956.

Gopal Krishna, Gokhale, *Speeches*. Madras, 1916.

Henry John Stedman, Cotton, *New India or India in Transition*. London, 1904.

Jawaharlal, Nehru, *The Discovery of India*, Calcutta, 1948.

———, *Toward Freedom*. New York, 194 1.

Lala Lajpat, Rai, *India's Will to Freedom: Writings and Speeches*, on the Present Situation. Madras, 1921.

Mahatma Gandhi, *His Life, Writings and Speeches*, Madras, 1918.

———, *Hindu Dharma*. Ahmedabad, Navajivan Publishing House, 1950.

———, *The story of My Experiments with Truth*. Ahmedabad, 1962.

N.C., Kelkar, Malaviya, the Honourable Pandit Madan Mohan, *His Life and Speeches*: Madras.

Rabindranath, Tagore, *Nationalism*. New York, 1917.

Sir Pherozeshah Mehta, Chintamani, C.Y., Editor, *Speeches and Writings of the Honourable Sir Pherozeshah Mehta*. Allahabad, The Indian Press, 1905.

Subhas Chandra, Bose, *The Indian Struggle*, 1920-1934. London, 1935.

Surendranath, Bannerjea, *A Nation in Making: Being the Reminiscences of Fifty Years of Public Life*. London, 1925.

T.L., Vaswani, *India in Chains*. Madras, 1920.

William, Wedderburn, *Speeches and Writings*, Madras, 1918.

INDEX